Fundamentals of Merchandising

Fundamentals
of
Merchandising

Jan Wiid (editor)

JUTA

Fundamentals of Merchandising

First published 2012

Juta and Company Ltd
PO Box 14373, Lansdowne, 7779, Cape Town, South Africa
© 2012 Juta & Company Ltd

ISBN 978-0-70218-693-6

Project manager: Karen Froneman
Editor: Glenda Younge
Proofreader: Kathy Sutton
Cover designer: Drag and Drop
Indexer: Jennifer Stern
Typesetter: ANdtp Services, Cape Town

Typeset in 9.5 pt on 13 pt Palatino

Printed in South Africa by

The authors and the publisher have made every effort to obtain permission for and to acknowledge the use of copyright material. Should any infringement of copyright have occurred, please contact the publisher, and every effort will be made to rectify omissions or errors in the event of a reprint or new edition.

Contents

Preface

Merchandising is a key element of any retail organisation. Merchandisers are responsible for ensuring that products appear in the right store at the appropriate time and in the correct quantities. Merchandisers also set prices to maximise profits and manage the performance of ranges, planning promotions and markdowns as necessary. The significance and importance of merchandising is stressed in this book and is reflected in the structure and layout.

Fundamentals of Merchandising will fill a specific gap in the South African marketplace for both academic and business readers. It is practically oriented and makes use of a number of South African examples to explain the theory, and applicable case studies are provided at the end of each chapter. The book is structured as follows:

Chapter 1 provides an introduction to retailing and discusses what retailing is. It describes the characteristics of retailers, the nature of retail competition, and classifies retailers and their competitive strategies. Chapter 2 examines the collection of marketing information, while chapter 3 focuses on product planning and selection and examines merchandise planning in terms of both Rand value and units.

Chapter 4 deals with the merchandise logistics. It discusses the retail supply base, supplier–retailer collaboration, types of supply chain, selecting suppliers, and negotiating the purchase and the merchandising process. Chapter 5 deals with inventory management and analysis. The emphasis is on merchandise control, inventory information systems and measuring merchandise performance.

Store decisions and design are the focus in chapter 6, where the importance of location, the store environment, and external and internal design are discussed. Chapter 7 addresses merchandise pricing and looks at pricing objectives, factors influencing pricing, pricing methods, different pricing policies, and the adjustment of the retail selling price.

Chapter 8 focuses on merchandise advertising and examines product promotions and advertising. It discusses planning, organising, executing and evaluating the advertising function, as well as sales promotion and publicity. Chapter 9 deals with visual merchandising. It addresses displays and visual merchandising in different store types (full- and self-service stores), and the design, arrangement, colour and lighting of displays.

I would like to acknowledge the main authors, Prof MC Cant, Mr W Grimes and Mr CN Diggines for their hard work and dedication.

JA Wiid
Pretoria
May 2012

About the authors

Content editor

Jan Wiid is a senior lecturer and professor in the Department of Marketing and Retail Management at the University of South Africa (UNISA).

Contributing authors

Mike Cant is a professor in the Department of Marketing and Retail Management at the University of South Africa (UNISA). He is the current chair of department (COD) of the department of Marketing and Retail Management.

Colin Diggines is a senior lecturer in the Department of Marketing and Retail Management at the University of South Africa (UNISA). His main areas of interest are in-service and services marketing, as well as branding and e-marketing.

William Grimes is a lecturer in the Department of Marketing, Logistics and Sport Management at the Tshwane University of Technology (TUT).

1

Introduction to retailing

Michael C Cant

1.1 Introduction

As diverse as we all are in South Africa, we all buy similar products, such as bread, milk and pap, and make use of transport to move from one place to another on a daily basis. When customers buy these everyday necessities they deal with retailers. We find retailers everywhere in our society, and we use them to satisfy our needs in a convenient manner. Can you think of the retailers you dealt with yesterday? These could have included a café, a petrol station, a drycleaner or even a fast-food outlet, such as Nando's. As you can see, retailers have a major impact on the lives of most customers. Retailing is an important part of any economy, and ultimately links consumers with manufacturers. Retailing is changing swiftly because of the fast-changing environment in which retailers operate (Cant, 2010).

In this chapter we discuss the nature of retailing, the classification of the different types of retailers, the evolution of retailing, as well as the changing nature of retailing. We also introduce the 'rights of retailing'. We begin by discussing the nature of retailing.

1.2 What is retailing?

Do you know the difference between a retailer and a wholesaler? A retailer may be seen as a business that focuses its marketing efforts on the final consumers with the intention of selling goods or services to them. This means that any business that sells a product or service to a final consumer, whether it is to a customer in a shop, by mail, over the telephone, door-to-door or by means of a vending machine, is a retailing business. Retailers usually buy items in bulk and sell these in smaller quantities to consumers for personal, family or household use. A wholesaler, on the other hand, sells the majority of its products to retailers, who in turn sell them on to consumers.

Retailing has a large impact on our society and the people in it. The large number of undertakings engaging in retail activities, the number of people employed by these businesses and the tremendous sales volumes they generate, indicate the importance of retailing in our society. Retailers play a major role in creating and adding value to final goods and services. This ensures that customers' needs and wants are satisfied.

Retailers provide a critical link between producers or manufacturers and end consumers, because they create the environment in which exchanges between producers or manufacturers and consumers take place. Consumers ultimately benefit from the marketing functions that the retailer performs. In the section that follows, the development of retailing according to the wheel of retailing will be discussed (Cant, 2010: 3–4).

1.3   The wheel of retailing

The wheel of retailing is a retail marketing process whereby original low-price discounters upgrade their services and gradually increase prices (http://www.all business.com/glossaries/wheel-retailing/4943201-1.html). As these evolve into full-line department stores, this creates a competitive opportunity for new low-price discounters to develop, and the process continues into the next generation. This opens the way for new competitors with the same recipe of lower costs for retailers to enter the market, which results in lower prices for consumers. This theory is relevant to South African conditions, especially in the fast-food industry. Wimpy, for example, started out by selling basic hamburgers at down-to-earth locations. Today Wimpy Bars are more upmarket, with improved décor and higher prices, leaving enough room for a new generation of fast-food stores to challenge them (http://www.wimpy.co.za/moments.htm). It should, however, be stressed that not all retailing institutions can be categorised according to the wheel of retailing. One example is the rise and decline of department stores and their subsequent revival. Some authors feel that in less developed countries, relatively small, middle- and upper-income groups have formed the major markets for 'modern' types of retailing. Supermarkets and other modern stores have been introduced in these countries, largely at the top of the social and price scales, contrary to the wheel pattern (Unisa, 2008: 29).

Other experts have also taken issue with the wheel model, contending that changes in the retail environment increase the likelihood that retailers will seek to remain where they are, rather than move up the wheel. Many authors describe retailing institutions as evolving from outlets selling a wide variety of products, to ones specialising in a narrower assortment of goods, then returning to a wider offering once again. These contractions and expansions are similar to the actions of an accordion.

This theory is relevant to the South African retailing environment. At first, general dealers selling a wide assortment of goods were established. Thereafter a contraction phase set in and specialist stores offering a smaller selection of goods became popular. During the 1970s we saw a return to businesses selling a wide assortment of goods with the introduction of the hypermarket. This was reversed again during the 1990s when there was a movement back to specialisation. In the new millennium we see a revival of the CBDs, which were neglected during the 1980s and 1990s. There is also a move towards bigger and more shopping malls in the suburbs.

Let us now consider the different methods of classifying retailers.

1.4   Classification of the different types of retailers

There are many ways of categorising retailers. One way is by looking at the level of control of the purchase experience and the number of different product categories (Cant, 2010):

❏   The level of control of the purchase experience refers to the degree to which the retailer controls the purchasing experience. A high level of control means that the retailer has a very tightly managed selling environment, and a moderate level of control means that there are a significant number of unmanaged variables.
❏   The number of different product categories refers to the number of different groups of related product lines. If there is a large number, the retailer has a broad range, but if there are only a few, the retailer tends to be a specialist.

Using this classification we can see that retailers with a high level of purchase control tend to follow a store-based approach, which allows them to design a definitive shopping experience. If the level of purchase control is moderate, the retailers tend to follow a more distance-based approach. Examples of these could be a chain of bookstores such as Exclusive Books, which has a high level of control, compared to Kalahari.net, an online retailer of books, which has moderate purchase control. A retailer offering a large range of products is termed a mass retailer (such as Game), while one offering a small range is called a specialist retailer (such as Musica). A retailer such as Kalahari.net is a delivery-based mass retailer, while one offering only music compact discs is called a delivery-based specialist retailer.

Another way of classifying retailers is by whether or not the retailer has an actual physical retail outlet. Let us look at this in the section that follows.

Store and non-store retailing

One may distinguish between two types of retailer: store retailers and non-store retailers. We will discuss each of these.

Store retailing

These are retail outlets that are housed in actual stores. Retail stores come in all sizes, from very small to very large. A store retailer may be classified by one or more of several characteristics. These characteristics are summarised in Table 1.1.

Table 1.1 Ways of classifying store retailers

Level and types of service	Size and assortment	Relative price, emphasis and position	Control of outlets	Types of store cluster
Self service	Speciality store	Discount store	Corporate chain	Central business district
Limited service	Department store		Voluntary chain	Regional shopping centre
Full service	Supermarket Convenience store Superstore Hypermarket Service business	Catalogue showroom	Franchise organisation	Community shopping centre Neighbourhood shopping centre

Source: Adapted from Kotler & Armstrong (1996: 427)

Store retailers can be classified according to the extent of the service they provide, the variety of the product assortment they sell, the pricing structures they implement and according to store cluster. An example of classification according to pricing structure is a discount store in which well-known national brands are sold and lower prices are automatically applied to the product range (such as in the case of Pick n Pay).

Stores offering a wide variety of products and services cluster together to attract customers. An example of this is the Menlyn Park shopping centre in Pretoria and the Canal Walk shopping centre in Cape Town.

Non-store retailing

Non-store retailing does not take place in an actual store. Three kinds of non-store retailing can be identified, namely direct marketing, direct selling and automatic vending.

Direct marketing uses the advertising media to call upon the customer to respond to advertisements. Direct marketing includes catalogue marketing (where catalogues are mailed to selected customers), telemarketing (where the telephone is used to sell to the customer) and electronic shopping (where orders are placed at retailers electronically with aids such as the Internet). Can you think of such a retailer?

Examples of direct selling include selling investments and timeshare, which is different from product demonstrations, for instance, at 'Tupperware parties'.

Automatic vending is the last form of non-store retailing. Automatic vending is a 24-hour method of selling convenience products, such as cigarettes, cold drinks and snacks, with the aid of a vending machine. Cellphone network airtime can now also be bought from vending machines, and many golf courses have vending machines that stock small golfing items, such as gloves and balls!

Now that we know how retailing is classified, we will examine the changing nature of retailing.

1.5   The evolution of retailing

How many street vendors did you pass on your way to work or class today? It is amazing to see how these vendors stock goods needed by many consumers, such as umbrellas on rainy days or ice-cold drinks when it is very hot! Many even stock rugby shirts and accessories during specific rugby competitions, such as during the Currie Cup.

As you can see from the above, non-store sales are becoming an important part of retailing. Internet shopping, mail-order catalogues, TV shopping programmes, door-to-door selling and vending machines are all examples of non-store retailing.

Another major trend in the evolution of retailing is the growth of service retailing. Although most people tend to associate retailing with the sale of products, the sale of services is a vital part of many retail businesses. Diverse businesses, such as banks, hospitals, insurance companies and hotels are also retailers, since they all ultimately provide services to the consumer. Can you think of any others?

A successful retail business strikes a balance between the customer's merchandising needs and the retailer's performance standards. Merchandising needs are the specific goods and services a customer is looking for, while performance standards are the specific goals the retailer wishes to achieve, such as sales targets and/or required profit margins.

Retailing is also becoming more customer-focused. It is no longer enough to simply offer customers a building (store) with merchandise, sales people and credit. Customers must have defined reasons to seek out retailers in this intensely competitive marketplace. The key to the future success of retailers relates to a strong customer focus, focused product development, database marketing (where customers can be identified more easily and quickly with the aid of computers) and innovative advertisements, to mention but a few. Retailers today do not operate in a closed environment, but in a continuously changing and challenging one. They face a dynamic environment in a tough international economy. Environmental elements, such as consumer behaviour, competition and intermediaries or distributors, are changing rapidly and have a huge impact on retailing. Retailing is a business of managing change. Retailers must be able to analyse and understand environmental changes, and anticipate and adapt to the changes made by others.

South Africa has one of the most interesting and exciting retail landscapes in the world today. Its apartheid laws kept the retailers and consumers of different races apart, which resulted in inadequate shopping facilities in the traditional black areas, and an oversupply of retailing outlets in the traditional white areas. Since then new markets, which are providing new opportunities and challenges for the retailer, have emerged. There is sufficient evidence to indicate the growing disposable income of the so-called 'black market'. Understanding the changing nature of retailing is, however, not enough (Unisa, 2008: 22–23).

Although these changes must be taken into consideration, one also needs to grasp the very basics of retailing, namely the six 'rights' of retailing, which we deal with next.

1.6   The six 'rights' of retailing

When customers have certain needs, they want certain products or services to fulfil these. They usually have a pretty good idea of where they can find these goods or services. Retailers must ensure that enough of these products are available when customers need them. Customers will most certainly attach a certain value to these products, and these values will be reflected in the price of the products. Retailers must, therefore, have the right price for the products. Having considered all these factors, retailers must still ensure that customers enjoy the shopping experience so that they will return for future purchases (Cant, 2010: 8–9).

Retailers need to take six specific 'rights' of retailing into account, namely the right product, in the right place, at the right time, in the right quantity, at the right price, with the right service, as shown in Figure 1.1.

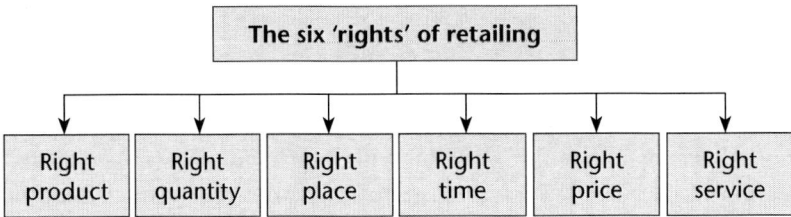

Figure 1.1 The six 'rights' of retailing

The 'rights' of retailing should not be considered in isolation. A retailer may have the right product, for example, but it may not be available at the right time or at the right price. We shall briefly examine these rights:

The right product

The retailer must provide the customer with the right product. If the consumers' needs are not being met, they will seek other retailers.

The right quantity

If customers want a certain product and they cannot find it at a specific retailer, they will go to another retailer to obtain it. The right quantity ensures that retailers have enough of a product to satisfy consumers' needs.

The right place

Having the right product, in the right quantity, is not enough if customers do not know where the retailer is or do not have access to them. The right product should, therefore, be available in the right quantity at the right place. The right place is one where customers can get hold of the product easily and without any unnecessary effort.

The right time

Retailers must have the right quantity of the right product in the right place at the right time. The right time to sell is when consumers are willing to buy. Time affects different consumers in different ways, therefore retailers must develop retailing strategies that coincide with consumers' buying times.

The right price

If retailers charge unreasonable prices for their products, their customers will probably not buy them. The right price will be the price that customers are willing to pay for the perceived value they receive from the product. They will also be willing to pay more for more valuable products. The right price for retailers is the price that generates sufficient money to ensure a reasonable profit. The right price is therefore the amount consumers are willing to pay and retailers are willing to accept in exchange for products and services.

The right service

The final 'right' of retailing is the right service. To be successful, every retail business needs to add value to its products by offering outstanding customer service.

1.7   Characteristics of retailers

Authors generally agree that retailers have specific characteristics.

Cox and Brittain (2004: 4), highlight the following characteristics that they deem to be important in retailers:

❑   They must be well-located and convenient for customers.
❑   They must carry a range of merchandise based on the market they are serving, i.e. they must meet market requirements.
❑   They should buy in larger quantities than they sell. This is called breaking bulk.
❑   Stock should be immediately available at prices that generally do not fluctuate too much.
❑   They must help to affect a change in ownership of goods, i.e. from the retailer to the customer.
❑   They should have a wealth of information for both their suppliers (regarding the needs and demands of the customers) and their customers (on availability and other related matters relating to the supply of goods).

❐ They must offer product guarantees, after-sales service and deal with customer complaints.

❐ They should offer a range of payment options, such as credit, lay-bye, hire purchase.

The characteristics of retailers are ever-changing and adapting to economic and social developments in a particular market area.

1.8 Retail environment

No retail organisation operates in isolation, and all retail organisations are influenced by numerous variables, both directly and indirectly. For example, rising interest rates mean less disposable income for consumers to make retailing purchases, while changes in technology mean that many consumers would rather shop from the comfort of their homes on the Internet, which influences how many consumers visit a particular shopping centre.

As can be seen from the above, the retailing environment is very dynamic and is constantly changing. Once a retailer understands the basics of retailing and knows exactly where the retail outlet is heading, they need to analyse the variables in the internal and external environments that could affect the success of their enterprise (Cant, 2010: 10–33).

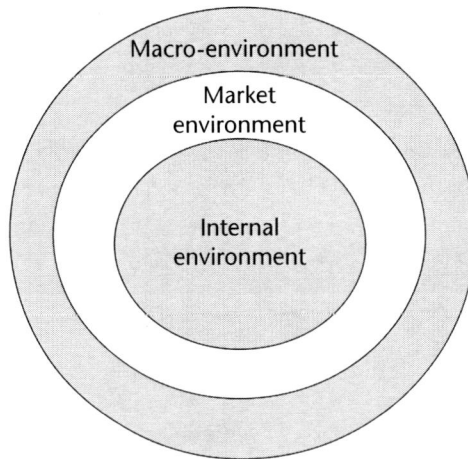

Figure 1.2 The retailing environment

We discuss the various sub-environments of the retailing environment, namely the macro-environment, market environment and the internal environment, below.

The macro-environment

There are, however, several factors that lie beyond the control of an individual retailer. These uncontrollable factors shape and constrain a retailer's activities. These uncontrollable factors (illustrated in Figure 1.3) are found in the external macro-environment and consist of the institutional or political, economic, social, technological and physical environments. Each of these factors or mega-trends will now be discussed.

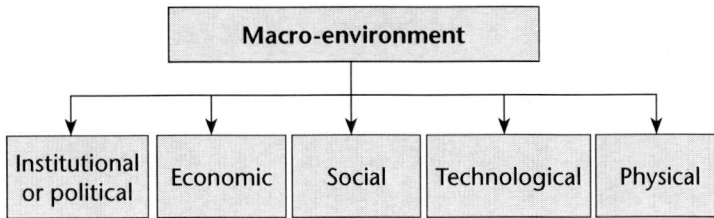

```
                    ┌─────────────────────────┐
                    │    Macro-environment    │
                    └─────────────────────────┘
```

Institutional or political	Economic	Social	Technological	Physical

Figure 1.3 The macro-environment

The institutional or political environment

The government can exert pressures on the country, steering agricultural and economic policy in a particular direction. Some of the policies of the South African government are based on maintaining the free-market system and private ownership. The government intervenes in the annual budget, taxation, import control, export incentives, price control for certain goods and services, health regulations, as well as other incentives to encourage development in a specific direction or region. These factors have a direct influence on the retailing industry and certainly influence ultimate profits. The government announces petrol price changes and also controls tax rates. For example, it set value-added tax at 14%. See the excerpt below from Minister Trevor Manuel's 2009 budget with regards to the fuel levy:

> As road-users, Madam Speaker, we have gained some advantage since mid-2008 from lower international oil prices. As road-users we also know that there is a substantial increase in spending on maintenance and construction under way, and we still face a heavy burden of road accidents and associated compensation claims. These are costs that have to be covered, and so there will be increases in the fuel levies on 1 April this year, of 23 cents and 24 cents per litre in respect of the general petrol and diesel levies, and 17,5 cents in the road accident fund levy.

Source: info.gov.za/speeches/2009

Retailers cannot, for example, control interest and tax rates or petrol prices, which directly influence the retailing industry. If the petrol price increases (as it did on 1 April 2012 due to the increase in fuel levies), distribution costs also increase. Similarly, an increase in interest and tax rates can result in a decrease in consumer spending.

The economic environment

Since 2009, articles such as the following have become commonplace:

> According to debt counsellors Debtbusters, more than 11 million people, nearly a quarter of the country's population, struggle with debt, and banks are sitting on a total (probably

bad) debt burden of more than R35 bn. The debt burden weighing on South African households is increasing, even though interest rates (as of 18 November 2010, 5,5%) and inflation (3,5%) are at historic lows.

The most financially vulnerable were the lowest income group, although high levels of financial vulnerability were found among the middle income group too.

Source: southafricaweb.co.za/article

New vehicle sales recorded further declines in February, falling by 36,3% year-on-year following a 35,5% decline in January as both local and global economic conditions continued to deteriorate. Domestically, consumer income remains under strain from high prices, high interest rates and heavy debt burdens, while the fall in commercial vehicle sales suggested that fixed investment activity is also losing momentum as recessionary conditions globally and locally start placing serious pressure on companies, prompting some firms to postpone or scrap new capital expenditure projects.

Source: odysseylife.co.za/documents

The inflation rate, interest rates, the economic cycle, unemployment, Gross National Product (GNP) and national debt are all part of the economic environment. Consumers' buying habits are strongly related to consumer income. Certain economic indicators have a direct influence on consumer income. If tax and interest rates increase, consumers will spend more and save less. Generally, debt will increase. Retailers must monitor trends in consumer income, savings, debt and expenditure patterns.

Consumers who save more money have less discretionary income (i.e. less spending money) while the availability of credit enhances consumer expenditure. Obviously this will happen when interest rates decrease. The important economic factors that retailers should be aware of will be discussed next.

Gross National Product

The Gross National Product (GNP) of a country is the total value of all goods and services produced by the citizens of that country in a specific period. Retailers prefer GNP to grow at a moderate and steady rate, as a too-rapid growth leads to inflation, while a too-slow growth rate may cause a recession. Retailers can use GNP figures to predict future national disposable income levels, which in turn can be used to predict future sales levels. When the GNP increases, there is usually a decrease in unemployment. More jobs are created, resulting in more salaries and wages being paid. Thus more consumers have money to satisfy their needs, and more products are sold.

Interest rates and the rate of inflation

An interest rate is the price paid for the use of money. When consumers borrow money from a bank, for example, they pay interest according to a determined interest rate. Consumers and retailers use other people's money to purchase merchandise. Consumers might use credit cards, and retailers' bank credits. When interest rates increase, so does the price of merchandise. As prices rise, the demand for products declines – in other words, fewer consumers buy them. Retailers need to be aware of fluctuating interest rates because they have to pay overhead expenses. As interest rates increase, the demand for the retailers' products declines (because consumers have to pay more interest on credit) but their expenses, such as the interest on a capital loan, increase. Inflation basically means that the prices of goods and services rise in general. An inflation rate of 10% means that products that cost R100 last year will cost R110 this year (http://www.mg.co.za/article/2009-01-28-sa-inflation-brakes-big-rate-cutlikely). The inflation rate in South Africa in February 2012 was 6,1% (http://www.mg.co.za/article/2009-03-02-stats-sa-unemployment-rate-down). Another factor in the economic environment that plays a vital role is the economic cycle, which will be discussed next.

The economic cycle

The economic cycle reflects economic trends over time. It is measured using the GNP or Gross Domestic Product (GDP) as an indicator of the state of the country's economy. The upswings and downswings of the economic cycle have become part of retail planning. Retailers need to predict economic upswings because consumers tend to be more optimistic about the future and therefore spend more money. This is when GNP increases. During economic downswings (which is where we still find ourselves in 2012), people tend to be more pessimistic and spend less money. During recessions when economic downswings are at their lowest, consumer spending and GNP are low and unemployment high. We now discuss national debt as a factor that influences the economic environment.

National debt

National debt is the money the government owes other countries. When the government spends more money than it receives, the national debt increases. As the debt level increases, the government is compelled to increase interest rates to fund the debt. As interest rates increase, consumers spend less money (see interest rates). National debt increases when the government has deficits, and decreases when it has surpluses. It therefore has a deficit when there are more imports than exports – when expenses are higher than the funds generated through, say, taxes. Unemployment is also discussed under 'economic environment'. The last element of the economic environment is unemployment.

Unemployment

South Africa's unemployment rate dropped from a peak of 31% in 2008 to 25% in the third quarter of 2011 according to Statistics South Africa data published in November 2011. The unemployment rate indicates the percentage of people in a country without work. If unemployment decreases, more people have jobs and therefore an income.

People who have an income tend to have money to spend. When unemployment rates increase, however, retail sales decrease.

As can be seen from the above discussion, the economic environment can be extremely turbulent. GNP, interest rates and the rate of inflation, the economic cycle, national debt and unemployment are all factors that play a role in the economic environment. The next component of the external retailing environment to be discussed is the social environment.

The social environment

In the social environment, the demographic details of the population are important for retailers because their potential customers are part of this environment. Each country has inhabitants or citizens. They are usually distributed all over the country and form part of various groups, as determined by factors such as social class, age groups and gender. Retailers should take note of social trends and use them to make future projections. The population growth rate, the geographic shift of the population, consumers' educational levels, different age groups, household incomes, family structures and consumers' gender are all part of the social environment.

Population growth and size

The population growth rate indicates at what rate the population is increasing, while population size indicates the number of people living in a country. To plan correctly, accurate projections about the population growth of South Africa are necessary. If there is an increase in the population growth rate, retailers will have to supply products and services to fulfil the needs and wants of the additional customers. Two factors determine population growth. Firstly, one has to determine the difference between the emigrants and immigrants of the country, and secondly, the difference between the number of births and deaths. Of interest to retailers is that an increase in the birth rate means a corresponding increase in the market for baby products and services. In 1999 the South African population was 43,1 million, but by mid-2011 it was estimated to be 50,59 million. Population growth is being threatened by the Aids crisis, however. If one takes the direct influence of Aids into account and assumes that the net migration rate will be low, it is estimated that South Africa's population will increase by 14 million by the year 2031 (www.southafrica.info/about/facts.htm).

The geographic location and shift of the population (urbanisation)

The geographic location of the population indicates where in the country the people are living: are they living in urban or rural areas, and more specifically, in which provinces do they reside? The geographic shift indicates trends in urbanisation. Retailers should be concerned not only with numbers of people and their ages, but also where they live. Consumers will not travel great distances to make retail purchases. When more people move to urban areas, more retail outlets are required to cater for the bigger demand. Population density is important in location decisions.

In Gauteng, the population density is estimated at 659 persons per square kilometre, while in the Northern Cape it is only 10 persons per square kilometre (47% of South Africans live in rural areas) (www.southafrica.info/about/facts.htm). The private minibus transport system has increased the mobility of people living in township areas, thus giving them access to urban areas. Retailers have to realise that the bigger markets will be in urban areas. Several factors have to be considered (e.g. the influence of a decreasing population growth, combined with urbanisation). This does not, however, mean that retailers are excluded from rural areas. There is a need for retailers in these areas. Retailers should also consider the education levels of consumers, which will be discussed next.

Education levels of consumers

Retailers need to determine the level of education of consumers. Educated consumers are better informed and more sophisticated when choosing between brands, stores and services. They are more alert to changes in price, quality, packaging and advertisements. The education level of consumers will, for example, also determine the level at which a retailer must communicate with them to ensure that they understand the message correctly.

According to a survey published by the South African Institute of Race Relations, the racial make-up of students attending universities and universities of technology over the last 15 years has changed dramatically. In the early 1990s approximately 60% of students enrolled at tertiary education institutions were black (African, coloured, and Indian). A decade later that proportion had increased to over 75%. The number of enrolled African students almost doubled in the decade after 1994 (http://www.sairr.org.za/sairr-today/tertiary-education-transformation-thenumbers-tell-the-true-story-07-03-2008.html).

The age distribution of consumers is another demographic factor that retailers need to consider.

Age distribution of the population

All people fall into one or other age group, and as they age, their needs change. Retailers should be aware of these changes. People are generally living longer than they did in the past, which means that a new or bigger market exists for older people. Senior citizens tend to spend more money on health products. However, retailers should realise that older people might not have as much money to spend on products associated with, for example, holidays and expensive vehicles. Teenagers also constitute an important group for certain retailers.

In South Africa, the average age of the white population is increasing, and it is predicted that by 2011 this group will have zero population growth. The average

age of the Asian and coloured population groups is also increasing, and by 2015, the economically active age groups in these population groups will have diminished in size. The average age of the black population is younger. Retailers need to know who their shoppers are, as this will enable them to formulate an effective communication strategy.

At this point we should ask the following question: How do consumers' needs change as they grow older? If the biggest potential market is babies, obviously the biggest market will be parents buying baby products, such as baby clothing, baby food, toys and accessories. When these babies grow older, the biggest market will change – parents will be buying different types of toys and clothes and necessities such as school clothes, schoolbags and stationery. When children become teenagers, the markets for music and fashion become important. As customers reach middle and old age, more emphasis is placed on products associated with security and/or status, such as short- and long-term insurance, housing and vehicles.

It is not enough to have knowledge of the population growth and size, geographic shift, educational levels and age distribution of consumers. Retailers should also be able to determine consumers' household and disposable incomes.

Household and disposable incomes

Retailers must know what the average income of households is and in which income group the majority of the consumers fall. People or households must have purchasing power to represent a market. Current buying patterns and personal savings trends influence the way consumers spend their money. Consumers have learnt to be much more disciplined with their spending.

Let us now consider how lower tax rates can result in a higher disposable income for individuals, and how a higher disposable income, in turn, can influence the retailing industry.

Individuals pay a smaller percentage of their personal income to the Receiver of Revenue when tax rates decrease. This results in a higher disposable income as consumers have fewer 'expenses'. If consumers have more spending money they obviously spend more. Think about it. If you had R100 more a month right now, the chances are you would spend at least some of it on goods and services. When consumers spend more, retailers sell more. A higher disposable income influences the retailing industry positively. Retailers should also have an idea of the family structures in the country.

Family structures

Family structures indicate the composition of families. Retailers should note, for example, how many single people there are, and how many married couples there are without children, and with children. Trends in marriages and divorces should also be monitored. When people marry they generally furnish their new homes and buy appliances. When married couples divorce, other markets, such as one-bedroom flats and their associated necessities can be exploited. There has been an increase in divorce rates in the past decade. When people stay single, different needs arise. Single-parent families and working women have also altered family structures.

Changes in family structures influence retailing. The needs of a single, young man or woman, for example, differ from those of a married couple with two children. Single, young people might have a need for smaller flats as opposed to larger houses. People also have different furniture needs. A single male, for example, would probably be quite happy with a couch, a music system, television and M-Net to watch sport, while a single female may prefer a cosy lounge with designer curtains, decent pots and pans, and a smart dinner service. Their refrigerators will be smaller than those of bigger families. Single people might have only single beds, while a married couple with two children would more likely have a double bed and at least two other single beds or, possibly, a bunk bed. This has further implications for linen, such as sheets, blankets, duvets and duvet covers.

People also have different clothing needs, as well as recreational and relaxation needs. Single people might dine at expensive restaurants or go to the movies to relax, while married couples might be more inclined to watch videos and eat at family restaurants, depending on the ages of their children. Transport needs also vary – a young up-and-coming business executive, for example, would probably opt for a smart status car (a BMW or Mercedes-Benz), while a young, struggling, married couple with three small children might opt for a second-hand station wagon. Young, single people may be interested in having only the basics, such as a few coffee mugs and assorted dishes, while a married couple will probably have a wider variety of crockery. Let us now look at the gender composition of the population.

Male–female composition of the population

The male–female composition indicates the percentage of males to females in the whole population. Many women have entered the labour market and are building their careers. The increased rate of working women has created unique opportunities for retailers. Retailers will want to know what percentage of the population is male and what percentage female, and what future trends are predicted. The female labour force in South Africa is expanding much faster than the male labour force. More married women are entering the labour market. An average increase of 1,3% and 1,8% for women and men respectively in the labour force was calculated by Statistics South Africa in 2011 (http://www.statssa.gov.za/publications/P0211/P02111stQuarter2011.pdf).

The implications for retailers will mean longer trading hours are necessary to accommodate the larger numbers of career women. This also implies that more men will be doing the household shopping because of limited time. Because both husband and wife are working, nobody in the household is available to do the shopping during working hours. Retailers will lose sales if they do not accommodate this phenomenon – hence the longer trading hours.

The next component of the external environment to be discussed is the technological environment.

The technological environment

Technology has changed dramatically in recent times. Technologically advanced products can become obsolete quickly as the rate of technological development accelerates. The advancement of computer applications, communications and electronics cannot be denied. In the rapidly changing consumer markets, retailers need to keep up with the latest innovations. Technology is now a fundamental competitive tool in retailing.

New technologies have given rise to new forms of retailing, have made retail transactions more efficient, thus increasing retail productivity, and have improved the control of retail operations. We go on to discuss these new forms of retailing and the control of retail operations.

New forms of retailing

Online retailing with the aid of computer link-ups is an example of a new form of retailing. Consumers are able to make their own choices from the available brands, styles, colours and sizes that are available. Online retailing appears to be taking off, although many consumers consider shopping through the mail, by telephone or through interactive devices to be risky. Many consumers do not like buying from non-store retailers because they prefer to examine a product physically before purchasing it. Let us look at a few technological advancements that have led to more efficient retail transactions:

Computers

Computers have become a must in any competitive business. The role that computers play in providing businesses with a competitive advantage is well documented. Think, for example, of retailers such as Edgars and Woolworths that use computers to process orders and outstanding accounts. The advancement of computer technology cannot be ignored. Computers have changed the face of retailing. Using computer technology will undoubtedly help a retail business to keep in touch with the rapidly changing environment. Certain trends in computer technology have emerged and offer huge opportunities for the retailer. There are, however, several advantages and disadvantages in using computers.

Advantages include:

❏ Computers can provide the retailer with better information.
❏ Computers process data and instructions quickly and therefore provide decision-makers with up-to-date information.
❏ Computers generate accurate information.

◻ Computers can eliminate many of the dull, monotonous tasks involved in compiling and maintaining routine records.

◻ Cash management and inventory control are two of the basic functions performed by computers that improve the internal control of the retailer.

◻ Computers can reduce customer service time, gather and present customers with useful purchase information, and help retailers to offer customers more convenience.

◻ Improved inventory control is one of the biggest advantages of using computer technology.

◻ The use of computers allows employees to focus on other more important tasks, thus increasing sales productivity and customer satisfaction.

Disadvantages include:

◻ The cost of computer systems is quite high.

◻ Obsolescence is another important consideration. A computer bought today may be obsolete tomorrow.

◻ If mistakes are fed into the computer, mistakes will come out ('garbage in, garbage out'). Computers sometimes make expensive mistakes if they are incorrectly programmed.

◻ Computers may alienate customers. Computer mistakes may be regarded as unreasonable actions taken by the retailer and not simply as errors.

◻ Some employees may feel anxious about or threatened by computers.

Universal product coding (UPC)

Universal product coding is the small black and white bars on product items. These bars are codes containing information about the product and the manufacturer. The information from the bar is transferred to a point-of-sale system when the barcodes are passed over a scanner. The information provided by the scanner accurately identifies sales and the merchandise that has been sold. This helps to determine exact stock levels, and when to reorder. Retailers can follow a just-in-time (JIT) reordering philosophy. This means that they can time the reordering of merchandise so as to receive it just before it is needed. Article numbering involves allocating a unique identifying number to each unit of sale. The variation in size, colour and packaging has a separate number. UPC makes communication between manufacturers, retailers and wholesalers possible.

Optical scanning

Optical scanning is the process whereby data from barcodes are entered at the point-of-sale terminal. The scanner reads the barcodes and passes the data on to the computer memory where the data are converted into information regarding size, weight, price and so on. Once a transaction has been completed, the data are entered into the inventory and accounting systems. However, retailers should ensure that the correct barcodes are used because incorrect codes may have a negative effect on the business. All products are coded at stock-keeping unit level. Every colour, flavour, fragrance or size must have its own unique barcode. Good point-of-sale systems are able to provide accurate stock reports, and show balances on merchandise, sales and margins by classification. These balances may be used to evaluate current inventory levels, sales volumes and profit margins. Optical scanners also save labour by eliminating the need to mark prices on each item. Instead, prices are indicated on cards attached to the shelves on which the products are placed. Price information is retrieved from the computer. This reduces delays and errors that can be made by people operating the tills, thus increasing customer service. The intelligent use of scanner information can place a retailer well ahead of its competitors. Retailers who use scanners provide a much faster service than those who do not. Most retailers in South Africa today make use of this technology.

Electronic funds transfer (EFT)

Electronic transfer of funds at the point of sale eliminates cash and other paper-based transactions. An EFT system is operational when pay terminals are connected directly to the computers of financial institutions. Electronic point-of-sale terminals are activated by a plastic card (such as a credit card) and a customer's personal identification number. When a point-of-sale terminal is used, funds may be transferred immediately to the retailer's bank account for the amount of the sale, either from the customer's bank account or through the extension of credit by the financial institution.

Electronic data interchange (EDI)

Electronic data interchange (EDI) is the system that links the databases of retailers and suppliers. EDI is defined as the transfer of formatted data between computer applications running on different machines and using agreed standards to describe and format the data contained in the messages. EDI thus enables companies with different computer systems to send and receive electronic documents that comply with standard formats. Various transactions, such as purchase orders, invoices, shipping confirmation, receiving notices, price changes and special promotions are examples of some operations that an EDI system can handle.

Space management

The cost of space rentals is increasing, which means that retailers need to use space optimally. Space management is essential and has become computerised. Direct product profitability (DPP) is a more sophisticated measurement of the profitability of an item in the store than the conventional gross margin method. It takes into account all the hidden costs of stocking individual products, such as shelf space, shelf packaging labour, storage costs, as well as the price and gross margin. DPP is used to determine whether a product is worthwhile keeping in stock and helps to control space management.

Security and shrinkage control

Closed-circuit television cameras, short frequency radios and detectors that detect firearms and other similar weapons have become more common. Electronic product tags and video cameras, which make store surveillance possible, all help to reduce shrinkage. Optical scanning may also be used for this purpose.

The Internet

The use of the Internet has increased tremendously. Firms that use the Internet are developing entirely new ways of doing business. They are dealing directly with suppliers and individual online shoppers. The Internet is a powerful and cost-effective way to communicate with clients and associates, disseminate information on products and learn the latest on what is happening in a given field. Two primary uses of the Internet are electronic mail (e-mail) and the web page. E-mail is a highly effective way of communicating with other people anywhere in the world, and the message that is sent may be accompanied by word-processing or spread-sheet files. Retailers can put the Internet to good use. Having said that, bear in mind that thousands of web pages are being designed and that everybody wants to utilise this technology. Retailers have to do something unique to attract customers to their web pages. Retailers have to make it worthwhile for customers to visit their websites; they should offer customers a different experience to visiting the store. Providing information via the Internet is a better proposition than trying to sell merchandise via the Internet, because selling becomes expensive if the high rate of returns and shipping costs associated with Internet selling are taken into consideration. Websites also need to be carefully designed. Although an attractive website may initially attract customers, what they are actually interested in is gathering information and they may go to another website if it downloads too slowly.

Multimedia

Computer technology has various possibilities when it comes to showing customers exactly what is on offer. The retailer may use videos and CD-Rom drives to create unique catalogues.

Improved control of retail operations

Technology has certainly streamlined the control of retail operations. Stock control is more effective, sales and inventory levels are always available, and the ordering, receipt and pricing of merchandise are controlled with the aid of computers. Scanners, for example, can now provide information on stock levels more easily and quickly because of technology.

The physical environment

In this dimension of the macro-environment, the focus is primarily on the natural environment. Issues such as pollution, the ozone layer, the greenhouse effect and the depletion of natural resources are some of the most prominent issues that have come to the fore in the last decade. The major areas of concern are:

- ❒ An impending shortage of raw materials;
- ❒ The increasing cost of energy;
- ❒ The increasing levels and consequences of pollution;
- ❒ Increasing pressure from the general public and the business community on governments to become more involved in environmental issues.

These factors will play an ever-increasing role in the activities of businesses, especially in the development and marketing of their products.

Now that we have discussed the variables in the macro-environment, we shall move on to the variables in the market environment.

Market environment

The marketplace or market environment surrounds the retail organisation, and has a direct influence on its activities, while the retail organisation in turn also exerts an influence on the variables in the marketplace.

Four market environmental variables will be discussed in this section, namely, competitors, suppliers, consumers and intermediaries. These variables are illustrated in Figure 1.4.

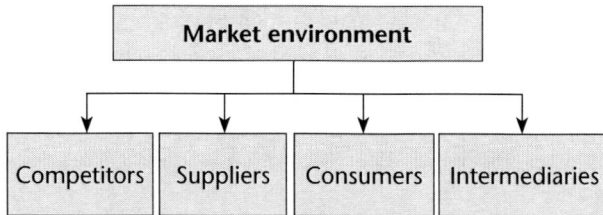

Figure 1.4 The market environment

Competitors

Why do consumers perceive one supermarket as giving better service than the others and at lower prices? To what extent is the one (say Pick n Pay) really different from the others (such as Shoprite Checkers or Spar)? The answer lies in competitive positioning. Competitive positioning refers to all the steps a business takes to distinguish itself from its competitors. The aim is for the retailer to utilise its strengths in such a way that consumers regard the company as distinctly stronger in terms of these criteria.

An organisation's strengths and weaknesses can be adequately assessed only in the light of the findings of an in-depth competitor analysis. The question one may rightfully ask is whether a certain aspect or dimension of an organisation may be regarded as a strength if its competitors are as good, or even better at that aspect than the organisation. Consequently, the positioning of the business in the marketplace will depend to a large extent on where competitors are positioned or aim to be positioned.

Three groups of competitors exert an influence on the organisation, namely, existing direct competitors in the marketplace; new competitors entering the marketplace (i.e. other organisations in the competitive market space); and businesses offering substitute products (new entries based on new ways of reaching customers).

Next we discuss the importance of suppliers as a market environmental variable.

Suppliers

When we think of Company ABC, which advertised products in the press but did not have those advertised items in stock, do we think that 'the company has very unreliable suppliers', or do we think that 'the company itself is unreliable'? As consumers do not distinguish between an organisation and its suppliers, it is vitally important that a retail organisation has reliable, dependable suppliers who supply stock of consistently high quality.

Relationship marketing and channel management have become buzz words over the last few years as more and more organisations realise that all the parties in the value chain should work more closely together to ensure a better deal for the final customer. For the retailer, the value chain stretches backwards to the manufacturers of the product items in their product assortment or even further back to the raw material suppliers. The retailer is, in many cases, the best situated in the chain to initiate, develop and manage the relationships between channel members. Supplier relations will be discussed in more detail in chapter 2.

Consumers

Consumers can be defined as people who identify a need or desire, make a purchase and then dispose of the product during the consumption process. This explains why consumers with their own particular needs, buying power and behaviour are the chief components of the market environment. Knowledge of the market's needs and wants are, therefore, of the utmost importance and pivotal to the success of the retail market offering.

Five main groups of markets exist, namely the consumer market, the industrial market, government markets, resale markets and international markets. Each of these will be discussed briefly:

❑ *Consumer markets* are markets in which individuals and households purchase products and services for personal consumption. In the case of the retailing industry, these are the people at whom retailers aim their market offering. Marketing managers evaluate the number of consumers as well as their buying power in a particular area. Buying power is the personal disposable income of consumers, which can be used to purchase consumer goods and services.

❏ *Industrial markets* are consumer groups composed of organisations that purchase goods and services for use in the production of other goods and services that are sold, rented or supplied to others.

❏ *Government markets* refer to the purchases made by the national government, the nine provincial governments and the local authorities in South Africa.

❏ *Resale markets* refer to businesses that purchase products and services in order to resell them at a profit.

❏ *International markets* refer to foreign buyers, and include consumers, manufacturers, resellers and governments.

A primary objective shared by retailers is the desire to satisfy the needs and wants of customers. Unless retailers make a serious attempt to define customer needs and wants, and direct their actions towards meeting these, they will not be in business for long.

Independent retailers are the masters of their own businesses, but those who serve their customers best and most efficiently will succeed where others fail. The successful store centres all its activities on the customer. There have to be people who want the store's products and services for the store to exist. Unwanted products cannot be forced on customers – this seems trivial, yet many businesses attempt to do it.

One good way to understand customer demands (both conscious and subconscious) is to analyse customer buying habits. The five concepts to help retailers know and understand customers are illustrated in Figure 1.5, and are known as the five customer demands.

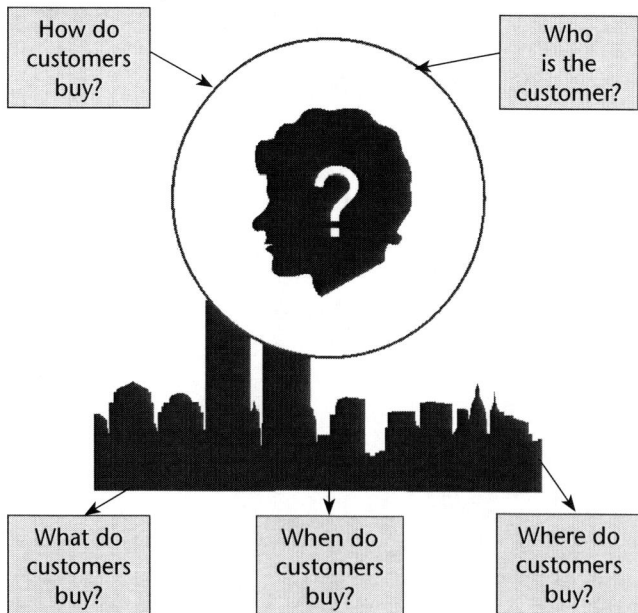

Figure 1.5 Understanding customer demands

The answers to these concepts or questions become the foundation for defining the customer. The five questions – Who? Where? When? What? How? – provide the framework for understanding customers. Clarity about these questions is vital for understanding your customer. Let us consider each of these questions next.

Who is the customer?

This concept leads to several important questions about the customer. What is the sex of your customer? Age? Income? Education? Occupation? What special interests, activities and values do your customers have? What influences their purchases? How do your customers make decisions on what products to purchase? The answers to these questions help retailers to define who is likely to shop in their stores.

A definition of customers (usually called a customer profile) helps retailers to determine what makes their customers (or potential customers) different from other people. A customer profile focuses on those groups (or segments) of customers to whom retailers can direct their efforts most profitably. The same product is not purchased by everyone, nor do all people shop in just one store. If retailers can identify and define the people who will be interested in their merchandise, they can make better decisions and policies to satisfy their customers' demands.

Example of developing a customer profile

The owner of a shoe store developed a customer profile and could therefore determine that most of his customers are female and are working women, earning a certain level of income. Using this information, the store owner could determine the type of women's shoes to stock, the appropriate pricing structure, as well as the level of customer service to be offered to the customers.

Where do customers buy?

Some people prefer to shop at independent retailers; others prefer department stores such as Edgars. Some will travel while others prefer to purchase in their neighbourhood. Some customers like shopping centres and malls, while others prefer local shopping strips. Also, the same person will buy different items in different places (e.g. chocolates at the closest corner store, but furniture or appliances at a particular store, even if others are closer). Reasons why customers purchase goods at certain shops could include one or more of the following:

- The convenient area in which the shops are located;
- The grouping of certain shops close to one another;
- Sufficient parking;
- Competitive prices;
- Services provided by a particular store;
- The service and expertise of the sales staff.

Retailers can use this information to determine the importance of their locations and to assess competition. By knowing who their customers are and where they prefer to shop, retailers can help to ensure that they are in the right place. A clothing shop, for example, might find it advantageous to locate beside a shoe store because it would be convenient for customers to visit both stores while shopping for an outfit.

Example of where customers buy
Joe had a flower stall on the street corner. He was concerned about the location of his stall, due to his fluctuating sales figures. He investigated his customers' buying behaviour and could determine that his customers preferred buying flowers on a single shopping trip to the neighbourhood shopping centre. Joe decided that he would have to relocate his stall to the neighbourhood shopping centre to ensure that customers purchase flowers while they are in the centre. He determined that since many women shopped at the greengrocer, it would be to his advantage to position his store close to the greengrocer, so that he could market his flowers to women on their one-stop shopping trips.

When do customers buy?

Do customers buy at a particular time of the year, a particular time of the week, or a particular hour of the day? Answers to these questions will influence inventory policy, promotion policy, store hours, number of staff and so on. Some products are bought when there is an absolute need and others are bought when a need is anticipated. Milk is often purchased 'on the way home' following a reminder that it is needed for dinner. On the other hand, umbrellas are bought in anticipation of rainy weather, so that they will be on hand when needed. Retailers should also consider whether their consumers buy regularly or irregularly. Retailers want to stock the right merchandise at the right time.

Example of when customers buy
Sibizo had a bakery and realised that he had a large number of women from the opposite office block frequenting his store at tea time in the mornings. Most of these women were in search of slices of cake and savoury tarts. In the afternoons Sibizo had large numbers of school children from the nearby school coming to his store. They were interested mainly in his delicious pies. Based on these factors Sibizo changed his baking times so that he would have cakes and tarts ready before tea time for the office workers, and pies ready in the early afternoon for the school children. By doing this, Sibizo satisfied his customers by having what they wanted ready at the right time.

What do customers buy?

Retailers, like other business people, want to provide their customers with the right products and services. In order to do this, they need to know what products and services their customers want. They can then make every attempt to supply these products in the quantity and quality demanded. When supplying a product or service to customers, a concept known as the total product must be kept in mind by the retailer. The total product indicates all the benefits a customer receives or experiences in the use or application of a physical product or service, which satisfies that customer's need. These satisfactory benefits could be derived from different methods of packaging, customer service, advertisements, financing options, delivery services, storage facilities and other attributes. Just as people buy for both conscious and subconscious reasons, they also buy more than just the physical product you sell. Retailers should consider what services (delivery, sales help, charge accounts, parking, etc.) customers want included as part of the 'total' product they are buying and use this information to develop store policies.

Example of what customers buy
Thandeka had a little gift shop and realised that she had very few business people purchasing gifts from her shop. When investigating this, she found that the business people did not have the time to shop for gifts during her existing trading hours. Thandeka decided to extend her trading hours by two hours and add an extra service for these very busy customers. Thandeka devised a catalogue from which business shoppers could choose gifts. Customers could call her with a gift order; she would wrap the gift and deliver the gift to the addressee at a small additional cost. All of this could be paid for by credit card. By doing this, Thandeka ensured that her customers had a total product offering focused on convenience.

How do customers buy?

Retailers can benefit from knowing how much influence they have over the customer's purchase decision. Do your customers buy from a retailer because of the store's name and reputation or on the basis of the brand names the store carries? Are your customers price-conscious or style-conscious? Knowing how your customers buy will help you to establish realistic policies and stock the right merchandise.

Example of how customers buy
The camping store that has built a reputation for knowledgeable sales help and reliable service need not buy more expensive merchandise simply to show known brand names, because the customer service offered attracts customers into the store. On the other hand, a high-fashion clothing store will want to display clothing from well-known designers in order to attract customers into the store.

After answering these five questions, retailers should meet the demands that they have identified.

Intermediaries

A good example of an intermediary is an estate agent, who acts as the go-between in a transaction between the buyer and seller of a house and earns a commission for their efforts. Intermediaries play a vital role in bridging the gap between consumers and the manufacturer, and include wholesalers, retailers, commercial agents and brokers. Financial intermediaries, such as banks and insurers, also play a role in the transfer of products and services from the manufacturer to consumers. In the case of restaurants, it could be said that food wholesalers and financial intermediaries, such as banks, play an important role in bridging the gap between the consumer and the restaurant. Without reliable wholesalers providing high-quality produce at reasonable prices, and banks providing the necessary funding in order to start a restaurant or restaurant franchise, the success of the restaurant could be negatively affected.

The dynamic and ever-changing nature of new trends in turnover and consumption are responsible for the development of new types of intermediaries. An example of contemporary trends in the South African context includes extended shopping hours and the increase in the number of spaza shops and franchises.

Now that the variables of the market environment have been discussed, we focus on the variables in the retailer's internal or micro-environment.

The internal or micro-environment

The internal environment consists of all the variables that need to be controlled by management in order for the retail organisation to be successful. Many management theorists regard the retailing environment as consisting only of external variables. Consequently, only external variables are considered when the organisation's information needs are discussed. It is, however, as important to analyse the internal environment as it is the external environment. In this regard, remember that we believe that the strategy and product(s) of the firm must be developed (or adapted) according to the situation in the external environment – not vice versa. The aim is to align the strengths of the organisation with the opportunities presented in the external environment.

Identifying the strengths and weaknesses of the firm is, therefore, an important dimension of the strategic planning exercise of any business. Important factors in the internal environment of a retailer include:

- ❏ The mission and objectives of the business;
- ❏ The management of the organisation, which includes the functional management (such as marketing, finance, purchasing and operations [production], and human resources management);
- ❏ The physical and intangible resources of the firm;
- ❏ The marketing strategy (the target market and marketing plan – also called the four Ps: product, place [distribution], promotion and price) and the organisational structure;
- ❏ The past and present results of the business;
- ❏ The business culture;
- ❏ The strengths and weaknesses of the organisation;
- ❏ Its unique or core competencies.

In this chapter, we will focus on one variable only, that is, the analysis of the human resources of the organisation, and why this variable is so vitally important to the success of the retail organisation.

Analysing human resources

How many of us will ever see George Steyn, the CEO of the Pep Group, when we go shopping at Pep Stores? None of us! We only see the staff of that particular store. It is for this reason that employees are critical to a retail store's success as employees are the face of the organisation. They may attract customers, but they may also drive them away. Employees are directly or indirectly in contact with customers. Whether they sell products, work behind the counters or are responsible for displays, they sell the business with its products and services to customers – hence the need to employ the right personnel. Not everyone will be suitable for a particular business. A retailer cannot employ someone and hope to change them to suit the business. The people working for a retailer are in contact with customers and will, therefore, affect their perceptions of the store, which means that they could influence customers to never visit the store again!

Unlike merchandise prices that a retailer can reduce if a particular item is not selling well, a retailer cannot simply dismiss an employee who is not performing well. This emphasises the fact that a retailer must employ the right person from the start. If the retailer employs someone who is incapable of doing the job, this increases the workload of the other employees. Money may therefore be wasted on unproductive employees. It is important for anyone involved in human resource management to consider the following aspects:

❐ Human resource planning;
❐ Recruitment and selection of potential employees;
❐ Training and development of employees;
❐ Motivating, evaluating and remunerating personnel.

We discuss each of these aspects in more detail.

Human resource planning

Human resource planning entails addressing three aspects: job analysis, job description and job specification. A job analysis may be described as the orderly and systematic evaluation of all the facts about the job. It determines the tasks, duties and responsibilities of the job, and the skills, experience, education and physical abilities the employee should have to meet the minimum job requirements. A job description specifies the duties an employee has to perform in order of priority. These should be stated clearly, since some duties cannot be measured quantitatively. Being nice to customers is too broad a description. It is necessary to specify something more concrete such as welcoming customers to your store within 30 seconds of their arrival.

Employees' duties should be prioritised, and they should not be expected to do too many diverse tasks as this could confuse them and result in them forgetting their priorities. Retailers should decide on the most important duties and place them in order of priority. Deciding on which duties are important will depend on what a retailer wishes to achieve in their business.

A job specification clearly states the minimum qualifications, competencies and abilities a person must have to be considered for a job. Qualification criteria include education and training requirements and/or basic knowledge and skill requirements. Certain characteristics are important for salespeople. These include a positive attitude, healthy ego, friendliness and goal orientation. The qualifications a person needs in order to do the job should be listed. These will vary from one retailer to the next. However, a retailer should not be too specific in this section, since potentially excellent salespeople may not have all the qualifications. Hence the basic requirements should be specified. If you page through a newspaper you will see the types of qualifications applicants need to have before they can apply successfully for certain jobs.

Recruitment and selection

Two of the most crucial elements when obtaining human resources for a business are the recruitment and selection of potential employees. It is essential to employ the right people, as employees affect profitability in many ways. Recruitment describes all the activities performed in the process of identifying and attracting a pool of candidates, from which some will later be selected to receive job offers. There are two sources from which potential employees may be drawn, internal sources and external sources.

Internal sources of potential employees

Promotion within a firm can be an extremely powerful tool to motivate and retain quality employees. Someone who knows the existing working environment may make a better contribution to the job than someone from outside. The advantages of internal recruitment are that the retailer knows the employee, the cost of recruitment is low, the transition to the new job is accomplished with the least disruption and internal promotion may motivate others to work harder for future promotions.

External sources of potential employees

Walk-ins, schools, public employment offices, private employment agencies, employee referrals, advertising and temporary employment agencies are external sources of employees. A walk-in basically means that an individual walks into a business to seek employment. Secondary and tertiary institutions provide various levels of skilled people. Although the people who come out of these institutions do acquire a certain amount of practical knowledge, they often lack practical experience in the retailing field. Public employment offices and private employment agencies may offer an additional service of supplying employees. Employees may also know of suitable applicants and refer them to the retailer. Some retailers advertise their need for employees in newspapers and trade magazines. Employment agencies help to fill temporary positions by providing temporary personnel. Kelly Girls or Quest Personnel, for example, provide these kinds of services.

During the selection process the individual best suited to the job from the list of qualified applicants is identified. Matching job requirements to employee attributes is the objective of this process. There are several methods of gathering additional information on prospective employees. These include application forms, personal interviews, reference checks, psychological and aptitude tests, and physical examinations.

Training and development

Once an employee has been recruited, the process of training and development starts. New employees require initial training and follow-up training may be done to reinforce their skills. Later on, employees may be exposed to developmental training that contributes to job growth. Finally, management development programmes enable them to reach their full potential.

New recruits should be trained to prepare them for the duties for which they have been hired. If employees do not undergo training they have to learn by trial and error, which wastes time and money. Training to improve skills may be done throughout the business because environmental factors change constantly and retailers need to update employees' knowledge and skills constantly. The development process starts with an employee's first day or two on the job. It is during this time that new employees may feel lost because they are confronted with a new physical layout, different job title, unfamiliar fellow employees, different supervision, changed working hours or schedules, and a unique set of personnel policies and procedures. Steps may be taken to help the newcomer adjust to these new surroundings. A clear explanation of performance criteria and the way in which an employee's work will be evaluated should be included in the discussion. New employees should be encouraged to ask questions and they should be given a written list of company procedures and practices.

Other more common training objectives pursued by retailers are to:

- Increase sales;
- Lower costs;
- Increase profits;
- Lower the rate of employee turnover;
- Reduce errors;
- Upgrade skill levels;
- Improve job performance;
- Develop positive work attitudes;
- Maintain good morale;

❑ Motivate employees;
❑ Improve quality of service;
❑ Make employees more productive.

Job descriptions and specifications also regulate the type of training appropriate for non-managerial employees. On-the-job training may be effective if it does not hinder the normal working activities, but needs to be properly planned. When using the apprenticeship method of staff training, new employees watch someone with experience doing a specific task before being assigned to the task themselves. In this way the employee learns by watching first and then doing a task. After a while the employee will receive a component or two of the work to do and later the whole task. New employees will model themselves on the owner of the retail business.

Experienced employees in the business may be assigned to the task of training new employees. The experienced employees may then be the role model for the new ones.

Motivating, evaluating and remunerating personnel

Keeping salespeople motivated and positive is a challenging task. To understand motivation we should consider Maslow's hierarchy of needs. Maslow stated that higher needs become important only after the basic needs have been fulfilled. People at different levels of Maslow's triangle will be motivated differently. Some people prefer belonging to a group, which can be stimulated by group contests. Others strive for achievement and a certain level of self-esteem. These individuals are motivated by individual goals and incentives. Motivation and incentives should be appropriate for each individual, so the retailer should determine each individual's motivation needs. A combination of affiliation motivation (where team or group building is enhanced) and achievement motivation (where the individual is awarded) is necessary.

When a retailer evaluates the performance of employees, they should determine whether the employees are performing their jobs according to established standards. A sensible performance evaluation programme calls for periodic and objective appraisals of each worker's performance. Employees' weaknesses and strengths should first be determined, because these form the basis for determining compensation, possible promotion and further training. Employees should be evaluated quarterly, bi-annually or annually. New employees are often evaluated during their first year. Retailers have learnt that the most important employee factors to evaluate are performance demonstrated skills and personal attributes.

There are distinguishable categories of remuneration that the retailer needs to consider. These categories are direct compensation, indirect compensation and rewards. Direct compensation refers to the actual salary or wage the employee receives in exchange for work done. Direct compensation may be in the form of a straight salary, a straight commission, a combination of the two or a salary and bonus plan. Indirect compensation and rewards refer to the various fringe benefits an employee may be offered. Rewards are incentives that the employer may offer an employee for exceptional performance. A salesperson might, for example, receive an overseas trip for exceeding a sales budget.

Employees should be happy in their working environment to ensure positive long-term relationships with the business. Employees will be happy when they enjoy their work. This includes the benefits they receive when working for a retailer. Before an employee starts working, they should be informed about all the benefits they will receive. Benefits are certainly a positive attribute that will attract potential employees to work for the business. Salaries and wages should be competitive and comparable with similar job descriptions in other stores. If salaries are comparable, other benefits might be the deciding factor for applicants.

Bear in mind, however, that the more benefits the retailer offers, the less profit there may be. Benefits should be carefully considered, and the retailer should ensure that they are able to pay those promised.

Retailers should ensure that they pay their salespeople well. If employees start resigning at regular intervals, retailers should find out why. If employee turnover becomes higher than inventory turnover, the retailer has to do something about this immediately. If they are caught in this spiral of declining sales with fewer employees, they could be heading for disaster.

1.9 Summary

In this chapter we discussed the nature of retailing and classified the different types of retailers. We investigated the evolution of retailing through the wheel of retailing and looked at the ever-changing nature of retailing. We introduced the six 'rights' of retailing and examined the components of the retail environment, namely the external or macro-environment, the market environment and the internal or micro-environment.

1.10 Self-evaluation questions

1. Explain, with the aid of examples, the different types of retail stores that you will encounter in South Africa.
2. Describe the different types of non-store retailing in South Africa.
3. Why is it important for managers to understand the environment in which their businesses operate?
4. Use the wheel of retailing theory to explain the changes in the FMCG industry in South Africa.
5. Explain why the international environment must always be considered when evaluating the macro-environment.
6. Evaluate the use of technology in South African retailing. Identify the advantages and disadvantages of using technology in a retailing operation.

1.11 Bibliography

Cant, M. (2010). *Introduction to retailing,* 2nd edition. Cape Town: Juta.

Cox, R. & Brittain, P. (2004). *Retailing: An introduction,* 5th edition. United Kingdom: Pearson Education.

Kotler, P. & Armstrong, G. 1996. *Principles of Marketing,* 7th edition. Englewood Cliffs: Prentice Hall.

Unisa. Centre for Business Management. (2008). Only study guide: Programme in Retail Management module 1. Pretoria: Unisa.

Websites

http://www.allbusiness.com/glossaries/wheel-retailing/4943201-1.html Accessed: 29 March 2009.

http://www.info.gov.za/speeches/2009/09021114561001.htm Accessed: 12 April 2012.

http://www.mg.co.za/article/2009-01-28-sa-inflation-brakes-big-rate-cutlikely Accessed: 29 March 2009.

http://www.mg.co.za/article/2009-03-02-stats-sa-unemployment-rate-down

http://www.odysseylife.co.za/documents Accessed: 12 April 2012.

http://www.sairr.org.za/sairr-today/tertiary-education-transformation-thenumbers-tell-the-true-story-07-03-2008.html Accessed: 29 March 2009.

http://www.southafrica.info/about/facts.htm Accessed: 7 May 2012.

http://www.southafricaweb.co.za/article Accessed: 12 April 2012.

http://www.statssa.gov.za/publications/P0211/P02111stQuarter2011.pdf Accessed: 8 May 2012.

http://www.statssa.gov.za/publications/P0211/P02113rdQuarter2011.pdf Accessed: 12 April 2012.

http://www.tradingeconomics.com/south-africa/inflation-cpi Accessed: 7 May 2012.

http://www.wimpy.co.za/moments.htm. Accessed: 29 March 2009.

CHAPTER 2

Collecting marketing information

Jan A Wiid

Learning objectives

After studying this chapter you should be able to:

- Explain the concept of a retail information system (RIS);
- Discuss the components of the retail information system;
- Explain the concept of retail marketing research;
- Discuss the retail research process;
- Understand the concept of research design;
- Explain the difference between secondary and primary data;
- Elaborate on the nature of questionnaire design in detail;
- Discuss the importance of a sample plan.

2.1 Introduction

People require information for a number of reasons. For instance you would seek information for entertainment and enlightenment by watching television, seeing movies, browsing the Internet, or reading newspapers and books. In retailing, however, the retailer seeks and uses information for the purpose of decision-making. One of the most effective ways of doing this is to base fundamental decision-making and problem-solving on reliable information.

Since the retail field is very competitive and retailers' strategies and ideas are quickly copied by competitors, retailers can be successful only if they have all possible relevant information available to make effective decisions. The retail information system can supply the necessary and relevant information to the retailer so that they can develop and implement strategic plans, monitor the enterprise's current activities and adjust them, if necessary. The aim of the retail information system is to anticipate the information needs of the retailer, and gather, organise and store relevant data and make it available to retail decision-makers on an ongoing basis. It is therefore important for the retailer to install an effective information system so that sufficient appropriate information is available on a continuous basis.

The purpose of this chapter is to give an overview of retail information systems (RIS) and retail marketing research as part of the retail information system.

2.2 What is a retail information system?

A retail information system (RIS) – also referred to as a retail decision support system – can be defined as a structure or a system that is designed to accumulate, produce and supply relevant information to a retailer whenever information is required for decision-making (Terblancé, 2002). It is therefore important to distinguish between data and information. Data refers to all available statistics, opinions, facts and predictions. Information, on the other hand, refers only to data components that have been manipulated or processed to make them meaningful.

Consider the following story: Two people who took a tour in a hot-air balloon encountered unexpected wind that soon blew them off course. When they managed to lower their balloon, they shouted to a farmer on the ground, 'Where are we?' The farmer answered, 'You are right above a corn field!' The balloonists looked at each other, and one groaned, 'Some information! Highly accurate, but totally useless!' To be useful, information must be relevant, complete, accurate and current. And in business, information must also be obtained economically, that is, cost-effectively (Oz, 2004).

Meaningful information is made available for decision-making by means of a structure or system. A system is an array of components that work together to achieve a common goal, or multiple goals, by accepting input, and processing and producing output in an organised manner. A system often consists of several subsystems that all contribute to the main goal. Consider the different departments of a retail store. The marketing department sells and promotes the merchandise, while the procurement department negotiates with suppliers and buys merchandise. The finance department is responsible for budgets and payments. All of these departments work towards a common goal, which is to maximise profits.

An information system consists of data, hardware, software, telecommunications, people and procedures.

Table 2.1 Components of an information system

Data	Input that the system takes to produce information
Hardware	A computer and its peripheral equipment: input, output and storage devices; hardware also includes data communication equipment
Software	Sets of instructions that tell the computer how to take data in, how to process it, how to display information, and how to store data and information
Telecommunications	Hardware and software that facilitate fast transmission and reception of text, pictures, sound and animation in the form of electronic data
People	Information systems professionals and users who analyse organisational information needs, design and construct information systems, write computer programs, operate the hardware and maintain software

Procedures	Rules for achieving optimal and secure operations in data processing; procedures include priorities in dispensing software applications and security

Source: Adapted from Oz. (2004). Management information systems, 4th edition. Boston: Thomson Course Technology, p. 17

All information systems operate in a similar way. Data is entered into the system, where it is processed or manipulated, an output is generated and, lastly, the data and information is stored. In a retail organisation, data of products purchased are recorded by a scanner. The inventory systems process the data to create information. The information tells the retailer what items need to be stocked. Analysts can analyse the stored data statistically and write research reports addressing important questions, such as: What are the trends in customer purchases and are there regional differences?

| INPUT | ➲ | PROCESS | ➲ | OUTPUT |
| (data) | | | | (information) |

The retail information system consists of four components. Note the continuous interaction between these components.

Internal reporting (record) subsystem (Internal secondary data) Accounting reports Production reports Sales reports Quality-control reports Engineering reports Goods returned reports		Retail intelligence subsystems (External data – secondary or primary) Consumers Competitors Suppliers Distributors Professional associations Government bodies
Analytic (statistical) subsystems (Modelling framework) Statistical methods Forecasting techniques Dynamic modelling Game theory Elasticity models		Retail research subsystems (Research process) Problem definition Research design Data collection Data processing Data analysis Reporting

Figure 2.1 A retail information system

Source: Adapted from Tustin et al. (2005). Marketing research in practice. Pretoria: Unisa Press

❑ *Internal reporting subsystem: (records search)*. All organisations generate a large amount of information. Various types of information are available within the organisation in the form of sales reports, stock reports, debtors' and creditors' statements. This data remains data unless there is a proper information system that can process the data into useful information for decision-makers.

❑ *Retail intelligence* is general information about developments in the retailing environment of the organisation that helps managers to develop and change retail plans. This subsystem is the set of procedures and sources used to acquire the information. Information is obtained from libraries, government agencies, clients, suppliers, middlemen, personnel, competitors and trade sources on a regular and systematic basis.

❑ *Analytical models* are various statistical and quantitative methods that researchers use internally to generate primary information. Mathematical techniques are used to solve problems.

❑ *Retail research* is the use of scientific procedures to obtain primary information.

2.3   What is retail marketing research?

Retail marketing research is the systematic collection and analysis of information that is relevant to the retail strategy (Wiid & Diggines, 2009). Retailers cannot always make meaningful and accurate decisions using available data. Marketing research is used to collect data and process it into information that is useful and relevant for decision-making; it is a tool to produce useful information for decision-making.

Many aspects of retailing can be researched, such as the location of the shop, shop management, the products and services on offer, pricing, the image of the shop, and promotion strategies. The scope of the research to be done is determined, to a large extent, by the risks associated with the decision. If, for example, a decision must be made on where to locate a new branch, this decision involves great risk, and costly large-scale research, which takes time, is needed. The decision to purchase and display a certain brand for resale purposes involves a smaller risk so research on a smaller scale may be sufficient.

Retailers sometimes tend to use non-systematic research methods. This is due to time and cost constraints or the absence of research skills. The following are examples of non-systematic research:

❑ The use of intuition. (I think we should buy 200 pen-and-pencil sets and sell them as Christmas presents for R40 each.)

❑ A continuation of what was done before. (We have never granted credit, so why should we do it now?)

❑ The imitation of a successful competitor's strategy. (XYZ has had great success with the sale of gourmet foods. We must also stock these products.)

❏ The development of a strategy based on conversations with several individuals about their perceptions. (My friends, Peter and John, think that my prices are too high. I should lower my prices to improve my sales and profit.)

❏ The assumption that past trends will continue in the future. (The wholesale price of television sets declined by 25% during the past year. I shall wait another six months before I buy television sets, because the wholesale price may drop further.)

Retailers who use non-systematic research to collect information for decision-making run the risk of making the wrong decisions and developing and implementing incorrect strategies. The marketing research process discussed below must be followed when collecting information for decision-making. It is a systematic approach to marketing research, which reduces the risk of making wrong decisions.

The retail research process

The retail marketing research process consists of a series of activities that must be performed. This process enables the retailer to collect and process data systematically and to decrease the risk associated with decision-making (Tustin et al., 2005).

Any marketing research project consists of two parts, namely, a preliminary and a formal marketing investigation (Wiid & Diggines, 2009).

The preliminary marketing research investigation consists of the following steps:

1. Defining the nature and the extent of the problem or opportunity
2. Developing an approach to the problem (setting research objectives)
3. Designing the research
4. Conducting secondary research.

In practice an expensive and time-consuming formal marketing research investigation is often undertaken, while the information needed to solve the problem or to make use of the opportunity is in the secondary sources. The purpose of the preliminary marketing research investigation is, in fact, to research the secondary sources of information.

On completion of the preliminary marketing research investigation, the retailer may have resolved the issue by using the secondary information that was collected. Therefore no further marketing research needs to be undertaken.

If the issue is not resolved, a formal marketing research investigation must be undertaken if it is economically justified and if the retail enterprise is able to act accordingly.

The formal marketing research investigation consists of the following steps:

1. Choosing the method of collecting the primary data
2. Designing the sampling plan
3. Collecting the primary data
4. Processing and analysing the data

5. Interpreting the results and making recommendations
6. Implementing the findings.

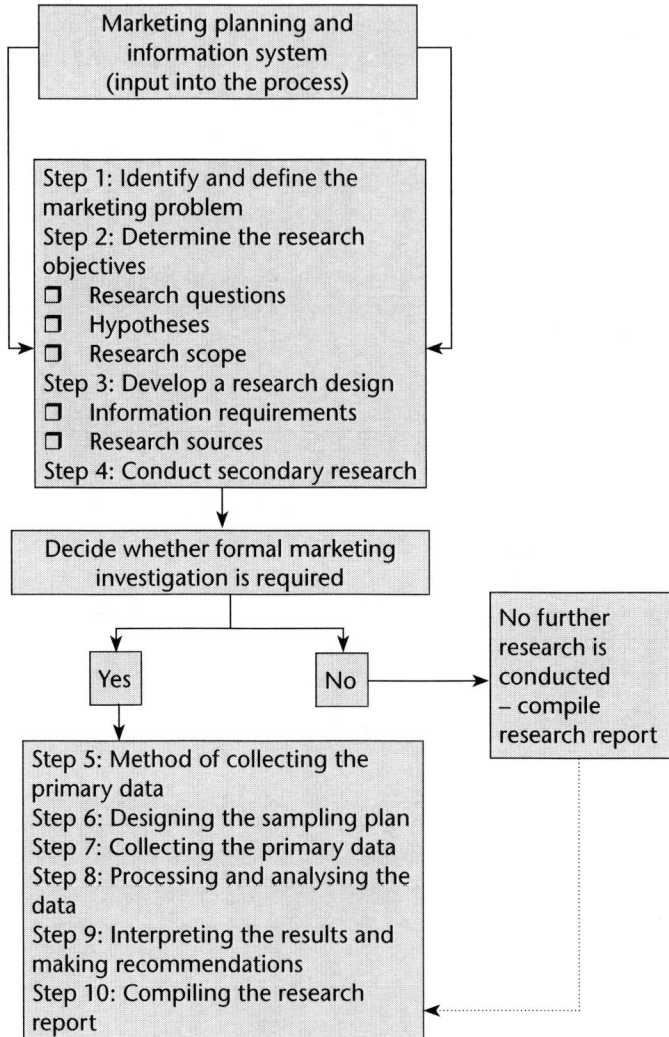

Figure 2.2 The retail marketing research process

Source: Adapted from Wiid & Diggines (2009). Marketing research. Cape Town: Juta, p. 30

It is important to understand that the various activities in the marketing research process follow on from one another. For example, secondary data cannot be investigated if the research problem has not been defined, and primary data need only be collected if the secondary data prove to be insufficient to generate sufficient information to solve the problem and to make the strategic decision. We shall discuss each component in the marketing research process.

Defining the research problem

When defining the research problem, a clear statement is given of the subject to be researched. Without a clear and precise statement of the subject to be researched, irrelevant and confusing data could be collected. A clearly defined problem statement therefore limits the scope of the marketing research investigation and gives the research project a specific direction. A clear definition of the research problem is the core of the marketing research process and indicates the kind of information that must be collected and the objectives of the research.

The following are examples of problem statements:

- ❑ Out of three potential locations for our new shop, which one should we choose?
- ❑ What should our hours of business be?
- ❑ Why is our biggest competitor so successful? How can we entice their customers away?

Develop an approach to the problem

This step includes a brief statement of purpose and the formulation of objectives and hypotheses. Research objectives give an indication of what must be achieved by the marketing research. It is usually expressed using the infinitive of the verb, for example to explore …; to describe …; to determine … etc.

The research design

Research design implies research planning and is an exposition or blueprint of the marketing research investigation that follows. The purpose of the research design is to plan and structure the specific marketing research project in such a way that the eventual validity of the research results and findings is increased. The research design is, therefore, the plan for carrying out the research investigation (Saunders, Lewis & Thornhill, 2009).

During this step the data needed and the broad framework of the procedures for the collection, processing and analysis of the data are specified. The retailer must therefore determine beforehand what type of data they will use, where they will find it, what methods and techniques they will use to collect the data, what their target market is and how the collected data will be analysed.

Once the research design has been planned, a time schedule is drawn up and the cost of the marketing research is estimated – this involves comparing the desirability and practicability of the research with its potential value.

Collecting secondary data

During this step the retailer physically begins to collect data. Secondary data is data that was collected previously for a purpose other than solving the particular problem currently under investigation. Secondary data sources may be internal (records of the enterprise, such as accounting reports, credit and sales reports, inventory records, point-of-sale scanning data, salesperson performance reports, customer complaint files, budget reports, invoices, balance sheets and income statements) or external (from outside the organisation, such as commercial publications, wholesalers, consumer and industry experts) (Cooper & Schindler, 2008).

The retailer must analyse the secondary data in terms of its relevance, accuracy, reliability and timeousness and, depending on the research problem and objectives, they must decide whether or not the formal marketing research investigation must be undertaken. If, at this stage, it is clear how the problem should be solved or how the opportunity should be exploited, no further marketing research is required.

Should the problem or opportunity not be solved after the collection of secondary data, the formal marketing research investigation should be undertaken – provided that it is economically and practically viable.

If the problem or opportunity has been solved by means of secondary research, the next action would be to communicate the findings to the decision-maker. Communication is usually in the form of a research report.

Table 2.2 Advantages and disadvantages of using secondary data

Advantages	Disadvantages
❑ When suitable secondary data is available, the retailer saves time, money and effort that they would have expended to gather primary information. ❑ Secondary data can be gathered quickly. Company or library records can be analysed immediately, while the generation of primary data may take many months. ❑ For most retailing problems, there are several sources of secondary data, hence a large quantity of data. It is therefore possible for a retailer to obtain various perspectives on solving the retailing problem. In the case of gathering primary data, there is limited available data and only one perspective is obtained. ❑ By using secondary data, the retailer can obtain information they would not normally be able to gather themselves in a formal marketing investigation, for example census statistics. ❑ A search of secondary data helps the retailer to define the problem more specifically. ❑ It is inexpensive to gather secondary data.	❑ The secondary data may favour the enterprise that published the information, and may thus be unreliable. The information may be correct, but certain facts that could harm the enterprise publishing the information may have been omitted, and it is this information that could be important to the retailer. ❑ The source of the secondary data may not be reliable since the information was not researched systematically. ❑ It is difficult to obtain secondary data that is suitable for the current marketing problem being investigated. The data may not be suitable for the retailer's target market, or the sample used may not be big enough to reflect the retailer's target market accurately. ❑ The secondary data may be outdated and no longer applicable to the current situation (for example, new fashions), since factors in the external environment change quickly.

The method of collecting primary data

Primary data, in other words data specifically intended for solving the problem or taking advantage of the opportunity, are collected during the formal marketing research investigation. Primary data are data that were not collected previously and that have to be extracted through original research. Primary data can be obtained through internal and/or external sources. Internal sources are, for example, the staff of the enterprise, and external sources are, for example, the consumers, clients, wholesalers and competitors (Saunders, Lewis & Thornhill, 2009).

Table 2.3 Advantages and disadvantages of primary data

Advantages	Disadvantages
❑ The gathered data are adapted to the specific purpose for which the retailer needs them. In other words, the data are relevant to the problem being researched. ❑ The data are current. ❑ Since the retailer gathers the data themselves or hires a market research company to do so, the source is known, reliable and controllable. ❑ The validity and reliability of the data can also be determined, if necessary.	❑ Primary data are more expensive to obtain than secondary data. ❑ The gathering of primary data is more time-consuming. ❑ Some types of primary data cannot be gathered by a single retailer, for example, census information. ❑ If the problem is not defined specifically enough, irrelevant data can be gathered.

Primary data can be collected by observation, experimentation, simulation or the survey method. Each method of data collection requires a different technique. There is not one best method of solving the problem. The method selected to collect data is, however, influenced by the research objectives, the type of research undertaken and the availability of time, funds, staff and facilities. Each method of data collection has advantages and disadvantages and the retailer must select the method that will generate satisfactory, useful and reliable data as cheaply and quickly as possible.

For each method of data collection, namely observation, simulation, experimentation and the survey method, an instrument can be designed. The two most important research instruments for collecting primary data are the questionnaire and mechanical or electronic equipment.

Mechanical or electronic equipment can be used to collect primary data during observation, experimentation and simulation. These include instruments such as galvanometers, cameras, electronic and mechanical meters and computers. These instruments range from simple counters (for example, the number of people who go through a turnstile) to sophisticated instruments measuring reaction (for example, instruments that measure the emotional reaction to a specific advertisement).

The questionnaire is the most commonly used instrument for collecting primary data and is used mostly in the survey method (Cant, Van Heerden & Ngambi, 2010).

Designing the questionnaire

The purpose of questionnaires is to collect specific information accurately and reliably. A questionnaire should fulfil the following five functions (Cooper & Schindler, 2008):

1. The questions put to the respondent must be clear.
2. The questionnaire should encourage the respondent to answer the questions openly and truthfully and it must assure them that all answers will be dealt with confidentially.
3. It must stimulate the respondents' thought processes and encourage them to recall their actions with the help of relevant information.
4. It must contain clear instructions.
5. The objectives of the interview must be stated clearly so that the results can be measured against these.

Designing a questionnaire is a difficult task. There are no fixed rules, but by following a few guidelines the questionnaire survey method can be reasonably successful. These guidelines are discussed below.

Determining the required information

The formulation of survey objectives provides a clear indication of the type of question that should be included in the questionnaire to meet these survey objectives. The information to be collected must, therefore, eventually satisfy the research objectives of the preliminary investigation.

Collecting information by using a questionnaire

There are three methods of collecting information when using a questionnaire: by post, by telephone and through personal interviews. The method used will depend on the person collecting the information. This choice then influences the design of the questionnaire (Cant, Van Heerden & Ngambi, 2010).

❑ The postal survey (including electronic media, e.g. Internet, cellphone, etc.): Because it is virtually impossible to clear up ambiguity or unclear questions in postal surveys, the design of the questionnaire must receive particular attention.

❑ The telephone survey: The advantage of the telephone survey is that it can be dealt with quickly, is relatively cheap and can be conducted fairly easily. Not everybody, however, has a telephone so a representative cross section of the population cannot be interviewed.

❑ The personal interview: Generally, more information can be collected by using this method and it is easier to do a statistically valid sample. The most important limitations are the relatively high cost, the time spent on planning and conducting the survey, and the possibility that mistakes may crop up during the interview.

The contents of individual questions

Once a decision has been made about the type of information required and the method to be used to collect the information, the individual questions for the questionnaires are formulated. The following aspects can be used as guidelines when determining the contents of individual questions.

- Is the question necessary?
- Are several questions necessary instead of just one?
- Does the respondent have the information being asked for?
- Is the question within the respondent's field of experience?
- Can the respondent remember the information? It is advisable to limit the questions to recent events, actions and phenomena.
- Will the respondent have to go to a lot of trouble to be able to answer the question?
- Will the respondent provide the information?

Types of questions included in the questionnaire

When the researcher decides on the type of question to be included in the questionnaires, the likely response or answer of the respondent must be taken into consideration. There are various types of questions that can be used in questionnaires. These can be divided into three basic groups: informal, open and closed questions.

Informal questions
There is no specific format for informal questions, and the type of questions may differ from interview to interview. These questions are not specifically structured so there is no prescribed wording that the interviewer (fieldworker) must follow. The fieldworker is, however, given certain objectives to fulfil regarding the information that is required, and several practical examples of questions are given, which can be used to increase the possibility of success. There are three types of informal interviewing:

1. *Depth interviews* – psychoanalytic techniques are used by asking intensive questions that investigate the respondent's experiences, attitudes or other reactions. This type of interview is usually quite time-consuming and is dealt with by one interviewer.
2. *Focus groups* – a number of people are interviewed simultaneously and group discussion of a given topic is encouraged. The person conducting the interview acts as mediator, and can start the discussion by asking a structured question. Depending on how the discussion goes, they can ask more questions to stimulate the discussion further so that the required information can be obtained.
3. *Projection techniques* – the respondent is asked to 'project' their own opinion on a situation. An example of this technique is a cartoon with an ambiguous meaning; two characters appear in the cartoon, but there is a caption for only one of the characters. The respondent is asked to provide a caption for the second character.

Open questions
These are structured questions, while the answer is unstructured. The respondent's answer may contain any information they have. A question such as 'What do you think of XYZ's current television advertisement?' is an example of an open question and may invite a variety of answers from different respondents (Bryman & Bell, 2007).

Closed questions
There are a variety of closed questions in which both the question and the answer are structured. Five groups of closed questions can be used, namely dichotomy questions, ranking, checklist and multiple-choice questions and scales.

Table 2.4 Five groups of closed questions for use in questionnaires

Dichotomy questions	The respondent has only two alternatives such as 'yes' or 'no'. This type of question is easy to ask and easy for the respondent to answer. These can be used only for collecting simple facts.
Ranking	This type of question obtains the opinion of the respondents by asking them to arrange a list of items in order of preference or according to regular use. The advantage of these questions is that it is easy to tabulate the items and to provide the respondent with a definite list of items. The disadvantage, however, is that the information can be misleading if some of the items on the list are not familiar to the respondent or if they are not part of their everyday use.
Checklist	The respondent is expected to choose the facts or products listed that are relevant to them, such as their income group, or the type of car they drive. This method is ideal for collecting factual information, and the researcher must ensure that all possibilities are included in the checklist.
Multiple-choice questions	A number of alternative answers are provided for each question. The respondent chooses the one alternative that is most relevant to them.
Scales	Respondents must express their opinion on a certain matter using a series of categories, such as when respondents must evaluate a number of retail stores. In the use of scales a neutral alternative is usually included for those who do not hold a definite opinion on a certain matter or event. Scales can be used to do comparative evaluations of people's motivations, attitudes and behaviour, which is sometimes of vital importance in marketing research.

The wording of questions

There are a number of important aspects regarding the wording of questions, which must be taken into consideration. The following points are important:

❒ Define the problem clearly. Aspects such as who, where, what, when, why and how must be clear in the specific question.

❒ Must the question be subjective or objective?

❒ Must the question be positive or negative?

❒ Use simple words that are familiar to everyone.

❒ Avoid ambiguous questions.

❒ Avoid questions that indicate the answer, such as 'This is a very reliable car, isn't it?'

❒ Avoid generalisations and ask the question in specific terms.

❒ Avoid unfair questions or first explain those questions that the respondent may regard as being unfair.

❒ Use alternative methods of asking questions. There is no correct way of asking questions. It is therefore advisable to ask half the questions in one way and the other half in another way.

The order of questions

The order in which questions are asked in a questionnaire is important for a number of reasons:

❒ The first questions must stimulate the respondent's interest.

❒ Questions that may cause problems must be asked later.

❒ Bear in mind the influence questions may have on those that follow.

❒ Arrange the questions in such a way that the respondent will regard them as following a logical pattern.

Layout and reproduction of the questionnaire

The following aspects regarding the layout and reproduction of the questionnaire are important:

❒ The physical appearance and layout of the questionnaire influence the attitude of the respondent towards the survey.

❒ Checking the questionnaire is made easier if the questionnaire is numbered and coded beforehand.

❒ The manageability of the questionnaire is important – the physical size of the questionnaire facilitates the fieldwork and the office work of the survey.

Provisional testing of the questionnaire

The questionnaire should be tested on a small scale before it is used on a large scale to collect primary data. During the pre-test the success of the various aspects mentioned above can be tested and the necessary changes can be made. After each meaningful revision of the questionnaire it must be tested again until it is finally approved.

Designing the sampling plan

During this stage the scope of the formal marketing research investigation is determined. In other words, the retailer must identify the individuals or respondents who will be involved in the research. If the survey population (universe) is too large for a comprehensive survey, a scientific sample must be taken of the population (Cant, 2010). Naturally, the requirement is that the sample must represent the universe as well as possible. Three basic aspects that must be considered during this stage are the definition of the universe (which includes a definition of the sampling frame and the sample units), the method of sampling and the size of the sample.

Collecting primary data

Primary data are data that are collected to solve the specific problem being researched. This step in the marketing research process involves the physical implementation of the research design (research plan) used in the collection of data. Since the retailer now knows who will be involved in the investigation (sample units), the method and techniques of data collection and the research instrument (questionnaire) must be implemented to collect the data. The investigation or fieldwork therefore involves the actual collection of the primary data from the sample units or the respondents (Berndt & Petzer, 2011).

The investigation is often the most expensive aspect of the research process and there is a good chance that mistakes will be made. Thorough attention must be paid to the selection, training and supervision of the fieldworkers. The investigation must be planned meticulously and clear instructions and appropriate methods of motivation must be used to maximise the co-operation and honesty of the respondents and the fieldworkers.

Processing and analysing the data

Once secondary and primary data have been collected, the data must be prepared and processed to relate the collected information to the research problem. Collected data must be edited, codified and tabulated to facilitate processing and analysis. During large surveys that require computer processing, questionnaires are coded beforehand so that data can be fed into the computer as quickly as possible. This is considered when the questionnaire is being designed.

The data is analysed after the data processing. The retailer must study the processed data and convert it into relevant information for decision-making. The possible alternatives to solving the research problem must be defined clearly and the advantages and disadvantages of each alternative must be compared. There are various methods of data analysis ranging from very simple to highly sophisticated methods. A number of computer programs are available to assist the data processing and analysis. Specialist firms are often called in to help (Creswell, 2009).

Interpreting the results and recommendations

Once all necessary information has been collected and analysed to obtain possible alternatives for solving the marketing problem, recommendations must be made. The recommendations must be based on the best alternative or strategy that will solve the retailer's problem. The success of the marketing research process is determined by the interpretation of the results and the subsequent conclusions and recommendations (Berndt & Petzer, 2011).

The interpreted information and the conclusions and recommendations must be communicated to the decision-maker. Communication is usually in the form of a research report. The research report must be understandable, relevant, clear, concise, structured, topical, accurate and comprehensive, so that meaningful decisions can be made about the marketing problem or opportunity.

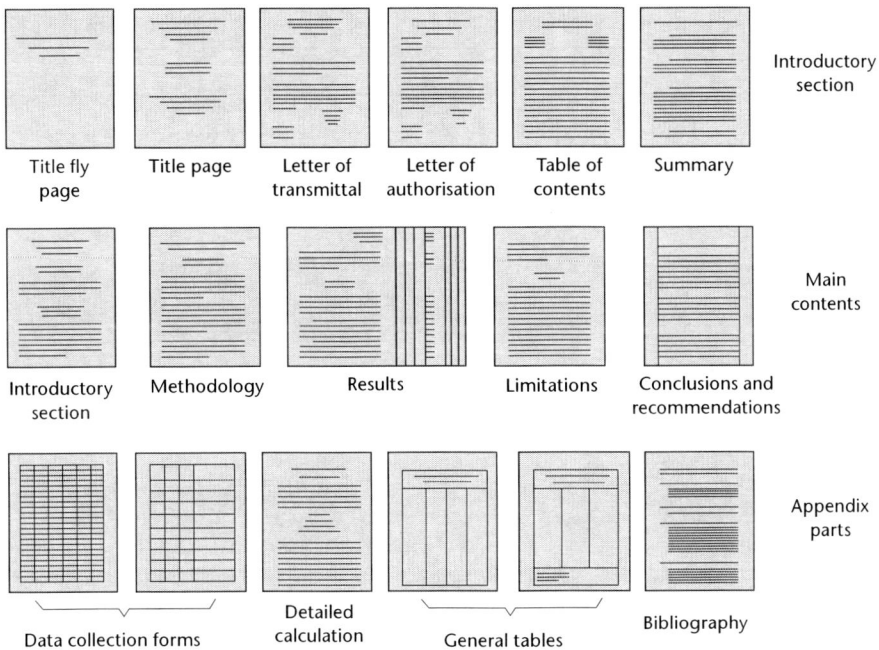

Title fly page	Title page	Letter of transmittal	Letter of authorisation	Table of contents	Summary	Introductory section

Introductory section	Methodology	Results	Limitations	Conclusions and recommendations	Main contents

Data collection forms	Detailed calculation	General tables	Bibliography	Appendix parts

Figure 2.3 Format of a research report

Source: Adapted from Wiid & Diggines (2009). Marketing research. *Cape Town: Juta, p. 261*

Implementing the findings

The recommendations must now be implemented, even if they conflict with the retailer's idea of what is the best. The retailer's idea of what is best is based on their own intuition, while the findings of the marketing research survey are based on concrete facts that were collected and analysed systematically.

2.4   Summary

Sometimes retailers do not have reliable and adequate information to make a meaningful decision about a retail problem. To collect valid and reliable information for decision-making, several systematic and step-by-step procedures are required and are known as the marketing research process. Retailers who use non-systematic research to collect information for decision-making run the risk of making incorrect decisions and developing and implementing the wrong strategies. The marketing research process is a systematic approach to marketing research, which reduces the risk associated with wrong decisions.

The marketing research process will differ from problem to problem. Although this is the case, any marketing research project consists of two parts, namely a preliminary and a formal marketing research investigation. On completion of the preliminary marketing research investigation, the problem/opportunity may be solved and the formal investigation does not need to be undertaken. The formal investigation, however, cannot be undertaken successfully unless a preliminary investigation is first undertaken.

Primary information is gathered if secondary information does not solve the marketing problem, and it is gathered to solve a particular marketing problem. The main methods or sources of gathering primary data are the survey method, observation, experimentation and simulation. Primary data have the advantage that they are current, but they are time-consuming and expensive to gather.

A retail information system should gather relevant information systematically, continuously and periodically, in order to analyse and report back to retail decision-makers.

Mini case study
Coca-Cola launched Bibo and Nestea (an iced tea brand) in Mozambique in the same type of pouch packaging, without any research having been conducted before the time. Only afterwards did they discover that women, in particular, did not want to buy their iced tea in the same packaging as their children's drinks, so the launch of Nestea was a flop. Proper marketing research may very well have prevented these unsuccessful product launches.

2.5   Self-evaluation questions

1.   Coca-Cola made a huge mistake by not conducting research. What should they have done? Explain the process in detail.
2.   Guide Coca-Cola in their design of a questionnaire, as well as the questions for their research.

2.6   Bibliography

Berndt, A. & Petzer, D. (2011). *Marketing research*. Cape Town: Pearson Education.

Bryman, A. & Bell, E. (2007). *Business research methods,* 2nd edition. New York: Oxford University Press.

Cant, M. (2010). *Introduction to retailing,* 2nd edition. Cape Town: Juta.

Cant, M.C., Van Heerden, C.H. & Ngambi, H.C. (2010). *Marketing management: South African perspective.* Cape Town: Juta.

Cooper, D.R. & Schindler, P.S. (2008). *Business research methods,* 10th edition. New York: McGraw Hill.

Creswell, J.W. (2009). *Research design: Qualitative, quantitative and mixed method approach,* 3rd edition. London: Sage.

Evans, J.R. (1989). *Retail management: A strategic approach,* 4th edition. Basingstoke: Macmillan.

Oz, E. (2004). *Management information systems,* 4th edition. Boston: Thomson Course Technology.

Saunders, M., Lewis, P. & Thornhill, A. (2009). *Research methods for business students,* 5th edition. Harlow: Pearson Education.

Terblancé, N. (2002). *Retail management.* Cape Town: Oxford University Press.

Tustin, D., Ligthelm, A.A., Martin, J.H. & Van Wyk, H. de J (eds). (2005). *Marketing research in practice.* Pretoria: Unisa Press.

Wiid, J.A. & Diggines, C.N. (2009). *Marketing research.* Cape Town: Juta.

3

Merchandise planning and selection

Colin N Diggines

Learning objectives

After studying this chapter you should be able to:

☐ Describe what merchandise planning entails;
☐ Discuss the steps to be followed when developing the merchandise plan (merchandise budget) in Rand;
☐ Explain the methods that can be used to plan stock levels;
☐ Conduct basic merchandise-planning calculations;
☐ Discuss merchandise planning in units and distinguish between the three merchandise lists.

3.1 Introduction

Consumers are more knowledgeable with less available time to spend on the things that they want to be doing. When they go to the shops with a list of goods to purchase they expect, and in some cases nowadays even demand, that the products be available in the style, colour and quantity they want. It is up to the retailer to ensure that they are able to meet their customers' 'reasonable' requirements by having the merchandise available in their stores.

Merchandise management includes the planning and controlling of the retailer's merchandise inventory. It is an extremely important task if the retailer wants to offer the right product, in the right place, at the right time, in the right quantities and at the right price. Merchandise planning consists of establishing objectives and devising plans to achieve these objectives. In the merchandise-planning process, planning in Rand occurs in the form of merchandise budgets and planning in units by developing merchandise lists.

Merchandise control includes the development of inventory information and analysis systems, in units or in Rand, for the gathering, recording, analysis and use of merchandise data to determine whether the set objectives have been reached. Merchandise planning thus involves establishing performance guidelines, while merchandise control means determining how well those guidelines are followed. Only the merchandise-planning process will be discussed in this chapter.

3.2 Merchandise planning

The primary objective of merchandise planning is to satisfy both the customer's merchandise needs and the retailer's financial needs. To achieve this objective, the retailer must develop merchandise plans that create an acceptable balance between merchandise in stock and sales. To maintain this balance between stock and sales, the retailer has to plan each merchandise category with regard to inventory investment, inventory assortment and inventory support.

☐ *Inventory investment* involves planning the total Rand investment in merchandise inventory so that the enterprise can realise its financial objectives.

☐ *Inventory assortment* involves planning the number of the various product items (brand, style, size, colour, material and price combinations) the retailer should keep in stock within a particular product line, and determining whether this assortment meets the merchandise needs of the target market.

☐ *Inventory support* refers to planning the number of units of each product item the retailer should have available to meet the sales forecast.

Planning in both Rand value and in units is important in merchandise planning and needs the retailer's full attention. Figure 3.1 illustrates the merchandise-planning process in its entirety. It is important from the outset that you understand the distinction between the two components.

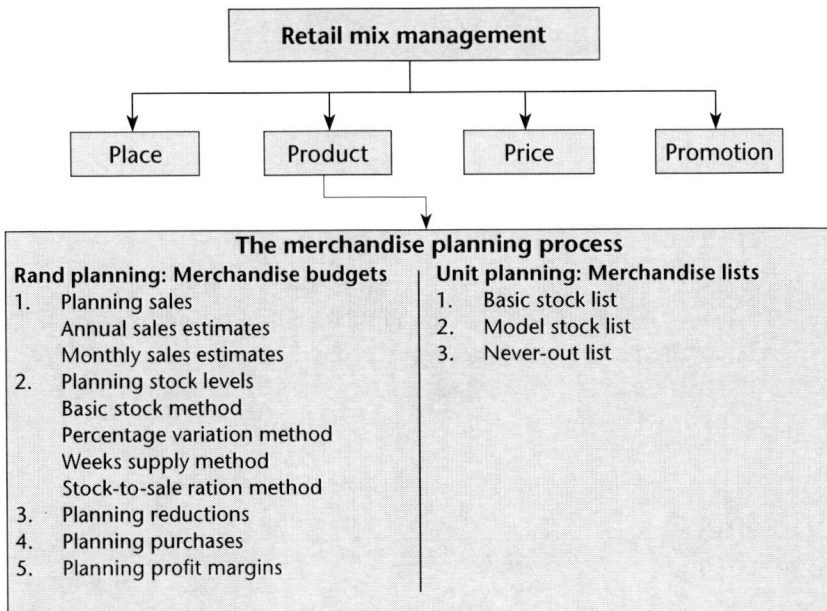

```
                    ┌──────────────────────────────┐
                    │     Retail mix management     │
                    └──────────────────────────────┘
         ┌──────────────┬──────────────┬──────────────┐
    ┌─────────┐   ┌─────────┐    ┌─────────┐   ┌─────────────┐
    │  Place  │   │ Product │    │  Price  │   │  Promotion  │
    └─────────┘   └─────────┘    └─────────┘   └─────────────┘
```

The merchandise planning process	
Rand planning: Merchandise budgets	**Unit planning: Merchandise lists**

1. Planning sales
     Annual sales estimates
     Monthly sales estimates
2. Planning stock levels
     Basic stock method
     Percentage variation method
     Weeks supply method
     Stock-to-sale ration method
3. Planning reductions
4. Planning purchases
5. Planning profit margins
	1. Basic stock list
	2. Model stock list
	3. Never-out list

Figure 3.1 The merchandise-planning process

Source: Adapted from Levy & Weitz (2012). Retailing management, *8th edition. New York: McGraw Hill, and Berman & Evans (2012).* Retail management: A strategic approach, *11th edition. New Jersey: Pearson*

3.3   Merchandise planning in Rand

Merchandise planning in Rand is used to plan the total Rand value of stock that a retailer must carry. Merchandise planning in Rand helps the retailer to determine how much should be invested in merchandise during a specific period of time. This planning in Rand takes place when a merchandise budget (merchandise plan) is compiled. A merchandise budget (merchandise plan) is a financial plan for managing merchandise inventory investments.

A successful merchandise budget (merchandise plan) must meet the following requirements:

☐   The merchandise budget must be drawn up early enough to allow time for revision. Proper planning might entail a number of revisions and drafts before the best one is finalised. Plans that are rushed with no time for revision are destined for failure.
☐   The merchandise budget must be simple, so that all the managers can understand it, but it must also be comprehensive. The best advice is to keep it simple. The document needs to be understandable to people at all levels to ensure its correct implementation.
☐   The budget must represent the judgement of both the buyers and the sales personnel. Numerous inputs are required from different sources to ensure that all angles and perspectives are addressed.
☐   The budget must be drawn up for a period for which it is possible to make reliable estimates. The business environment is highly dynamic and many changes are experienced. Reasonable planning periods need to be established.
☐   The budget must be flexible to be able to adapt to changing conditions in the market. As mentioned in the previous point, the retail environment is dynamic with both positive and negative changes being experienced. The plan must be flexible enough to allow measures to be taken to respond to unexpected events that may arise.

When developing a plan, it is always best to follow a systematic approach to the planning to ensure that all elements are properly covered. Compiling the merchandise budget (merchandise plan) consists of the five sequential steps identified in Figure 3.2.

Each of the five steps in the compilation of a merchandise budget (merchandise plan) will be discussed in more detail.

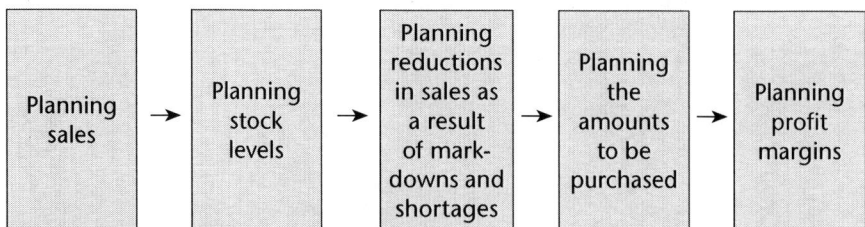

Figure 3.2 Steps in compiling the merchandise plan

Step 1 – Planning sales

The planned or forecast sales for the following planning period are the most important element of the merchandise plan/merchandise budget because all other amounts contained in the merchandise plan are derived from the planned sales. For this reason it is essential for forecast sales to be determined accurately and for the development of the merchandise budget to begin with planning sales. The retailer must decide whether they will estimate the sales of the entire store, of a certain department, or of an individual product line or product item.

It is considered better to establish separate estimates for different merchandise categories or product lines in order to obtain more accurate estimates, and to ensure a greater degree of control over the drafting of the merchandise plan and its execution.

The rationale behind starting the merchandise plan with a sales estimate is that the volume of expected sales determines the following factors:

❑ *Variable costs.* Variable costs, such as delivery costs and sales commission, vary in direct relation to sales.

❑ *Fixed costs.* Fixed costs, such as rent, water and electricity do not usually change if sales increase, but these costs may rise if there is a large increase in sales.

❑ *Greater need for funds.* If sales are going to increase, extra funds are needed to purchase stock and other resources to ensure that deadlines are met.

❑ *Increase or decrease in other expenses.* Examples of other expenses include storage costs, delivery costs and salaries.

In the estimation of sales volumes, retailers need to consider the following:

❑ *Past sales figures.* Past sales figures must be analysed because they can give an indication of future sales. Sales records indicate what products, styles, colours, prices and quantities were purchased by customers in the past, and can be used to determine the type and quantity of goods they will purchase this season.

❑ *General business conditions.* When economic conditions are good and there is little unemployment, sales will increase. In times of recession, sales will drop. Retailers must thus gather information on economic conditions, and do their own research on national and local economic conditions, and on changes in consumer markets.

❑ *Competition.* A retailer's planned sales can be influenced by the opening of a new store by a competitor, the expansion of an existing competitor, or a change in the marketing communication strategy of an existing competitor. Each one needs to be carefully monitored.

❑ *Trends in consumer demand.* The start of a fashion trend will increase the demand for that particular fashion item, and planned sales will thus have to increase. It is important to be mindful of the planning term – short term and long term.

❑ *Changes in policy.* Changes in the layout of the store can make a specific merchandise line more accessible to the customers, which will bring about increased sales. When the image of a store is improved, it will lead to a drop in the sales of low-priced articles, and an increase in the sales of higher-priced articles.

When engaging in sales planning the retailer can develop annual, monthly, or seasonal estimates of future sales. Let us consider each of these estimates in more detail.

Estimating annual sales

By investigating the past sales figures and plotting these on a graph, retailers can determine past sales patterns and from that identify possible future sales trends. This approach to estimating sales is known as time-series forecasting. Time-series forecasting, as a method of sales forecasting, is used frequently by retailers as it is economical and simple to use. However, while it is suitable for forecasting the sales of staple products, it is not suitable for forecasting the sales of fashion articles.

Before moving on let us first ensure that you understand the difference between staple merchandise and fashion merchandise.

❑ *Staple merchandise* refers to merchandise that is in continuous demand over a long period. Consumers buy these items on a regular basis and a change in price does not always result in a decrease in demand. Examples of staple merchandise include bread, milk, soap, toothpaste and deodorants. Forecasting the demand for staple merchandise is relatively easy as the demand for the products is so consistent.

❑ *Fashion merchandise* is merchandise that is in demand for only a short time. Sales of these items are highly cyclical and change as people's tastes and lifestyles change. Examples of fashion merchandise include cellphone models, hairstyles, shoes and clothes. The erratic nature of fashion merchandise makes it difficult to forecast demand accurately.

This topic of estimating annual sales will be addressed using the following practical example. Figure 3.3 is a diagrammatic representation of a cycle retailer's sales of road bikes and mountain bikes for the years 2005 to 2011.

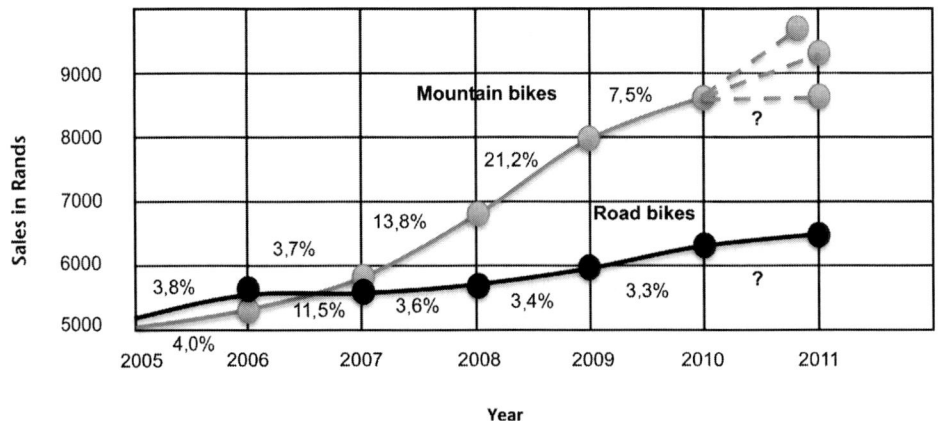

Figure 3.3 Example of mountain bike versus road bike sales

As may be deduced from the graph, the sales of both road and mountain bikes increased, although the amount and stability of the increases differed for the two products.

The sales figures show that the sales of road bikes increased constantly over the six years, but at a decreasing rate. It is thus possible to conclude that road bikes are in the maturity stage of the product life cycle, and that the future sales of this product will be reasonably stable and predictable.

Conversely, the sales figures for mountain bikes indicate that although sales increased over the six years, the increases differed drastically from year to year. Sales of mountain bikes increased at a growing rate and it may thus be concluded that the product has moved through the growth phase of its product life cycle. In 2010, the sales figures for mountain bikes showed that although sales had increased, this was at a decreasing rate (7,5% compared to 21,2% the year before), which indicates that the product may have reached the maturity phase of its product life cycle. Therefore, the sales estimate for 2011 will probably be less accurate for mountain bikes than for road bikes, because retailers are unable to predict with certainty whether the product's sales will increase, remain constant or drop.

An estimate of the sales in 2011 can be made by means of judgemental or qualitative methods. Two examples of these methods are fixed and variable adjustment procedures.

❐ *Fixed adjustment method*

Under this method, the retailer adjusts the previous year's sales figures by a certain fixed percentage in order to predict the following year's sales. The direction of the adjustment (plus or minus) and the size of the adjustment are based on the retailer's experience with past sales of each merchandise category. The use of the fixed adjustment method works well in the forecasting of future sales when a stable sales pattern has been identified. When the past sales differ dramatically from one sales period to another, however, this method cannot be used. It is unacceptable to simply add a standard fixed percentage, for example 4%, 6% or 8%, to the sales of the previous year 'to beat last year's sales'. This approach does not take into consideration the fact that different merchandise categories are in different phases of their product life cycles and have to be analysed and adapted separately. Beating last year's sales is a suitable sales objective for the enterprise as a whole, but is not an acceptable method for estimating the sales of individual merchandise categories.

❐ *Variable adjustment method*

Using this method, the retailer determines a certain percentage change in the sales, based on past sales figures. This percentage is then adjusted upwards or downwards depending on the nature of the merchandise concerned and the influence of environmental conditions.

The following external environmental factors can be considered when deciding on this percentage adjustment:

- The general prosperity of local and national markets;
- The inflation rate;
- The possible development of recessionary conditions;
- Discernible trends in the growth or decrease of the target market population;
- Changes in the demographic characteristics of the target market;
- Developing legal or social restrictions;
- Changes in the competitive environment;
- Changes in the needs and lifestyle of the consumer.

Internal factors that can be considered are:

- Changes in the size and location of the sales space allocated to a specific merchandise category;
- Changes in the type and degree of promotion done;
- Changes in the retailer's policy, for example longer business hours, better service, and so on.

In summary, it may be said that the estimated annual sales of a specific merchandise category consist of the previous year's sales figure plus or minus a fixed or variable percentage adjustment. The retailer needs to be extremely diligent when deciding on which method to use.

Estimating monthly sales

Estimating monthly sales comprises three steps, namely estimating annual sales, estimating monthly sales and the adjustment of these monthly sales by means of an index of monthly sales.

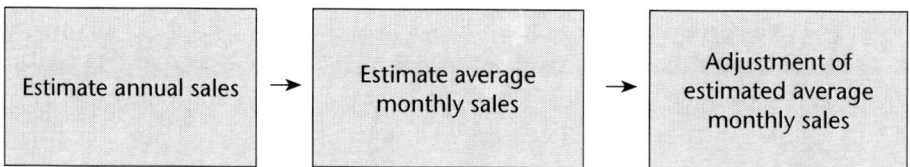

| Estimate annual sales | → | Estimate average monthly sales | → | Adjustment of estimated average monthly sales |

Figure 3.4 Estimating monthly sales

❑ *Step 1 – Estimating annual sales*
The procedure for estimating annual sales was discussed earlier in this chapter and will not be discussed here again. Refer back to this section to refresh your memory if necessary.

❑ *Step 2 – The determination of estimated average monthly sales*
The average sales for each month are calculated by dividing the estimated annual sales by the number of months in the year, that is, by 12. This method of estimating monthly sales is adequate provided the sales of the product concerned are constant for every month of the year and there are no seasonal fluctuations. If there are

seasonal fluctuations in sales, the estimated sales figures must be adjusted to accommodate these monthly fluctuations in sales.

❑ *Step 3 – Adjustment of estimated average monthly sales*
Estimated average monthly sales are adjusted by using an index of monthly sales, which is based on past monthly sales. By using an index, the retailer can determine a sales norm for an average month, by which all other monthly sales can be adjusted. The average month is represented by an index value of 100, and any month with an index value of less than 100 has monthly sales under the norm. Months with above-average sales have an index value above 100. The retailer must do numerous calculations to determine the index of monthly sales, and once the sales index has been calculated, it is applied to adjust the average planned monthly sales.

Step 2 – Planning stock levels

The second step in the development of the merchandise plan is the determination of the quantity of stock needed to generate the planned sales. The stock level must be planned in such a way that sufficient stock is available at the beginning of the month to meet the demand, while not investing too much capital in stock and avoiding out-of-stock situations. The merchandise plan must also indicate the amount of stock that must be carried over at the end of the month to the following month. Four methods can be used to plan stock levels, namely the basic stock method, the percentage variation method, the week's supply method, and the stock-to-sales ratio method.

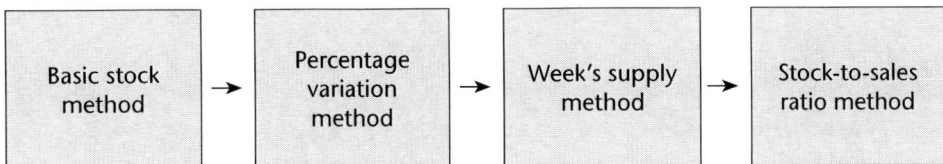

Basic stock method	→	Percentage variation method	→	Week's supply method	→	Stock-to-sales ratio method

Figure 3.5 Methods to plan stock levels

Basic stock method

The basic stock method is developed to meet sales expectations and avoid out-of-stock situations. Each month is started with stock levels equal to the estimated sales for that month, plus additional basic stock that serves as 'safety stock' in case actual sales for the month exceed estimated sales, or in case shipments are delayed or damaged and have to be returned. The disadvantage of this method is that more money has to be invested in stock and the inventory carrying costs are higher. This method is used especially by retail enterprises or departments with a low stock turnover rate.

Example
Suppose for the three-month sales period of October, November and December, the estimated sales for each month are R9 450, R27 150 and R44 400 respectively. Based on past sales records it can be concluded that the stock turnover rate (number of times the average stock on hand is sold out during a given time period) during this three-month sales period equals two. To calculate how much stock has to be available at the beginning of October, for example, the following calculation can be done:

Average monthly sales for October, November and December
= R9 450 + R27 150 + R44 400
= R81 000 ÷ 3
= R27 000.

Average stock for October, November and December
= R81 000 ÷ 2
= R40 500.

Basic stock = R40 500 – R27 000
= R13 500.

Stock needed for the beginning of the month October = Planned monthly sales (R9 450) + Basic stock (R13 500) = R22 950.

From the calculation it can be seen that a basic stock or safety stock of R13 500 is added to each month's planned sales to calculate the stock that is needed at the beginning of each month. The stock needed at the beginning of November and December can be calculated in the same way.

Percentage variation method

This method attempts to adjust stock levels in accordance with actual variations in sales. This method is used particularly for merchandise with a high turnover rate (usually more than six times a year) as it results in fewer fluctuations in stock compared to the basic stock method.

In this method the stock needed at the beginning of a month is calculated as follows:

Stock needed at the beginning of October = Average stock for October, November and December x ½ (1 + planned sales for October/Average monthly sales for October, November and December).

That is: *Stock needed at the beginning of October = R40 500 x ½ (1 + R9 450/R27 000) = R27 337,50.*

The stock needed at the beginning of November and December can be calculated in the same way.

Week's supply method

This method determines stock levels in direct relation to sales. This method uses the envisaged annual stock turnover rate to determine the amount of stock needed to cover a pre-determined number of weeks. If the stock turnover rate is 8 times per year, stock must be stored for 6,5 weeks (52 weeks divided by 8). If the average weekly sales are R3 000, the quantity of stock to be purchased for the sales period of 6,5 weeks is R3 000 x 6,5 = R19 500. This method is used particularly by retailers with merchandise categories with stable sales and stable stock turnover rates.

Stock-to-sales ratio method

This method requires that retailers keep a certain ratio of merchandise to planned monthly sales. This ratio can be 2 to 1, 3 to 1, and so on. A stock-to-sales ratio of 2 to 1 means, for example, that stock of R10 000 is required for planned monthly sales of R5 000. For this method to be effective a reliable stock-to-sales ratio has to be found. The retailer's past sales records are the best source of information for calculating this ratio.

Step 3 – Planning reductions in sales

It sometimes happens that the sales for a certain month are less than the retailer had planned either because it may have been necessary to mark certain articles down in order to attract consumers to the store and stimulate the sales of certain merchandise, or because merchandise was stolen or damaged, and could not be sold. The retailer's merchandise plan must thus provide for these markdowns and shortages, for example by allowing 5% of the month's sales as cover for the above. The percentage used can be derived from past sales figures. If the past sales figures indicate that markdowns of 6% were allowed in a certain month, and that there were shortages of 2,5%, the total planned reduction in stock for that month is 8,5% of the planned monthly sales.

Step 4 – Planning purchases

Careful planning of purchases ensures that the correct quantities of stock are available at the right time.

No retailer can afford to have too much or too little merchandise in stock, because too little stock leads to a loss in sales, and too much stock means that the capital tied up in stock cannot be invested in other projects.

The retailer calculates the quantity of merchandise that must be purchased by using the following equation and information obtained from the merchandise plan:

Planned purchases for the month = Planned sales for the month – (planned stock levels at the beginning of the month – desired stock levels at the end of the month) + shortages and planned markdowns for the month.

The closing stock of a certain month is usually equal to the opening stock of the subsequent month.

When the above equation is used, the planned purchases for the month are usually calculated based on retail prices. Since retailers do not purchase their stock at retail prices, the amount obtained from the above equation must be translated into cost price, or the amount at which the retailer purchases his merchandise.

Example
Work through the following example as a practical explanation of this concept:
Suppose that the planned sales for the month (at retail prices) were R5 000, the planned stock levels at the beginning of the month were R2 000 (at retail prices), the planned stock levels at the end of the month were R1 500 (at retail prices) and the shortages and planned markdowns for the month were R600.
The planned purchases for the month (at retail prices) are thus:
R5 000 – (R2 000 – R1 500) + R600 = R5 100
The buyer must now determine how much he can spend on purchases for the month at cost price. This is done by adjusting the planned purchases for the month (at retail prices) by the amount of the planned initial mark-up. If the initial mark-up is 40%, the planned purchases for the month (at retail prices) must be multiplied by the complement of 40%, that is, 60%.
R5 100 x 60% = R3 060 stock can thus be purchased at cost price, and this is the actual amount that the buyer can spend on purchasing stock for the month.

Step 5 – Planning profit margins

Planning the profit margin is the last step in the process of developing a merchandise plan or merchandise budget. To allow for a big enough profit, the gross profit must be sufficient to cover the operating expenses associated with buying, stocking and selling the merchandise, as well as producing an acceptable operating profit. The retailer attempts to achieve an acceptable gross profit margin and operating profit by planning the initial mark-up percentage (the percentage difference between the cost of the merchandise and the original retail price) that will cover expenses, profit and reductions.

The required initial mark-up percentage for the next year can be calculated as follows:

Suppose the estimated total annual sales are R1 800 000, the reductions are 10% of sales, in other words R180 000, and anticipated expenses are 20% of sales, in other words R360 000. If the desired profit objective is 12% of sales, or R216 000, the required initial mark-up percentage is:

(R360 000 + R216 000 + R180 000)/(R1 800 000 + R180 000) = 38,2%.

Now that we have looked at the steps in the process, refer to Table 3.1 for a basic visualisation of a retailer's merchandise plan. Take note that each of the steps in the process that has just been discussed are covered in this example. Take the time to work through the basic logic of the process with the figures given in this table.

Table 3.1 Basic merchandising plan

Merchandise plan			Product classification: hand towels			
Factor	Year		Jan	Feb	Mar	Total
Sales in Rand	Last year (actual)		500	400	350	1 250
	This year (planned)		500	500	400	1 400
Stock, beginning of month in Rand	Last year (actual)		100	100	100	300
	This year (planned)		150	200	150	500
Shortages and planned markdowns in Rand	Last year (actual)	Markdowns	25	25	20	70
		Shortages	25	25	20	70
	This year (planned)	Markdowns	30	30	25	85
		Shortages	30	30	25	85
Retail purchases in Rand	Last year (actual)		550	450		
	This year (planned)		610	510		
Initial mark-up percentage	Last year (actual)		40	40	40	
	This year (planned)		40	40	40	

3.4   Merchandise planning in units

Various merchandise lists are used to plan the number of units to be kept in stock and for the control of the number of units in stock. Based on the kind of merchandise that is sold, retailers can use one or more of these lists.

Three types of merchandise lists can be used, namely a model stock list, basic stock list and never-out list. Let us take a brief look at each of these.

Model stock list

Model stock lists are used to plan the inventory of fashion articles. A model stock list is a pre-planned list of items, determined by a store or department's policy, which should always be in stock. This plan indicates whether it is the store's policy to keep the complete range of styles and brands or only popular items. The model stock list differs from the basic stock list because the merchandise items or stock-keeping units listed in it are not described or identified in such precise terms. Stock-keeping units can thus be identified in terms of general price lines, sizes, basic colours, styles or materials.

The model stock list is thus adaptable to fashion styles that can change within a selling season because it follows a more general approach to stock planning. If the model stock list specifies that 300 dresses in the price lines of R400, R550 and R700 should be kept in stock, the retailer can buy the latest fashions and still meet the criteria stated in the model stock list.

Basic stock list

Retailers selling staple products, such as food products, hardware and cosmetic products, use basic stock lists for stock control and planning. Staple products are product items with a very stable or very variable selling pattern, but one that is still predictable.

The basic stock list is used to determine how many different merchandise items should be in stock and how many units of each should be available. The basic stock list therefore lists the merchandise items and number of units that should be in stock. In this list each merchandise item or stock-keeping unit is described or identified in precise terms.

A basic stock list indicates the minimum amount of stock that should be available for every type of merchandise that is sold and the quantity that should be ordered. This list therefore indicates the items that should never be out of stock while the model stock list indicates the range of merchandise that should be kept. Items are counted on a regular basis and, in this way, the quantity in stock can be compared with the minimum quantity that should be in stock in order to determine when and how many units should be ordered. The basic stock list usually indicates the minimum acceptable stock level, the actual stock level, the quantity of stock that has been ordered, planned sales of the product, as well as actual sales. As consumers expect sufficient stock of staple products, it is very important to control the minimum quantity of these products that should always be in stock.

Never-out list

A never-out list identifies key best sellers that the retailer wants to ensure are never out of stock. A retailer may want to specify that 99% of all items on this list should always be available and displayed for sale. This list can include fast-selling staple products (such as bread and milk), key seasonal products (such as jerseys, heaters or umbrellas) or fashion articles (the latest trend).

3.5 Summary

The merchandise planning process includes the planning of merchandise in Rand value by developing a merchandise budget (merchandise plan) and planning in units by using merchandise lists. The primary reason for planning the merchandise mix is to satisfy consumers' needs at a profit.

The merchandise planning process in Rand consists of five steps, namely, planning sales, stock levels, reductions in sales, purchases and profit margins. This planning takes place to determine how much stock should be invested in at any particular time. Merchandise planning in units is necessary to determine how many different merchandise items (stock-keeping units) and how many units of each item should be kept in stock. A model stock list can be used for planning fashion articles, a basic stock list for planning staple products, and a never-out list for planning key products that are best sellers.

Mini case study

Read the following case study and work through the questions that follow:

New Tropika 1,5 ℓ take-home pack

Market background

Tropika is now conveniently packed in a new 1,5 ℓ take-home pack for the whole family to enjoy. Clearly (in a PET bottle) still the same great smoooth taste that is well known and expected from SA's leading brand in the fresh fruit juice category. In extensive research we have identified a market opportunity to have a quality juice offering positioned between the 1 ℓ and 2 ℓ, hence the introduction of the new Tropika 1,5 ℓ to meet consumers' needs. The 1,5 ℓ market segment is the biggest take-home pack size purchased.

The brand

Tropika is currently the market leader in the dairy fruit mix (DFM) category, short shelf life juice category and a dominant player in the total fruit juice market. The brand enjoys a heritage of more than a quarter of a century with our consumers, which keeps us as the Number 1 brand in the dairy fruit mix category.

Market description

The primary market is defined as the dairy fruit mix market and secondary market as the short shelf life juice market. However the brand is not restricted to this market but also competes for 'share-of-throat' against all fruit juice, squashes, cordials and soft drinks.

Market size and statistics

The DFM market in South Africa is an estimated volume of 64 million litres and has a value of over R602 million in the Top End channel.

➲

Target market

New Tropika 1,5 ℓ pack will be ideal for consumption by the entire family; however this will be targeted primarily at mothers with children. LSM: 5–10. Primary: ages 24–49. Mothers (take home). Secondary: ages 16–24 (impulse consumption).

Trade benefits

Launching the Tropika in a new 1,5 ℓ pack will provide us with a unique selling point, as well as categorise the Tropika brand as being innovative and the category leader. Six tasty current flavours to stimulate greater purchase frequency. Strong colour-coded impact to draw visual attention to shelf. Full marketing supports from the brand with the highest advertising spend in this category.

Marketing support

The new Tropika 1,5 ℓ is guaranteed to be a huge success due to the strong marketing support that will be provided through the following: ATL – TV advertisement communicating the new product launch. BTL – in-store campaign, in-store demos and promotion. POS – posters, wobblers, shelf strips.

Product description

The new 1,5 ℓ will be the same trusted dairy fruit mix formulation with a 45-day shelf life refrigerated. The new 1,5 ℓ pack is in the following popular flavour variants:

- Orange
- Pineapple
- Mango
- Peach
- Pear
- Tropical granadilla.

Distribution

Product will be distributed through the current Tropika distribution channels focusing on wholesalers and retailers.

Source: http://www.fastmoving.co.za/activities/new-tropika-1-5-litre-take-home-pack-1243 Accessed: 12 March 2012.

Questions

1. Would you classify the new Tropika 1,5 ℓ take-home pack as staple merchandise or fashion merchandise?
2. Using the information in the case study, describe how you would go about forecasting sales for the new Tropika product.

> 3. Which method would you use when planning stock levels for the new Tropika product? Give reasons for your answer.
> 4. Do you think the new Tropika product will be a success? Discuss how well you think the product will do or not do in a larger retailer such as Pick n Pay or a Checkers Hyper.

3.6 Self-evaluation questions

1. Distinguish between inventory investment, inventory assortment and inventory support.
2. Discuss the requirements that a successful merchandise budget (merchandise plan) should meet.
3. Explain the steps to be followed when compiling the merchandise plan.
4. Distinguish between staple merchandise and fashion merchandise.
5. Discuss the four methods that can be used for planning stock levels.
6. Crazy Bobs is a retailer that estimated its planned sales at R70 000 for the coming month (at retail prices). Their planned stock levels are estimated at R50 000 at the beginning of the month and at R30 000 at the end of the month, with planned reductions of R1 000, which were budgeted for. Calculate the planned purchases for the coming month at retail prices, and at cost price, if the initial mark-up is 30%.
7. Discuss merchandise planning in units and distinguish between the three merchandise lists that can be used.

3.7 Bibliography

Berman, B. & Evans, J.R. (2012). *Retail management: A strategic approach,* 11th edition. New Jersey: Pearson.

Cant, M.C. (ed.). (2010). *Introduction to retailing,* 2nd edition. Cape Town: Juta.

Cox, R. & Brittain, P. (2004). *Retailing: An introduction,* 5th edition. Harlow: Prentice Hall.

Dunne, P.M. & Lusch, R.F. (2008). *Retailing,* 6th edition. Mason: Thomson.

Levy, M. & Weitz, B. (2012). *Retailing management,* 8th edition. New York: McGraw Hill.

Websites

http://www.fastmoving.co.za/activities/new-tropika-1-5-litre-take-home-pack-1243 Accessed: 12 March 2012.

http://retail.about.com/od/merchandisemanagement/Merchandise_Planning_and_Management.htm Accessed: 12 March 2012.

4

Merchandise logistics

William S Grimes

Learning objectives

After studying this chapter you should be able to:

- Define the retail supply chain;
- Explain why supplier–retailer collaboration is important;
- Discuss the different types of supply chains;
- Discuss the advantages of branding from the customer's perspective;
- Explain the criteria for selecting the right supplier base;
- Discuss how to identify suitable sources of suppliers;
- Highlight the criteria for evaluating suppliers;
- Explain the merchandising process.

4.1 Introduction

Effective merchandising contributes to capturing the impulse of the consumer to buy more and to buy better. On-shelf availability remains a key challenge for retailers. Out-of-stock items will result in consumer dissatisfaction. Consumers will seek products elsewhere if they do not find the products on the shelves. In this case the store loses sales and profits. Research into consumer reactions to out-of-stock items also shows that the consumer substitutes the product with another brand.

It is important for the retailer to determine the amount of inventory needed to support the forecasted sales and assortment plan. The buyers of a retailer need to develop a plan based on expected sales. The buyers then need to identify suppliers and negotiate with the vendors.

4.2 Merchandise supply base

The retailer is part of the supply chain. The supply chain is a 'set of institutions that move goods from the point of production to the point of consumption'. The successful retailer must understand the importance of the supply chain. Although the retailer is at the end of the supply chain, effective co-ordination and co-operation of all parties in the supply chain will ensure successful retailing. The retailer must manage its supply chain. New members, methods and processes must be evaluated constantly in order to improve the effectiveness of the supply chain.

In the fast-moving consumer goods industry, inefficiencies in the supply channel contribute to higher prices, out-of-stocks and many undesired products that take up space and retail attention. These problems result in declining store loyalty, erosion of sales volume and an increase in competing retail formats.

In the fast-moving consumer goods industry, efficient consumer response is a customer-orientated, re-engineering, value-added management strategy. It is a process whereby the partners in the supply chain work together to avoid duplication of costs and improve overall service.

Supply chain management: The supply chain includes all the activities and exchanges involved in the extraction, processing, manufacturing and distribution of goods and services from raw materials through to the end consumer. The supply chain consists of a number of businesses that share information to ensure material flows down in order to make certain that the physical product ends up satisfying the consumer.

The retail supply chain includes more than stores. The nature of the retail supply chain will vary depending on product type and characteristics, as well as the preferences of the consumer. The retail supply chain in the fast-moving consumer goods industry has more than one intermediary distributor. For example, milk is produced on the farm, and then it is sold to a co-operative, which sells it to a processor, which sells it to a distribution brand, and only then is it sold on to a retailer. The supply chain in retailing is thus very complex. Various trade transactions take place before the consumer finally buys the product. Figure 4.1 illustrates the retail supply chain.

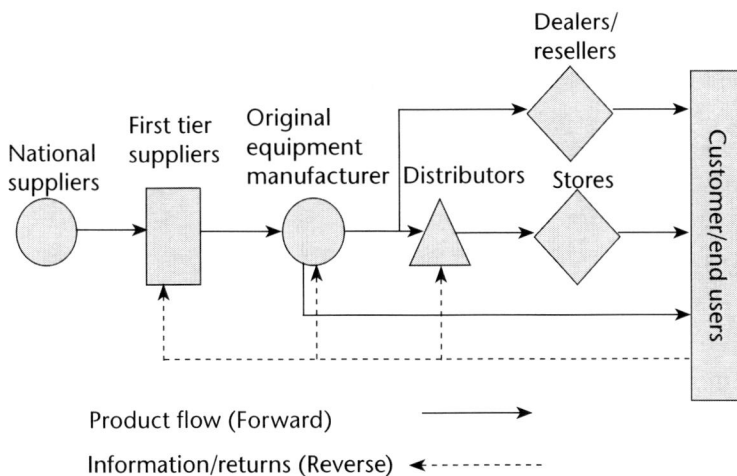

Figure 4.1 The retail supply chain

Source: Adapted from Ayers & Odegaard (2008). Retail supply chain management. *Copenhagen: Auerbach Publications, p. 5*

The supply chain is made up of processes. These processes include the sourcing of materials, designing products, manufacturing, transporting, and fixing and selling products or services to the various supply chain members. It is a process whereby physical products, information and finances flow forwards and backwards. Knowledge is the key that ensures improvement of the supply chain. The ultimate aim of the supply chain is to improve customer satisfaction.

4.3   Supplier–retailer collaboration

The overall supply chain must ensure that the right products are at the right place at the right time. In the fast-moving consumer goods industry, managers need to manage across boundaries. By working together managers can achieve a sustainable advantage, which will lead to enhanced customer value.

Co-ordination within the supply chain is a source of competitive advantage. The partners in the supply chain need to align their goals and actions. Unfortunately, however, in retail business, the retailer and the supplier do not always have the same goal. They can disagree on various issues, such as the assortment list, shelf allocation, distribution methods and responsibilities. As these differences can lead to poor performance, the supply chain members need to co-ordinate their goals.

The supply chain members can also differ in their attitudes to risk taking. This is especially true when they face risk situations, such as excess inventory or out-of-stock items. The chain members need to co-ordinate the various mechanisms, policies and contracts to manage the potential risk. Information sharing and incentive alignment can help to reduce their risk.

Those retailers who are able to maximise the efficiencies of their supply chain members will tend to be more profitable. There are various advantages for the partners in the supply chain if they work together. These include an increase in sales, reduced logistics costs, and a dramatic improvement in product availability and lead times.

If the supply base is not managed effectively, the inefficiencies of the supply channel will contribute to higher prices, out-of-stocks and many undesired products taking up space and retail attention. The result of these problems will be declining store loyalty, the erosion of sales volumes and an increase in the number of competing retailers.

4.4   Types of supply chains

Supply chain length

The retailer's supply chain can be either direct or indirect. A direct supply chain occurs when a manufacturer sell the goods directly to the final consumer or end user. A farmer who sells farm produce at a farm stall is an example of a direct supply chain.

The indirect supply chain may include a retailer or both a retailer and a wholesaler. If the farmer sells his produce to Pick n Pay, and the consumer buys these products from Pick n Pay, this is an example of an indirect supply chain. The desired length of the supply chain is determined by factors such as:

- Size of customer base;
- Geographical dispersion;
- Behavioural patterns, such as purchase frequency, average purchase size and the needs of the consumer.

Consider the example of a consumer wanting to buy eggs. It would probably be cheaper for the consumer to buy eggs directly from the farmer than from the local Pick n Pay. However, if one takes into account the cost of travelling to the farmer, it would most likely be cheaper to buy from the local grocer.

Supply chain width

Supply chain width can be explained in terms of intensive distribution, selective distribution or exclusive distribution. Intensive distribution means that every possible retailer is used to reach the target market. Intensive distribution is usually associated with convenience goods. The fast-moving consumer goods industry uses mostly an intensive distribution supply chain channel.

Selective distribution makes use of a smaller number of retailers. Goods such as electronic equipment are distributed through selective supply chains. Exclusive supply chains use only one retailer in a selected area.

4.5 Selecting suppliers

Mini case study
Walmart woos local suppliers
In a bid to expose South African suppliers to Walmart's philosophy of price-cutting promotions, the retailer plans to host 10 local suppliers at its US base in Arkansas in May 2012.
The retailer, which bought a controlling stake in Massmart in 2011, is courting local suppliers by drawing them into the long-period price-reduction business model. Massmart, which owns stores such as Game, Makro and Dion Wired, said suppliers and customers had benefited in its 10-week extended price-cut promotions.
Massmart merchandising executive Jon Martinek said: 'It is not only consumers who win. Suppliers also stand to benefit from these promotions, specifically if they are able to forecast production needs optimally.'
'The result is that we now receive proactive enquiries from suppliers requesting the opportunity to be included in these promotions,' Martinek said.
Although Massmart refused to name the suppliers, the retailer said the partnership helped with efficient production scheduling.
Don Frieson, an executive at Walmart, said suppliers could be successful in longer-term price reduction activities in two primary areas: cost-savings and growing the brand. ⟲

'Lowering prices and offering better value allows existing customers and a new pool of potential customers to make repeat purchases more often ... and outstanding cost-saving benefit through a more predictable supply chain,' Frieson said.

Retail analysts said the long-period price-cut promotion business model would help suppliers plan by producing enough stock and increasing volumes at a guaranteed price.

Others said, unlike the week-long or short-period promotions that South African consumers were used to, the long-period promotions would give consumers more time to plan their shopping.

Abri du Plessis of Gryphon Asset Management said that despite an outcry by the unions and some of the suppliers against Walmart's entrance into the country, the move had been a good one, especially for suppliers and consumers.

'Walmart's takeover would push local manufacturers to produce in more volumes and also apply some pressure in lowering some of the prices,' he said.

He also added that, given Walmart's sourcing knowledge internationally, the retailers would know where to look for better prices.

He said Massmart's extended price promotion would help drive down inflation, which would be a huge relief for consumers. This would also push other retailers, such as Shoprite and Pick n Pay, to lower prices and create space for competition.

Adrian Boland, a merchandising executive at Game Stores, said that as part of the process, suppliers received a two-month commitment, which ensured better planning and increased volumes.

Marlo Scholtz, an equity analyst at Sanlam Investment Management, said suppliers would benefit from this new extended price promotion as it would increase volumes in production.

Source: http://www.iol.co.za/business/companies/walmart-woos-local-suppliers-1.1281481

Questions
1. Explain how Walmart works with local suppliers to improve their performance.
2. Discuss the benefits local suppliers receive by working together with Walmart.

As the supply chain is so important for the success of the retailer, it is essential that retailers select suppliers that provide them with reliable service. Most retailers use a variety of suppliers. If the suppliers do not deliver the right products at the right time, the retailer will be out of stock of certain items. The out-of-stock items will lead to lower profits and less customer satisfaction. The supplier is expected to provide a dependable service, handle returns and provide adjustments to products and orders.

It is thus important to evaluate your suppliers in terms of reliability and availability of stock. If suppliers do not perform, the retailer can change to a different supplier. Ideally the retailer wants to establish long-term relationships with suppliers.

The availability and reliability of suppliers

Retailers should constantly evaluate their suppliers in terms of their reliability and the availability of their stock. When evaluating the availability of supply, retailers should ask the following questions:

- Is the product readily available through the retailer's normal channels of distribution?
- Are alternative back-up sources of supply available?
- Will the product be available on a continuous basis?
- What are the terms and conditions of sale under which the product is available?

The availability of supply can therefore be defined as the extent to which suppliers can supply merchandise through the normal channels of distribution on a continuous basis.

Retailers also need to establish the reliability of a supplier, for it is imperative that the product be delivered to the store at the right time, in the right quantities and in good condition. The following criteria can be used to assess a supplier's reliability:

- Does the supplier ship an order on time?
- Does the supplier fulfil orders adequately?
- Does the supplier maintain adequate stocks?
- Does the supplier adjust orders to meet the retailer's needs?

Once a retailer knows what their needs are as far as suppliers are concerned, they can identify suitable suppliers. This is the next topic of discussion.

4.6 Identifying suitable sources of supply

Once the retailer has identified the sources from which they can obtain merchandise, they can decide where to procure each product line. Retailers can buy merchandise from a wide variety of sources. Products that can be bought directly from the producers include fruit, vegetables, wood and flowers. Most products, however, are bought from the manufacturers of those products. Small retailers buy merchandise from wholesalers because manufacturers cannot handle their small orders. It is vital for retailers to establish and maintain strategic partnerships with these suppliers. Retailers are able to select merchandise from any one of, or a combination of raw resource producers, final manufacturers, wholesale intermediaries or resident buying offices.

Let us briefly examine each of these.

The raw resource producer

Retailers often procure supplies directly from the raw resource producer. Examples are retailers buying fresh fruit and vegetables directly from farmers. Buying directly from raw resource producers has the advantage of increased speed and reduced handling costs.

The final manufacturer

The final manufacturer differs from the raw resource producer in that they manufacture final products. If a retailer buys oranges from a farmer, the source of supply is the raw resource producer of oranges. However, if they buy orange juice from Liqui-Fruit®, they are buying it from the final manufacturer. There are several advantages to buying directly from the final manufacturer, namely:

- ☐ The retailer buys a fresher product;
- ☐ Delivery is much quicker;
- ☐ Prices are lower;
- ☐ Manufacturers can give more information about their products than can intermediaries;
- ☐ Adjustments are better;
- ☐ Products can be made to the retailer's specifications.

The wholesale intermediary

Wholesale intermediaries position themselves between the manufacturer and the retailer in the distribution channel, and can be classified into various groups.

Merchant intermediaries

Merchant intermediaries are wholesalers who are directly involved in the purchase and sale of goods as they move through the channel of distribution. They actually own the goods in which they deal. There is a distinction between full-function merchant intermediaries, who perform a full range of wholesaling functions, and limited-function merchant intermediaries, who limit their activities to certain wholesaling functions.

There are three types of full-function merchant intermediaries, namely:

- ☐ The *general-merchandise wholesaler* who offers different product lines;
- ☐ The *single-line wholesaler* who sells products such as hardware, groceries and pharmaceutical products;
- ☐ The *speciality-line wholesaler* who sells products such as frozen foods.

Limited-function merchant intermediaries are divided into:

- ☐ *Cash-and-carry wholesalers* where the retailer has to go to the wholesaler to select and assemble the merchandise, check out at a central station, pay cash and load and transport the merchandise;
- ☐ *Drop shippers* who distribute bulky products;
- ☐ *Truck distributors* who distribute merchandise from trucks;
- ☐ *Rack jobbers* who organise displays.

Agent intermediaries

Agent intermediaries specialise in buying and selling merchandise for others. They bring manufacturers and retailers together, but they do not take over ownership of the merchandise, and they provide only a limited number of functions. They usually work on a commission basis. Examples of agent intermediaries include estate agents, brokers, sales agents, manufacturer's agents, commission agents and auction houses.

Contractual intermediaries

The retailer agrees to purchase a certain amount of merchandise from the wholesaler in return for certain considerations, lower prices being the most important. The lower prices are made possible by the fact that the wholesaler has several retailers under contract, which allows them to realise certain economies of scale, similar to chain organisations.

The resident buying office

Resident buying offices are organisations that specialise in the buying function and are located in major wholesaling and producing markets. They provide information to retailers on the availability of products, the reliability of suppliers, the present and future market and supply trends, and the special deals, price promotions and services that various suppliers offer.

After determining the sources of supply, a retailer must evaluate these sources.

4.7   Criteria for evaluating suppliers

Despite popular belief, price is not the only factor to consider when selecting the best possible supplier for a retail organisation. The selection of suppliers involves nothing more than a systematic analysis of a number of important characteristics. Retailers must first decide what characteristics are important in suppliers. They can then determine which suppliers fulfil their needs. Finally, they should buy from the suppliers who are best qualified and provide the best terms. The following characteristics are important to most retailers:

Suitability of merchandise

Is the merchandise supplied by the supplier in line with the wants and needs of the store's customers? If the supplier sells merchandise similar to that which the retailer's customers have been buying, or if the retailer believes that their customers will buy these goods, the supplier is suitable.

Completeness of a line

When buying school clothing for your children, for example, do you want to go from shop to shop looking for all the items you need, or would you prefer to buy everything from one retail store? Of course you would prefer to get everything from one supplier! Similarly, if a supplier has desirable merchandise but their lines of merchandise are incomplete, this supplier might be eliminated. Smaller retailers usually choose to buy from suppliers that carry an assortment of the items they need. This saves buying time, reduces the cost of transportation and can result in better discounts. Generally, the more you buy from a supplier, the better the service it will provide.

Profitability of merchandise

Retailers buy merchandise that they can sell at a profit, so they are constantly on the lookout for reasonable prices. Retailers therefore need to find suppliers that can provide merchandise at prices, allowances and terms of sale that permit them to operate successfully.

At the same time, retailers should beware of buying inferior quality merchandise in an attempt to find low-priced goods.

Delivery

Timely delivery is vitally important in retailing. How frustrating, for example, to only receive one's Valentine's Day stock a month after Valentine's Day! Retailers have to determine how much time is required for the delivery of their orders. Small retailers who cannot estimate their requirements far in advance should consider the advantages of dealing with suppliers who can deliver goods quickly. Retailers also need to know that the supplier can provide the quantities they will need to meet customer demands. Smaller retailers who need only small quantities at a time cannot buy from suppliers who sell only in bulk.

Stability

Is a supplier likely to go out of business or discontinue a line of goods? Retailers need to be sure that suppliers will still be in business when it is time for goods to be delivered or re-ordered. The financial strength of a supplier, its ownership and its management indicate a great deal about its stability. Previous experience with the supplier or the recommendation of other businesses that have used this supplier can help to assess stability and reliability of service.

Promotional assistance

Are advertising and display materials furnished by the supplier or are advertising allowances available? It is not unreasonable for smaller retailers to expect suppliers to provide services such as promotional assistance, which reduces the retailer's costs and increases the chances of selling the supplier's merchandise.

Dependability of quality

Does the supplier maintain a certain standard of quality? Retailers rely on suppliers to ship merchandise to them that is the same quality as the samples they were shown. The same quality of products must also be supplied over time, as inconsistent quality can tarnish a retailer's name.

Returns

Does the supplier make adjustments when the incorrect merchandise is supplied or delivered late? When orders are placed, retailers should determine the supplier's policy regarding merchandise returns. Circumstances do occur which require the return of goods to suppliers. Reasons for returns could include goods that were damaged in transit or goods that did not arrive on specific delivery dates. Merchandise that arrives too early can interfere with receiving and ticketing procedures, take up warehouse space or become spoiled by excessive handling. Merchandise that is delivered too late may no longer be in demand and this may necessitate early markdowns. These events are costly to retailers. Some suppliers prefer to take back merchandise than see it marked down at the end of season. Others are prepared to grant an allowance or reduction in price for unsatisfactory goods so that the store can sell them at a lower price.

Distribution policy

Will the supplier offer exclusivity? A small retailer might find it advantageous to deal with a supplier that wants to limit the number of stores selling its merchandise. Another factor that must be considered is whether goods are available on consignment; this can help a retailer who is unsure of the saleability of a particular line of goods (for instance, in new stores), since the supplier takes back any unsold stock. Although profit margins for the retailer are generally lower on consignment goods, the risk is also less and nothing is paid for until it has been sold.

Support services

Does the supplier have knowledgeable and competent sales representatives? Do they provide information on market trends? Do they provide warehousing or other services? Retailers need to determine the support services that can help them and consider which suppliers are best able to provide these.

Prices and terms

How do the prices and terms of the supplier in question compare with other suppliers? The credit terms, discounts, amount of time allowed for paying accounts and transportation charges vary from supplier to supplier. These factors are important to smaller retailers, particularly those with limited capital, because they determine what the final cost of the merchandise will be.

Will the supplier guarantee prices? Retailers who can negotiate fixed prices can protect themselves against price increases and, in times of high inflation, this can be a significant advantage. Before making the final decision on whether or not to use a supplier, retailers should examine the conditions and terms available. Retailers should know what discounts they will receive, what method of dating will be used and what the transportation arrangements are for the merchandise they are purchasing. All of these factors affect the final cost of the goods.

4.8   Negotiating the purchase

After choosing the supplier, the retailer has to negotiate the purchase and its terms. Many purchase terms have to be specified, including:

- ❏   The delivery date;
- ❏   The quantity purchased;
- ❏   Price and payment arrangements;
- ❏   Discounts;
- ❏   The form of delivery;
- ❏   The point of transfer of ownership.

The delivery date and quantity purchased should be clearly stated. The retailer's purchase price, payment arrangements and permissible discounts are also important. They must determine the supplier's cost per item (including the handling charges) and which forms of payment are permitted (such as cash versus credit). Possible discounts and stipulations concerning the form of delivery (by ship, air, truck or rail) should also be determined.

Certain components that have to be considered when negotiating a purchase are discounts offered, shipping charges and promotional allowances. We shall discuss the latter two components below.

Shipping charges

Basic issues must be agreed upon between the retail organisation and the supplier when designating the shipping terms and conditions. These issues are important since any costs incurred will increase the retailer's cost of goods. The following terms must be determined:

- ❏   Who pays the freight charges?
- ❏   Who is responsible for filing claims?
- ❏   Who owns the merchandise while it is in transit?

If retailers pay the shipping costs, this increases the cost of goods. Retailers must always negotiate to reduce shipping charges, if possible. If the retailer becomes the owner of the merchandise before it has been transported, they are responsible for the merchandise during shipment, which means that they will have to pay insurance, which also increases the cost of goods.

If a supplier is given a preferred rate because of the huge volumes they ship, the retailer may ask how much it would cost to ship the products prepaid. If it is less than they would pay at the standard rate for shipping the product, they should offer to pay the shipment costs the supplier will incur. This means that the retailer will save on shipment costs.

Promotional allowances

Have you ever seen an advertisement placed by a large retailer, in which products from only one or two well-known suppliers are featured? In these cases, the suppliers featured in the advertisements are contributing to the retailer's advertising costs in return for being one of the only suppliers featured.

Advertising or promotional allowances are discounts that retailers earn by advertising the supplier's products in the local media. In essence, the retailer assumes part or all of the supplier's local advertising functions and is compensated by the supplier for the money spent and services performed in the form of an advertising allowance. Retailers give suppliers preferred selling space in return for a price reduction. Preferred sales areas include a free-standing display in a high-traffic aisle, an end-of-aisle display, a high-exposure area near a checkout counter and a special window display.

Negotiating the purchase is not enough. Retailers must build and maintain relationships with suppliers. We shall discuss this in more detail in the following section.

4.9 Building and maintaining relationships with suppliers

A retailer relies on suppliers to supply them with merchandise. However, the opposite is also true. Suppliers are just as dependent on retailers. This should give the retailer the ability to negotiate confidently with suppliers. It is important to build relationships with suppliers. This does not imply that retailers cannot evaluate suppliers every once in a while, but it does imply building a long-term relationship with them. Retailers cannot build relationships by changing their suppliers every month.

To develop a strategic partnership that will lead to a competitive advantage, the retailer and supplier must commit to a long-term business relationship, in which, as partners, they both make significant investments to improve their profitability. Thus a strategic partnership is a win-win relationship.

Maintaining a strategic partnership accomplishes both parties' goals. The four foundations of successful strategic partnerships are *mutual trust, open communication, common goals* and *credible commitments*. When a retailer starts a business, they have to build up credibility with suppliers.

Initially, retailers will struggle to obtain financing because no one really knows them, and they have no reputation for paying their bills on time. Sometimes, during the first year of a retailer's business they will be required to pay a large amount of the order before it is delivered.

Even when retailers have built some credibility, they still have to take special care to pay their suppliers on time. It may take a retailer two weeks after placing the order to actually put the merchandise on the selling floor, because processing the order, shipment, reception, control and pricing the merchandise all take time. Once relationships have been built between retailers and suppliers, the tasks of ordering and following up the purchase become so much easier.

4.10   Ordering and following up the purchase

When retailers have determined their merchandise needs, they place an order with the suppliers for the merchandise. The order must be followed up to ensure that the suppliers are, in fact, preparing the order.

Ordering

Ordering is the process in which a retailer places a purchase order to procure the merchandise from a supplier. Retailers should place their orders in writing. When placing a written order, it is advisable for a retailer to use their own order form. The order form is legally binding only once both parties have signed the document. The order form should contain the following standard information:

☐ The full names and addresses of the retailer, suppliers and the name of a contact person(s) should a problem arise;
☐ Various numbers, such as the order number, store and department number;
☐ Various dates, such as the order date, the delivery date on which the merchandise is to be shipped and the cancellation date;
☐ Various terms, such as discount terms, transportation terms, including a description of all shipping and handling terms, transportation charges, modes of transport, place of delivery, handling and insurance arrangements;
☐ A description of the merchandise, including the quantity, unit price, total price and description and/or numbers to distinguish the products.

The order form must be signed by an authorised person.

Following up orders

Retailers follow up their orders to ensure that suppliers have received them. The supplier usually notifies the retailer when they have received the order form. Routine follow-ups take place when the retailer reminds the supplier that they are waiting for an important order. Special follow-ups are linked to personal visits to the supplier, putting pressure on them to meet their obligations.

After the retailer has identified the suppliers and placed an order, they must receive and check the order. This is known as the merchandise handling process, and will be discussed next.

4.11 The merchandise handling process

The definition of merchandising stresses a number of key points. Merchandising has to acquire future purchase opportunities. Forward planning is, therefore, needed in relation to changing needs and demands. The merchandise needs to be acquired from either the wholesaler or the manufacturer. The merchandise then has to be treated in such a way to ensure that it is sold on time and in perfect condition. Availability is thus an important concept.

The role of the merchandiser has increased over the past few years and includes activities such as dealing with customer complaints, stock level assessment and even account queries. The merchandising function is becoming more responsible for managing bottom-line profitability. The merchandisers are responsible for inventory returns, carrying costs, in-stock position and distribution expenses.

Merchandising requires a systematic approach, as well as an adherence to the marketing concepts. Merchandising must ensure optimal levels of stock to improve cash flow and profitability. Merchandise replenishment is the process that ensures that the product is available at all times. It prevents out-of-stock situations and thus leads to increased sales.

The acquisition, ordering, handling and storing of merchandise

Merchandising is more than an arrangement of products on the shelves. It is an integral part of the business. The main purpose of retail marketing is to provide the consumer with a steady flow of goods and services. Decisions on where to hold stock, in what quantities and how it is distributed is a key element of logistics management for retailers.

Effective merchandising helps to capture the impulse of the consumer to buy more and to buy better. On-shelf availability remains a key challenge for retailers. Out-of-stock items will result in consumer dissatisfaction. Consumers will seek products elsewhere if they do not find the products on the shelves. In this case the store loses sales and profits. Research into consumer reactions to out-of-stock items also shows that the consumer substitutes the product with another brand.

In large-scale distribution activities, it is advisable for producers of mass consumption goods to train merchandising specialists. These merchandisers need to implement the merchandising techniques at the point of sale and manage the shelf space for optimal performance. They also have to be sales promoters.

Managing shelf space

The display and distribution of the products in the store are a fundamental activity of the merchandiser. The placing of products contributes to the perceptions that customers have of the store. The distribution of the products on the shelf is the responsibility of the merchandiser. The managing of shelf space is essential to prevent out-of-stock items and to increase sales and profits.

When managing the shelf space there are three criteria to take into consideration.

❑ The perception and attitudes of the consumers are influenced by the presentation and aesthetics of the store. This includes the quality of displays, the ease of finding products and the legibility of the products and labelling.
❑ When managing the shelf space, the merchandiser must also consider the constraints of handling products and re-supplying.
❑ The economic return on products is influenced by the position of the product on the shelf and the space allocated to it.

The placing of the product on the shelf should be arranged vertically according to value. The most profitable items should be placed at eye level to ensure maximum exposure. The less profitable items should be placed lower. New products should also be placed in front of the store. In the fast-moving consumer goods industry it is the responsibility of the in-store merchandiser to negotiate with the store manager for shelf space and position. There are various competing brands of a product and it is the responsibility of the in-store merchandiser to ensure that the most profitable items have the best shelf position.

Out-of-stock items

In an era in which retail competition has become more intense, it is important for retailers to find ways to enhance their performance. Out-of-stock items contribute to the poor performance of retailers. Out-of-stock means the lack of availability of products. Retailers can improve their earnings by up to 5% if they address their out-of-stock issues. The unavailability of products is the new battleground in the fast-moving goods industry. Shelf space for different products is a key decision in the fast-moving consumer goods industry, and this is the responsibility of merchandisers.

Studies that focused mainly on the fast-moving goods industry in the United States, Europe and Australasia have shown that an average out-of-stock rate is 8,3%.

Consumer reaction to shelf out-of-stock

Consumers' response to out-of-stock items can be summarised into five primary responses. All five responses result in losses for the retailer and the manufacturer. The responses are:

- ❏ Buy the product at another store.
- ❏ Delay the purchase to a later time or date.
- ❏ Substitute the product with another product of the same brand.
- ❏ Substitute the product with a different brand.
- ❏ Do not purchase the item.

Out-of-stock items contribute to negative experiences for customers. The average customer will not return to the store after three negative experiences.

The cost of shelf out-of-stock to the retailer

Shelf out-of-stock does not mean a loss in sales for only the retailer; it affects the entire supply chain. The cost of these losses can be divided into four areas:

- ❏ Retailer shopper loss. This is when the shopper permanently switches stores due to out-of-stock items.
- ❏ Retailer sales loss. This loss consists of three components. The consumer will buy the out-of-stock items from another store. They will cancel their purchase of an item. They will substitute the product with a smaller or lower-priced item.
- ❏ Manufacturer shopper loss. Consumers will switch to a competitor's brand within a category of a product.
- ❏ Manufacturer sales loss. In this case the consumer substitutes a competitor's item or cancels the purchase.

Causes of shelf out-of-stock

Research available has indicated that 72% of all out-of-stocks are caused by factors in store. The causes include bad store practices, late or insufficient ordering, incorrect sales forecasts or shelf-restocking problems. The problem is further increased due to store managers having to manage thousands of stock items, as well as hundreds of promotional items. The main causes of out-of-stock can be attributed to the following three general processes: ordering, replenishing and planning.

4.12   In-store merchandising

Effective merchandising helps to capture the impulse of the consumer to buy more and to buy better. On-shelf availability remains a key challenge for retailers.

Let us look at the process from receiving the product in the receiving bay to displaying it on the shelf. The process will differ depending on the type of retailer. The process explained here is taken from the fast-moving consumer goods industry.

Assessing current stock situation

The merchandiser must check the stock for which they are responsible, for damages, expiry dates and out-of-stock items. They should also check the overall cleanness of the shelves. The merchandiser must then complete the documentation for any returned goods. By evaluating items sold, the merchandiser can identify opportunities to increase stock levels. If the sales of the merchandiser's brand are better than those of the competitors, they can negotiate with the store manager for more shelf space or a better position on the shelves.

Drawing stock

Once the merchandiser has assessed the current situation, they must complete an order sheet for new stock. The order will be influenced by the allocated stock level on the shelves. The merchandiser must take damaged and expired goods to the warehouse and report these to the relevant stakeholders. The new stock is then drawn from the storeroom and taken to the shelves.

Ordering stock

After drawing new stock from the storeroom the merchandiser must inform the relevant managers of low stock levels. They must obtain a signed approval to order new stock. The quantity ordered will be determined by the stock level agreed with the store manager. The merchandiser will then order the stock from the manufacturer or relevant suppliers. Special note must be taken of the delivery date.

Receiving stock

Once new stock is ordered, it is the merchandiser's function to check with the stock controller that the correct stock has been delivered. The merchandiser must, therefore, be aware of the delivery date, so that they can be present when the stock is delivered to the storeroom. Once they have checked the delivery, they must report any discrepancies, and ensure that the correct documentation is completed. The stock must then be stacked correctly in the allocated place in the storeroom, and any damaged and expired goods in the storeroom must be rotated by the merchandiser.

General stock maintenance

Apart from the above functions of the merchandiser, the following general stock maintenance also needs to be completed:

- ❑ Conduct an eye-ball check to determine out-of-stock items and shelf health standards.
- ❑ Identify opportunities for cross merchandising.
- ❑ Assist in the management of stock.
- ❑ Draw stock from the stockroom, order new stock, and receive and rotate stock according to in-store procedures.
- ❑ Interpret planograms in accordance with in-store practices.

- Analyse forward share and market share.
- Apply colour-breaking principles according to store practices.
- Conduct competitor analyses to compare stock sold against the stock sold by competitors.
- Plan promotions according to retail promotion criteria.
- Understand merchandising and in-store terminology.

A planogram is a diagram or model that indicates the placement of retail products on shelves in order to 'maximise sales'. Planograms help organisations to plan how their stores are going to look.

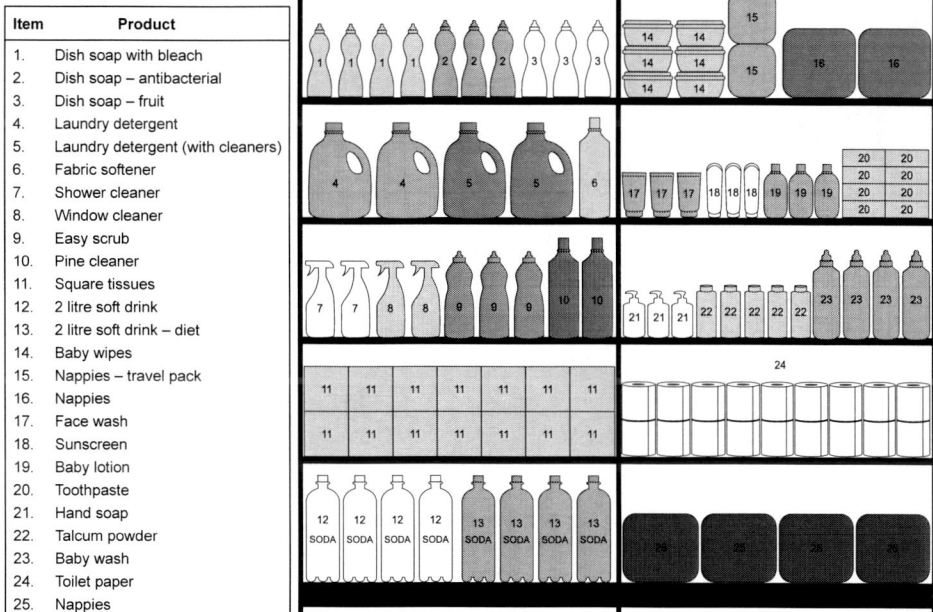

Figure 4.2 Example of a planogram

Source: http://www.dmsretail.com/retailplanograms.htm

4.13   Summary

Effective merchandising helps to capture the impulse of the consumer to buy more and to buy better. On-shelf availability remains a key challenge for retailers. Out-of-stock items will result in consumer dissatisfaction. Consumers will seek products elsewhere if they do not find the products on the shelves.

The overall supply chain must ensure that the right products are at the right place at the right time. By working together, managers can achieve a sustainable advantage, which will lead to enhanced customer value.

Retailers should evaluate their suppliers constantly in terms of their reliability and the availability of their stock.

The role of the merchandiser has increased over the past few years and includes activities such as dealing with customer complaints, stock level assessment and even account queries. The merchandising function is becoming more responsible for managing bottom-line profitability. The merchandisers are responsible for inventory returns, carrying costs, in-stock positioning and distribution expenses.

4.14   Self-evaluation questions

1. Define the retail supply chain.
2. Explain why supplier–retailer collaboration is important.
3. Discuss the different types of supply chains.
4. Explain the criteria for selecting the right supplier base.
5. Discuss how to identify suitable sources of supplies.
6. Highlight the criteria for evaluating suppliers.
7. Explain the merchandising process.

4.15   Bibliography

Ayers, J.B. & Odegaard, M.A. (2008). *Retail supply chain management*. Copenhagen: Auerbach Publications.

Cant, M. (2010). *Introduction to retailing*. Cape Town: Juta, pp. 35–34.

Corsten, D. & Gruen, T. (2003). Desperately seeking shelf availability: An examination of the causes, and the efforts to address retail out of stocks. *International Journal of Retail and Distribution Management*, 31(12): 605–617.

Dubois, P., Jolibert, A. & Muhlbacher, H. (2007). *Marketing management. A value-creation process*. Basingstoke: Palgrave Macmillan.

Dunne, P.M. & Lusch, R.F. (2005). *Retailing*. Mason, OH: Thomson South-Western.

Dupre, K. & Gruen, T.W. (2004). The use of category management practices to obtain a sustainable competitive advantage in the fast-moving-consumer-goods industry. *Journal of Business and Industrial Marketing*, 19(7): 444–459. [Online] Accessed: 20 May 2011.

Eastham, J.F., Sharples, L. & Ball, S.D. (2001). *Food supply chain management: Issues for the hospitality and retail sectors*. Oxford: Heinemann.

Walker, M. (1994). Supplier–retailer collaboration in European grocery distribution. *Logistic Information Management*, 7(6): 2327. [Online] Accessed: 18 May 2009.

Wong, C.Y. & Johansen, J. (2008). A framework of manufacturer-retailer coordination process: Three case studies. *International Journal of Retail and Distribution Management*, 36(5): 387–408. [Online] Accessed: 14 April 2009.

Websites

http://www.bizcommunity.com/196/160.html
http://www.dmsretail.com/retailplanograms.htm
http://www.iol.co.za/business/companies/walmart-woos-local-suppliers-1.1281481

5

Inventory management and analysis

Jan A Wiid

5.1 Introduction

If a store sells twice as many of one merchandise item than another store, is its performance twice as good? Although firms must generate sales to earn profits, and increasing sales is an important goal for most retailers, it is not the ultimate objective. The overall goal is to increase sales while also ensuring higher profits (Lusch, Dunne & Carver, 2011).

A product that generates higher sales does not necessarily generate higher profits, because the margin on the two items may differ. The margin is the difference between an item's selling price and its original cost to the retailer. Margin is an important measure of merchandise performance, since it indicates the extent to which the item can contribute toward meeting the firm's operating expenses and profit goals (Jacobsen, 2009). This chapter focuses on merchandising control and the analysis of merchandise performance.

5.2 Merchandise control

Merchandise control involves the development of an inventory information and analysis system to gather, capture, analyse and use merchandise data to determine whether merchandise objectives have been reached (Lusch, Dunne & Carver, 2011).

The merchandise control process complements the merchandise planning process. Merchandise control is, therefore, the sum of two types of inventory systems, that is, an inventory information system and an inventory analysis system. The inventory information system comprises the methods and procedures for gathering and processing merchandise data that is relevant to the planning and control of merchandise inventories (Terblancé, 2002).

The inventory analysis system includes methods for evaluating the retailer's past merchandising performance, and decision-making aids for controlling future merchandising activities. The merchandise control process should, therefore, use the retailer's information regarding her/his inventory and analysis system to control the investment in inventory, and the assortment of merchandise kept in inventory. A well-developed merchandise control system can thus assist in the merchandise decision-making process by supplying important information regarding the correct quantity and assortment of items that should be purchased, kept in inventory and sold (Gilbert, 2003). Figure 5.1 shows the elements of the merchandise control process.

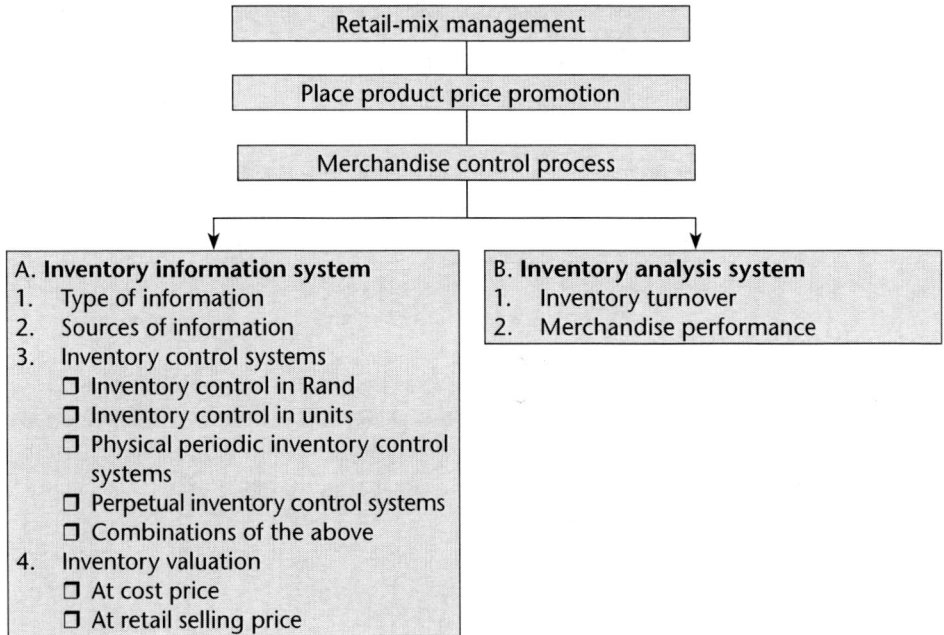

Figure 5.1 The merchandise control process

Source: Adapted from Lewison & DeLozier (1986). Retailing: Casebook and applications, 2nd edition. Basingstoke: Macmillan, p. 554

5.3 Inventory information systems

If retailers are to control their merchandise inventory effectively, they should be able to obtain information about the current and past state of the inventory effectively. For this reason a suitable inventory information system is required.

The inventory information system must make information available for the control of merchandise. This includes information on inventory investment, inventory assortment and inventory support. In order to complement the merchandise planning process, the retailer's inventory information system should be able to supply information about the Rand value and the number of units in inventory. In other words, information about the Rand value invested in inventory must be gathered and analysed, and information on the various product items and the number of units of each type of item in inventory must also be gathered. Information on sales, purchases and inventory levels of merchandise in physical units must, therefore, be gathered and analysed (Lusch, Dunne & Carver, 2011).

A retailer's source of inventory information is their inventory control systems. Inventory control systems differ with regards to when and how inventory is taken. Inventory control systems may provide information in units or in Rand, or they may be periodic physical inventory control systems or perpetual inventory control systems.

Inventory control systems

The purpose of inventory control is to control the size and composition of inventory in order to keep inventory-keeping costs as low as possible and to have the inventory available to sell in good time. This function includes the co-ordination of delivery, the physical condition, storage, distribution and recording of merchandise (Lantion, 2001). As mentioned earlier, the purpose of an inventory control system is to maintain sufficient quantities of merchandise for current needs without investing too much capital in stock (Axsäter, 2006).

Inventory control systems are organised to supply information about the status of merchandise for a certain period, for example, a month, a year or a selling season.

There are several inventory control systems and procedures to assist retailers in effective inventory and merchandise planning and control.

The most important inventory control systems, which also serve as inventory information systems and are used in the merchandise control process, are:

Inventory control systems in units or Rand value

Unit control is an inventory control system based on the number of items rather than the Rand value of the merchandise. This system indicates the number of units of each type of merchandise in inventory, on order and that have already been sold (Heintz & Parry, 2008).

Inventory control in Rand is an inventory control system that stores data on merchandise in terms of Rand value. The Rand value of merchandise can be expressed in terms of cost price or retail selling price.

When the retail selling price is used as a basis for inventory valuation, one thinks of the merchandise in terms of what it is worth and not in terms of the price at which it was purchased. In practice both systems should be used for effective purchasing so that buyers have enough information about inventory in order to make decisions.

Physical inventory control systems

When using a physical inventory control system, merchandise is counted physically to determine the quantity of inventory on hand. In this inventory control system the merchandise is periodically counted physically to calculate the sales for the period since the last physical count (Needles, Powers & Crosson, 2011). This sales figure in units can be calculated by adding the purchases in units for the period to the opening inventory on hand for the period, and then subtracting the closing inventory on hand that was determined by a physical count (Travis, 2010).

The reason for counting merchandise physically is to determine whether the true value of the inventory corresponds with its book value so that the correct information can be reflected on the balance sheet.

There are several proven methods for inventory control (Hendrick et al., n.d.).

1. *Tickler control.* With the tickler control system, sections of the inventory are checked at regular intervals in order to determine the extent of the retailer's inventory for a given period of time, as well as the sales in units made in that period. The inventory is, therefore, counted and recorded on a rotating basis. This system is used particularly for counting staple products.
2. *Visual control.* This system does not involve the regular counting of merchandise. This method is used particularly to check items stored in drawers or bins. A tag or label containing information about the required reorder is placed at a point regarded as the minimum inventory point. When inventory reaches this point, the reorder card appears. It is removed and sent to the buyers so they can use the data to reorder inventory.

When applying visual control as the inventory control system, inventory can be marked by means of a colour code. Each order received is given a certain colour code, which is attached to the merchandise. For example, the first shipment of a particular type of merchandise received is coded blue, the second green and so on. Buyers can, therefore, immediately determine which items have been in inventory for a long time and which items are selling slowly. These items may then be marked down and this ensures a better rotation of inventory. This method is used particularly for controlling perishable and seasonal products.

Perpetual inventory control systems

The physical counting of inventory is an expensive and time-consuming process. Therefore inventory is counted only once or twice a year. In order to be competitive, more recent sales and present inventory-level information than the previous physical inventory count is required. It is important to adjust inventory information monthly

(Needles, Powers & Crosson, 2011). For food and clothing, daily or weekly adjustments are perhaps necessary. A perpetual inventory control system supplies the most recent information and is intended to ensure a correspondence between the inventory records and quantities actually in inventory at a given time. Inventory is therefore taken and information collected on a continuous or perpetual basis by using various bookkeeping records to determine the amount of inventory on hand at any given time. All inventory information, such as purchases, sales and so on, is recorded in the inventory records immediately so as to have current inventory information available (Needles, Powers & Crosson, 2011).

One can distinguish between systems where inventory information is recorded manually and computerised systems (Hendrick et al., n.d.).

1. **Manual**. Merchandise data is written down continuously on perpetual unit control records drawn up for individual items. These records are adjusted constantly to reflect current orders, receipts, returns by customers, sales, shortages and damaged items. The following aids are used to facilitate the recording of inventory information and to ensure that mistakes do not occur:

    Sales slips. The salesperson writes the required information on the sales slip and sends it to the person responsible for the unit control of inventory. This information is then recorded on inventory cards. The information recorded on these cards includes the amount received, the number of units sold, the date of inventory adjustment and the balance. More information can be recorded on the cards if the retailer regards this as necessary.

    Stub control. A label is attached to the merchandise. When the merchandise is sold, the stub is removed and sent to the inventory control staff. This information is then also recorded on inventory control cards for each item.

    Point-of-purchase sheet. As items are sold, the information is recorded on inventory control cards where merchandise is displayed. This method is used in particular for items of high value, such as electrical goods.

2. **Computerised systems**. A computerised system has the same function as the system mentioned above, but is faster and more accurate.

    The use of computerised data processing equipment enables the retailer to convert information on sales, purchases and inventory levels of merchandise into useful information (Correia et al., 2010).

    Point-of-sale systems are examples of computerised systems used for inventory control. Point-of-sale systems include cash registers or computer terminals capable of transmitting information directly to the central data processing facility and therefore adjusting inventory levels immediately once a product has been sold. Information regarding merchandise being sold can be entered into cash registers or computer terminals or entered using optical scanners that read the information in the barcodes on the merchandise into the computer terminal or cash register (Correia et al., 2010).

Off-line point-of-sale terminals relay information directly to the supplier's computer who uses the information to ship additional items automatically to the buyer/inventory manager.

Retailers usually use perpetual inventory control systems to keep a record of staple products and products with low-unit values, while items with high-unit values are controlled by carrying out periodic physical inventory taking and perpetual inventory control. An effective inventory control system will provide the required information at the correct time to retailers for use in decision-making (Dopson & Hayes, 2011).

Combinations of the above inventory control systems

1. Perpetual inventory control system in Rand

This inventory control system provides the retailer with continuous information about the quantity of inventory, in terms of Rand value, that should be on hand at any given time, as determined by internal bookkeeping records (Travis, 2010). The procedure for calculating the inventory in terms of Rand value at any given time is as follows:

Opening inventory on hand + purchases = total inventory on hand – sales – markdowns = closing inventory on hand.

Merchandise data on purchases, sales and markdowns are obtained from internal bookkeeping records. The closing inventory as calculated does not include any shortages as a result of pilferage or damage to merchandise (Travis, 2010). To determine the shortages, the merchandise must be counted physically. Many retailers use an estimated shortage percentage, for example 3%, based on their past experience, to adjust the closing inventory. A final adjustment is then made at the end of the season or year by physically counting the inventory.

2. Physical periodic inventory control system in Rand

This inventory control system provides the retailer with periodic information about the quantity of inventory on hand in Rand by physically counting and valuing the merchandise in inventory (Travis, 2010). It enables the retailer to calculate the sales in terms of Rand value from the last time the inventory was physically counted, for example monthly, quarterly, yearly and so forth. The sales in Rand for the period can be calculated in the following way:

Opening inventory on hand + purchases = total inventory on hand – closing inventory on hand = sales and markdowns – markdowns = sales.

Information about purchases and markdowns is obtained from internal records. The figure for the closing inventory on hand is obtained by physically counting the inventory and valuing it. This sales figure includes all shortages that occurred in the specific period since they are included in the closing inventory on hand calculated by physically counting the inventory.

3. Perpetual inventory control system in units

With this inventory control system all transactions that change the quantity of units in inventory, for example the quantity purchased or sold, are recorded on a continuous or perpetual basis, for example daily. This information can be recorded manually or by using computerised systems (Nikolai, Bazley & Jones, 2010).

4. Physical periodic inventory control systems in units

This inventory control system is used when the retailer requires periodic information on the quantity of merchandise in inventory in units. The inventory is then physically counted periodically, or visual control is used (Nikolai, Bazley & Jones, 2010).

Inventory valuation

Information about the actual value of inventory is an essential element in effective financial planning and control. The way in which retailers determine the value of their inventory greatly influences the result of the financial statements, that is, the income statement and balance sheet. Inventory can be valued at cost price or at retail selling price (Brechner, 2012).

Inventory valuation at cost price

Small retailers usually prefer the cost price method of inventory valuation, as it is easy to understand and implement, and requires only a limited amount of record-keeping. With this method of inventory valuation, merchandise is valued at cost price each time the inventory is physically counted.

The cost price method of inventory valuation may cause a problem when merchandise is purchased at different wholesale prices during times of inflation. The retailer must decide what cost price value to use for evaluating the merchandise in inventory. The first-in-first-out and last-in-first-out method of inventory valuation can be used to solve this problem.

1. The first-in-first-out method of inventory valuation

By using this method, the retailer assumes that merchandise is sold in the order in which it was purchased. In other words, old inventory that was purchased first, is sold first. The cost of the oldest items in inventory therefore determines the retailer's cost of merchandise sold. From a financial point of view, this method of inventory valuation results in an exaggerated presentation of profit during times of inflation, which in turn increases the retailer's tax liability (Brechner, 2012).

2. The last-in-first-out method of inventory valuation

The cost price of the last merchandise purchased is used to price the inventory. In other words, the cost of the merchandise purchased last determines the retailer's cost of goods sold. During times of rising wholesale prices, the use of this method of inventory valuation will result in a tax saving because of lower gross profit (Tuller, 2008).

The disadvantages of valuing inventory at cost price lie in the fact that inventory must first be counted physically, which is time-consuming. Also, since inventory is only counted physically once or twice a year, monthly or quarterly financial statements cannot be prepared and effective planning and control cannot be carried out. These disadvantages of the cost-price method of inventory valuation can be overcome by using the retail selling price as the basis for inventory valuation.

Inventory valuation at retail selling price

The method of inventory valuation at retail selling price enables the retailer to determine the cost price value of inventory levels at the end of a period without physically counting inventory. The value of the inventory indicated in the financial statements is, therefore, based on the retail selling price of the merchandise (Biafore, 2012). In order to implement this method, the retailer must calculate the following:

❑ The total quantity of merchandise available for sale;
❑ The cost complement;
❑ The total deductions;
❑ The value of the closing inventory at cost price and retail selling price.

1. Total quantity of merchandise available for sale

The total merchandise available for sale can be calculated by using the following formula (Nikolai, Bazley & Jones, 2010):

Opening inventory + net purchases + additional price increases + freight cost = total merchandise available for sale.

Example		
	At cost price (R)	At retail selling price (R)
Opening inventory:	120 000	200 000
+ net purchases	80 000	140 000
+ additional price increases	–	2 000
+ freight costs	4 000	–
= total merchandise available	204 000	342 000

From the above example it can be seen that the opening inventory and purchases are indicated in terms of cost price and retail selling price. Net purchases consist of all purchases during the sales period minus any returns to the suppliers. All price increases during the period are added to the retail value of the inventory to reflect the market value of the merchandise. Freight costs are added to reflect the true cost of the merchandise.

2. Calculating the cost complement

The cost complement indicates the relation of the cost value to the retail value of all merchandise available for sale during the sales period. This cost complement is calculated as follows (Brechner, 2012):

$$\text{Cost complement} = \frac{\text{cost value of inventory}}{\text{retail value of inventory}}$$

If the values in the example above are used, the cost complement can be calculated as:

$$\frac{204\ 000}{342\ 000}$$

= 0,5965, which means that the cost of the merchandise equals 59,65% of the retail value of the merchandise.

3. Calculating the total deductions

At this stage the total deductions from the total merchandise available for sale should be calculated. Deductions include merchandise sold, marked down, sold at a discount, pilfered or lost (Fishman, 2011). The total deductions can be calculated as follows:

Sales for the period + markdowns + discounts granted + shortages = total deductions.

If the sales for the period were R160 000, the merchandise was marked down by R30 000, discounts amounting to R10 000 were granted and shortages of R2 000 estimated, the total deductions are as follows:

Example	
Sales for the period	R160 000
+ markdowns	R30 000
+ discounts granted	R10 000
+ shortages	R2 000
= Total deductions	R202 000

4. Calculating the value of the closing inventory

The value of the closing inventory at cost price and at retail selling price can now be determined. The retail value of the closing inventory is calculated by subtracting the total deductions from the total merchandise available for sale at retail selling price (Carmichael, Whittington & Graham, 2007).

Example	
Total merchandise available for sale at retail selling price	R342 000
– Total deductions	R202 000
= Closing inventory at retail selling price	R140 000

The cost price value of closing inventory is calculated by multiplying the closing inventory at retail selling price by the cost complement (Jones, 2008).

Closing inventory at cost price = closing inventory at retail selling price x cost complement.

R83 510 = R140 000 x 0,5965

Although the above amount is only an estimate of the actual cost price value of the closing inventory, the amount is reliable enough to be used in the financial statements.

Although more records must be kept, the advantage of this method of inventory valuation is that regular calculation of financial statements is possible because information about the cost price and retail selling price of merchandise is available. The method also gives an up-to-date valuation of inventory.

5.4   Inventory analysis systems

Information on inventory is useful only if it can give retailers insight into past mistakes and help them to plan for the future. Merchandise data collected and processed by the inventory information system can, therefore, be used for evaluating previous performance and planning future actions (Stellman, 1998). Determining the inventory turnover rate and determining the return on inventory investment are the most important methods for evaluating the retailer's previous performance in controlling merchandise inventory. The unit and Rand open-to-buy methods are two of the most important methods for controlling future merchandising activities.

Inventory turnover rate

The inventory turnover rate is the rate at which retailers sell out and repurchase inventory. It can be defined *as the number of times the average inventory on hand is sold during a specific period of time* (Stadtler & Kilger, 2005). The inventory turnover rate can be calculated for a week, month, sales season, year, or for any other period. It can also be calculated for the store as a whole, for each separate department, for each classification of merchandise or for a specific item of merchandise. Inventory turnover rate analysis is a valuable merchandising aid, which assists retailers to make purchasing, price, inventory-keeping and promotion decisions. The inventory turnover rate can be calculated by using the unit value or Rand value of inventory (Jones, 2008).

Determining the inventory turnover rate by using the unit value of inventory

Inventory turnover in terms of units refers to the number of times the average number of merchandise units on hand has been sold and replenished in a sales season. The average number of inventory units on hand is the quantity of inventory usually available during a sales season. The inventory turnover rate, based on the unit value of inventory, can be calculated by using the following formula (Fleay, Poustie & Mroczkowski, 2011).

$$\text{Inventory turnover rate} = \frac{\text{Sales in units}}{\text{Average number of inventory units on hand}}$$

Calculating the average inventory on hand

The average inventory on hand for a certain period of time can be defined as the sum of the inventory on hand at the beginning of the period and at the end of the period, divided by two. The average inventory on hand can be calculated in terms of units or Rand value. The above method for calculating the average inventory on hand can be used only for periods of a month or shorter. If a longer period is used, for example a quarter, season or year, the average inventory on hand should be calculated as follows (Brechner, 2012):

Add the opening inventory for each month in the sales period and the closing inventory at the end of that period, and then divide the total by the number of months plus one.

Example
The average inventory on hand at retail selling price for the sales season of June, July and August can, for example, be calculated as follows:

1 June	R60 000
1 July	R40 000
1 August	R50 000
31 August	R35 000
Total inventory	R185 000

$$\text{Average inventory on hand} = \frac{\text{total inventory}}{\text{Number of months} + 1}$$

$$= \frac{185\ 000}{4}$$

$$= \text{R46 250}$$

This method is more accurate, because monthly changes in inventory are taken into consideration.

Calculating the inventory turnover rate by using the Rand value of inventory

Inventory turnover rate in Rand value is a measurement of the number of times the average inventory is sold at retail selling prices during a given period. The following formula can be used for calculating the inventory turnover rate based on the Rand value of inventory (Spurga, 2004):

$$\text{Inventory turnover rate} = \frac{\text{sales of merchandise for the period in Rand}}{\text{average retail Rand value of inventory on hand}}$$

If the inventory turnover rate has been calculated correctly, the calculation of the inventory turnover rate based on the unit value and Rand value of inventory will give the same value.

Analysing inventory turnover rates

Inventory turnover rates by themselves are of little importance to the retailer and an analysis of these figures is, therefore, needed. Inventory turnover rates can be compared from year to year to determine whether the right merchandise is being purchased. The inventory turnover rate of one retailer can also be compared with that of another, and if the retailer's inventory turnover rate differs from that of their competitors, the cause should be determined (Kimmel, Weygandt & Kieso, 2011). The rate of inventory turnover differs from one retailer to another as a result of the following factors:

1. The assortment kept by the stores is different. Retailers who keep a wide assortment of slow-moving merchandise have a low turnover rate compared to those who stock only best sellers that sell quickly.
2. Some retailers are situated close to suppliers and can obtain inventory more quickly than retailers situated far away, who have to order merchandise well in advance.

Advantages of a high inventory turnover rate

A high inventory turnover rate usually reflects effective merchandise planning and control (Cant, 2010). The advantages of a high inventory turnover rate are the following:

1. Fresher merchandise, because merchandise must be replenished more frequently.
2. Fewer price reductions, because there is no time for merchandise to go out of fashion or to be damaged.
3. Lower inventory-keeping costs, since less merchandise is in inventory at a given time.
4. Larger sales because the assortment of merchandise can be adjusted to the consumers' changing needs and therefore results in larger sales volumes.
5. Higher returns on the inventory investment because sales increase and inventory decreases.

Disadvantages of a high inventory turnover rate

A high inventory turnover rate may indicate that the retailer is purchasing too small a quantity and this means that (Nigam & Jain, 2001):

1. Retailers do not make use of quantity discounts.
2. Transport and handling costs increase.
3. Bookkeeping costs increase because too many orders have to be processed.

Another disadvantage of a high inventory turnover rate is a loss of sales because of out-of-inventory situations that arise.

Merchandise strategies by which inventory turnover rates can be increased

The following strategies can be used to increase inventory turnover rates (Cant, 2010):

1. Improved buying

When retailers know what their customers want and follow an effective merchandise plan, inventory turnover rates will increase.

2. Improved pricing strategy

If prices are fixed too high, the inventory turnover rate will decrease because consumers will not purchase these products. If this occurs, prices should immediately be marked down. Merchandise that is slow to sell should also be marked down to get rid of the inventory.

3. Accurate inventory control

Accurate inventory control helps to increase the inventory turnover rate. The inventory control system indicates which merchandise items sell well and which do not. It also indicates the maximum number of units of an item that should be in inventory. It prevents the purchase of too much merchandise, which decreases the inventory turnover rate.

4. Effective inventory keeping

The inventory turnover rate can be increased by effective inventory keeping, which will reduce inventory damage.

5. Co-ordinated promotion

The inventory turnover rate can be increased by following a co-ordinated plan for advertising, displays and personal selling. The sales of merchandise advertised, displayed in shop windows and promoted by sales staff increase.

6. Restricting the merchandise assortment

The inventory turnover rate can be increased by restricting the merchandise assortment kept in inventory to only the most popular brands, styles, sizes, colours and price lines (Pride, Hughes & Kapoor, 2012).

7. Keeping less reserve inventory or safety inventory

5.5 Measuring merchandise performance

Measuring the performance of merchandise is necessary in order to gain an understanding of the products that have performed well and those that have not performed as per the target. Inventory turnover is a key to merchandise performance. Inventory turnover measures how long inventory is on hand before it is sold. Items that are on hand for a short time have a high turnover, while those that are on hand for longer have a low turnover. Turnover is a key to high performance, which means profits in retailing. Success in retail can be measured by the amount of profit generated in relation to the working capital invested, in other words, the return on investment. Certain costs in any business are fixed or at least are not easily flexed. Shop rents and head office costs fall into this category. Merchandise margins and product mix, however, are variable and their management can either enhance or destroy profitability (Rao, 2010).

Gross and net profit

The *gross profit* is the profit obtained through sales before operating expenses are deducted. It is the result obtained by deducting the cost of goods sold from total sales (OECD, 2010).

Gross profit margin

This ratio measures the relation between gross profit and net sales by using the following formula:

$$\frac{\text{Gross profit}}{\text{Net sales}} \times \frac{100}{1} = \%$$

Net profit is the profit or loss at the end of the financial period. It is the operating profit plus other income and minus other expenses. It is on this profit that tax is paid, and it is usually referred to as net profit before tax or net profit after tax.

Net profit margin

The relationship between net profit and net sales is measured by applying the following formula:

$$\frac{\text{Net profit}}{\text{Net sales}} \times \frac{100}{1} = \%$$

Gross margin return on investment (GMROI)

Information on inventory turnover and gross margin must be considered together to obtain a comprehensive measure of the productivity of resources invested in inventory.

Consider the experiences of three retailers that sold torches.

On 1 January, Store A purchased 100 torches from a wholesaler at R15 each. It displayed the torches for sale at R30 each, selling the last one just before the store closed on 31 December.

Store B also bought 100 torches on 1 January at R15 each, but sold the entire stock by 30 June at R30 each. It then received a new shipment of 100 torches on 1 July and sold out the second lot on 31 December.

Like the other two stores, Store C started the year with 100 torches that it had purchased at R15 each, but it sold them at R37,50 a piece. By closing time on 31 December, it had sold only 80 of the 100 units.

What returns did the three stores get from the money they invested in torch inventory?

On 31 December, Store A completely depleted the inventory of 100 torches it had bought from the wholesaler on 1 January. Thus, its average inventory for the year was 50 units (see Figure 5.2). The value of this inventory was R750 (50 x R15). This R750 investment earned the firm revenues of R3 000 (100 units x R30/unit) and gross margins of R1 500. The firm's gross margin of R1 500 on its investment of R750 gave it a gross margin return of 200% on the merchandise investment.

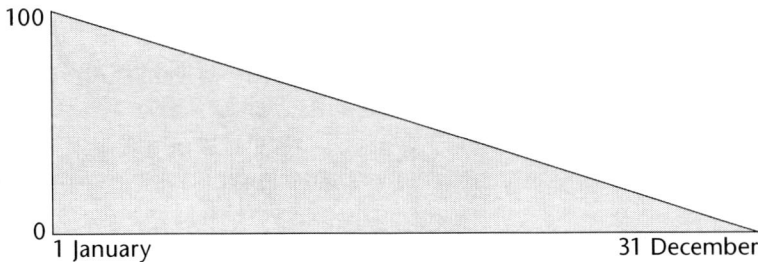

Figure 5.2 Store A average inventory ((100 + 0)/2 = 50)

Store B also had an average inventory of 50 torches (see Figure 5.3), so its investment in torch inventory was also R750. Unlike Store A, however, Store B sold 200 torches generating R6 000 of revenues and R3 000 of gross margins. The gross margin return on its investments was thus 400%.

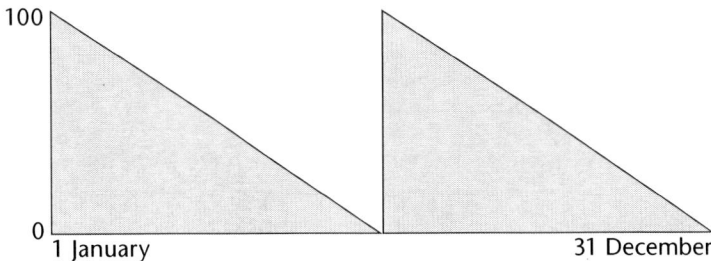

Figure 5.3 Store B average inventory ((100 + 0 + 100 + 0)/4 = 50)

Store C maintained an average inventory of 60 units (see Figure 5.4), so its inventory investment was R900. Since the store sold only 80 units during the year, its gross margins from torches totalled R1 800 (80 x R22,50). Store C, therefore, earned a gross margin return on investment of 200%, the same as Store A.

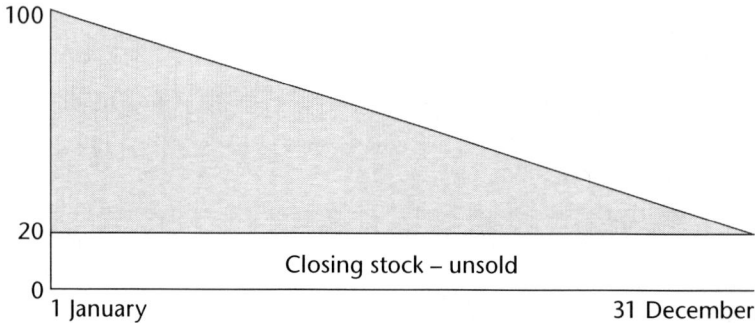

Figure 5.4 Store C average inventory ((80 + 0) / 2) + 20 = 60)

Measured by the criterion of gross margin return on investment, Store B performed the best of the three stores, and Stores A and C performed equally well. Store A and Store B both made the same unit margin on torches, but Store B generated higher returns because of its greater inventory turnover. Although both stores made R15 from each torch, the higher turnover at Store B increased its return on inventory investment.

But how did Store C get the same return as Store A despite its lower sales? The answer is in its greater unit margin. Although Store C had a lower inventory turnover, it generated gross margins of R22,50 on each sale compared to R15 at Store A. The higher margin compensated for the lower inventory turnover.

Calculating gross margin return on investment (GMROI)

The experiences of the three hardware stores reveal the importance of both the gross margins a merchandise item generates and the Rand amount of inventory investment in it when evaluating merchandise performance. Together they yield the gross margin return on investment (GMROI), an important yardstick for measuring merchandise performance (Friedlob & Plewa, 1996). GMROI is formally defined as follows:

$$\text{GMROI} = \frac{\text{Total gross margin (Rand)}}{\text{Rand cost of average inventory}} \times \frac{100}{1}$$

GMROI directly measures the amount of total margins an inventory investment generates. A GMROI of 100%, for example, means that each Rand invested in a particular inventory item generates one Rand of margin. If GMROI is 200%, a Rand invested in inventory generates two Rand of margin. Thus, a higher GMROI indicates a more productive item than a lower GMROI.

GMROI is one of the most important measures by which firms monitor and evaluate the performance of merchandise items. GMROI evaluates merchandise performance from a return on investment perspective. GMROI measures the gross margin returned per Rand invested in specific merchandise inventories. It measures the productivity of assets invested in merchandise inventory.

5.6 Summary

It is necessary to apply merchandise control in the management of merchandise. This merchandise control process consists of two systems, namely the inventory information system and the inventory analysis system.

The inventory information system uses various inventory control systems as sources of information. These include inventory control systems in units or in Rand, periodic physical inventory control systems and perpetual inventory control systems. Information regarding the actual value of inventory is essential for effective financial control of merchandise and inventory is therefore valued at cost price or at retail selling price. The inventory analysis system makes use of the inventory turnover rate and return on inventory investment to evaluate the retailer's previous performance.

Mini case study
Bass Pro runs a million-square foot distribution centre in Springfield, through which all their merchandise flows. Bass Pro's operations evolved from a 100% manual, paper-based system in their old facility to wireless data collection when they moved into their new distribution centre in 1992. The old system required workers to write on paper the item number, the shelf they took the item from, and where it was going. At the end of the day, the information was keypunched into the system. Not only did this create several points at which errors could occur, but Bass Pro could never be 100% sure what they had in the warehouse during the day.

5.7 Self-evaluation questions

1. Explain in detail the type of inventory control system that Bass Pro had used in the past and the inventory control system they use currently.
2. Explain with theory to the owner of Bass Pro what is meant by the 'inventory turnover rate' and calculate the inventory turnover rate for Bass Pro by taking the following sales figures into consideration:
   - Assume the cost of sales is R70 000;
   - Beginning inventory is R10 000;
   - Ending inventory is R9 000.

5.8 Bibliography

Axsäter, S. (2006). *Inventory control,* 2nd edition. Berlin: Springer Science + Business Media.

Biafore, B. (2012). *Quickbooks 2012: The missing manual.* Sebastopol, CA: O'Reilly Media.

Brechner, R. (2012). *Contemporary mathematics for business and consumers,* 6th edition. Mason, OH: South-Western Cengage Learning.

Cant, M.C. (2010). *Introduction to retailing,* 2nd edition. Cape Town: Juta.

Carmichael, D.R., Whittington, O.R. & Graham, L. (2007). *Accountants' handbook. Volume one: Financial accounting and general topics,* 11th edition. Hoboken, NJ: John Wiley & Sons.

Correia, C., Flynn, D. Uliana, E. & Wormald, M. (2010). *Financial management,* 6th edition. Cape Town: Juta.

Dopson, L.R. & Hayes, D.K. (2011). *Food and beverage cost control,* 5th edition. Hoboken, NJ: John Wiley & Sons.

Fishman, S.J.D. (2011). *Deduct it: Lower your small business taxes,* 7th edition. New York: Delta Printing Solutions.

Fleay, D., Poustie, N. & Mroczkowski, N. (2011). *TAFE accounting: Financial accounting applications,* 3rd edition. Melbourne: Cengage Learning.

Friedlob, G.T. & Plewa, F.J. (1996). *Understanding return on investment.* Hoboken, NJ: John Wiley & Sons.

Gilbert, D. (2003). *Retail marketing management,* 2nd edition. Harlow: Pearson Education Limited.

Heintz, J.A. & Parry, R.W. (2008). *College accountings,* 169th edition. Mason, OH: Thomson South-Western.

Hendrick, F.D., Barnes, F.C., Davis, E.W., Whybark, D.C. & Krieger, M. n.d. *Inventory manangement.* [Online] Available from: http://archive.sba.gov/idc/groups/public/documents/sba_homepage/pub_mp22.pdf Accessed: 15 March 2012.

Jacobsen, M.L. (2009). *The art of retail buying: An insider's guide to the best practices from the industry.* Singapore: John Wiley & Sons.

Jones, T. (2008). *Culinary calculations: Simplified math for culinary professionals,* 2nd edition. Hoboken, NJ: John Wiley & Sons.

Kimmel, P.D., Weygandt, J.J. & Kieso, D.E. (2011). *Accounting tools for business decision making,* 4th edition. Hoboken, NJ: John Wiley & Sons.

Lantion, C.C. (2001). *Student workbook: Fundamentals of management.* Iloilo: Rex Printing Company.

Lewison, D.M. & DeLozier, M.W. (1986). *Retailing: Casebook and applications,* 2nd edition. Basingstoke: Macmillan, p. 554.

Lusch, R.F. & Dunne, P.M. (2008). *Retailing,* 6th edition. Mason, OH: Thomson South-Western Higher Education.

Lusch, R.F., Dunne, P.M. & Carver, J.R. (2011). *Introduction to retailing,* 7th edition. Singapore: South-Western Cengage Learning.

Needles, B.E., Powers, M. & Crosson, S.V. (2011). *Financial and management accounting,* 11th edition. Mason, OH: South-Western Cengage Learning.

Nigam, B.M.L. & Jain, I.C. (2001). *Cost accounting: An introduction.* New Delhi: Prentice-Hall.

Nikolai, L.A., Bazley, J.D. & Jones, J.P. (2010). *Intermediate accounting*, 11th edition. Mason, OH: South-Western Cengage Learning.

OECD. (2010). *OECD transfer pricing guidelines for multinational enterprises and tax administrations*. OECD Publications.

Pride, W.M., Hughes, R.J. & Kapoor, J.R. (2012). *Business*, 11th edition. Mason, OH South-Western Cengage Learning.

Rao, S.R. (2010). *Evaluating merchandise performance*. [Online] Available from: http://www.citeman.com/9078-evaluating-merchandise-perrformance.html#ixzz1kSGDG2XG Accessed: 10 March 2012.

Spurga, R.C. (2004). *Balance sheet basics: Financial management for non-financial managers*. New York: Penguin.

Stadtler, H. & Kilger, C. (2005). *Supply chain management and advanced planning: Concepts, models, software and case studies*, 3rd edition. New York: Springer.

Stellman, J.M. (1998). *Encyclopaedia of occupational health and safety*, 4th edition. Geneva: ILO Publications.

Terblancé, N. (2002). *Retail management*. Cape Town: Oxford University Press.

Travis, R. (2010). *Synergistic management control systems*. Bloomington, IN: Author House.

Tuller, L.W. (2008). *The small business valuation book*, 2nd edition. Avon, MA: Adams Media.

6 Store decisions and design

CHAPTER

Michael C Cant

Learning objectives
After studying this chapter you should be able to:

- ❏ Explain the importance of location with regard to retailers;
- ❏ Discuss the importance of store atmosphere;
- ❏ Know why interior design is important;
- ❏ Discuss the role of exterior design in attracting customers;
- ❏ Describe the role and purpose of fixturing;
- ❏ Discuss why store position is crucial for success;
- ❏ Discuss how store architecture influences the business.

6.1 Location of retailers

The question often asked when it comes to retailing is: 'What are the three most important things in retailing?' The popular answer always is 'location, location, location'. Location is generally one of the most powerful considerations in a customer's store selection.

'Reilly's law of retail gravitation' was formulated in 1920 and holds that population and distance are the key factors for a retailer to consider when establishing the most suitable and profitable location. The higher the concentration of consumers within the area, the higher the likelihood of the retailer attracting customers. Special consideration should, therefore, be given to where a retail outlet should open, as the location is perhaps the key success factor for any retail establishment. Location decisions therefore have strategic significance as they can give a retailer a sustainable competitive advantage. Think of any McDonalds and where it is located, and you will see the strategic importance of location in terms of the number of cars passing the site, road access, visibility and the number of consumers in the area. It therefore stands to reason that the retailer in the location that is the most attractive to customers will make it more difficult for competitors (Levy & Weitz, 2009).

There are basically four types of store-based retail locations: business districts, shopping centres and malls, freestanding units and non-traditional locations. These are depicted in Figure 6.1. Please note that only store-based formats will be discussed as this is the focus of this chapter.

From Figure 6.1 it can be seen that retail formats are classified into two broad retail formats, namely store based and non-store based. The store based retail formats are discussed briefly below and are based largely on Lusch, Dunne & Carver, (2011).

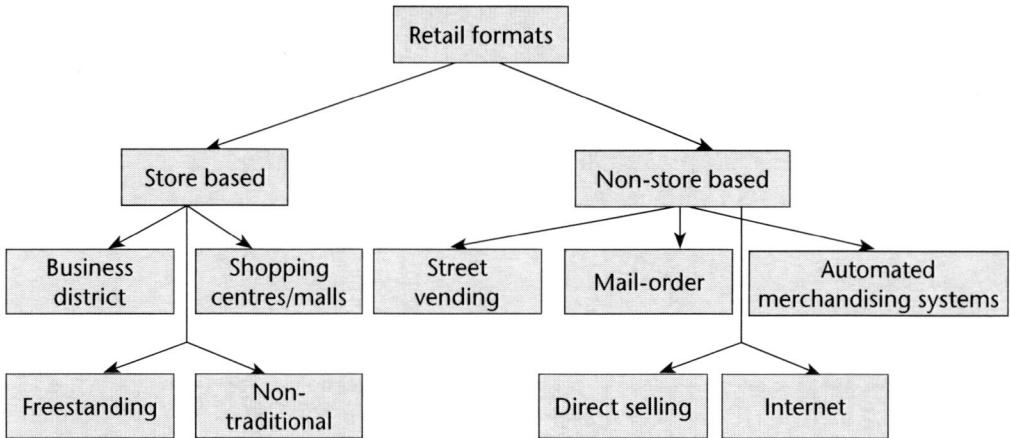

```
                              ┌──────────────┐
                              │Retail formats│
                              └──────────────┘
                    ┌─────────────┐       ┌─────────────────┐
                    │ Store based │       │ Non-store based │
                    └─────────────┘       └─────────────────┘
   ┌──────────┐ ┌──────────┐ ┌────────┐ ┌───────────┐ ┌──────────────────┐
   │ Business │ │ Shopping │ │ Street │ │Mail-order │ │    Automated     │
   │ district │ │centres/  │ │vending │ │           │ │merchandising     │
   │          │ │malls     │ │        │ │           │ │systems           │
   └──────────┘ └──────────┘ └────────┘ └───────────┘ └──────────────────┘
   ┌──────────────┐ ┌──────────┐   ┌──────────────┐ ┌──────────┐
   │ Freestanding │ │   Non-   │   │Direct selling│ │ Internet │
   │              │ │traditional│   │              │ │          │
   └──────────────┘ └──────────┘   └──────────────┘ └──────────┘
```

Figure 6.1 Retail formats for accessing your target market

Source: Adapted from Lusch, Dunne & Carver. (2011). Introduction to retailing, *7th edition. Mason, OH: South Western, p. 228*

Business/shopping districts

When cities were developed, a general trading area was selected and the specific shopping districts within the area were decided upon. In all cities you find a downtown central shopping district, which is traditionally the more popular location for retailers because of the high density of people living in and around the area (Lusch, Dunne & Carver, 2011). This downtown shopping area made it easy for people to shop on foot, at a time when owning your own vehicle was not as popular as it is today. However, as cities became over-populated and crowded people started to move away from the city – retailers followed.

The nature of residential areas is such that they are usually scattered and grow at different rates, so the levels of concentration of people are uneven. This made it difficult, if not impossible, for retailers to achieve their traditional closeness to their customer base at a scale that made a retail area sustainable. As a result, retailers started to position themselves away from the residential areas and simply waited for their customers to come to them.

Prospective retailers can select a location for their store in either the downtown part (as referred to above) or in shopping centres or malls. The *central business district (CBD)*, which is often in the geographic heart of a city, used to be the more popular retail location, but this has changed over the past decade or two for various reasons, some of which are given below (Cant, 2011):

❑ The rentals, and rates and taxes are generally higher in the CBDs, which results in higher selling prices (this is no longer the case in South Africa due to the decay in many CBD areas).
❑ Buildings have become unsightly and old and unattractive in many instances.
❑ Parking has become restricted and less available.
❑ Less wealthy people tend to live in the old buildings of the CBD.
❑ The shopping environment has become less attractive with many informal businesses on the streets among formal businesses and in open spaces.
❑ Due to the high incidence of crime in many of these areas, shoppers have tended to move away from these areas.

The fact that many CBD areas became overpopulated or unsafe or less financially feasible has led to the development of *secondary business districts* which attracted retailers. These areas are located away from the core of the city. Secondary business districts are smaller than CBDs, and generally develop around one (at least) department store or variety store at key crossroads. These locations generally attract business offices and smaller retailers, such as petrol stations, swimming-pool shops, pharmacies and hairdressers. It is usually easier to find parking in these locations and the rent is significantly lower than in the CBD (Cant, 2011).

In addition to the above there are *neighbourhood shopping streets* (also known as neighbourhood business districts). These streets are found in virtually every suburb and in areas in which houses are converted into business premises, or houses are demolished and replaced with small business premises. A neighbourhood business district is a convenience-oriented shopping area, which evolves to cater for the shopping needs of the local area and it usually contains numerous small stores, with the main retailer being a supermarket or a variety store, and is situated on a major road in a residential area. Typical outlets that can be found here include convenience stores, such as a café, a hairdresser, a dry cleaner, a bank, a small supermarket and a steakhouse. These locations offer retailers the opportunity to grow and become well-known and attract customers from other parts of the city (Lusch, Dunne & Carver, 2011).

Shopping centres and malls

For the retailer looking for an ideal location there are a number of options available. *Shopping complexes* are very popular in the larger cities. You will find that in the more affluent areas the shopping centres will tend to look more 'upmarket' and the mix of tenants and prices will also reflect this. 'A shopping centre (more commonly known as a mall) is a centrally owned or managed shopping district that is planned, has even-handed occupancy (the stores go together with one another in merchandise offerings) and is enclosed by parking conveniences'. These complexes usually have a name such as Woodlands Boulevard or Canal Walk and have corporate colours and management teams. The rent is generally very high and therefore the prices charged by retailers are also high (Colborne, 1996).

As part of the evolution of retailing, retailers located in the CBD areas started to consider suburban malls as an option to expand their businesses and to get closer to their customers who had been vacating the CBDs in order to get away from the hustle and bustle. As the competition from the regional malls expanded and the customers moved out of the CBD, many urban department stores have taken advantage of this trend and located their branch stores in suburban malls. The success of the suburban shopping mall has been due primarily to the following factors (Lusch, Dunne & Carver, 2011):

☐ Since 1945, a major shift of the population to less populated areas has taken place, i.e. away from the city centres. It therefore stands to reason that retailers should follow their customers and move to these locations.
☐ More people could afford their own vehicles and therefore drive to the CBD. This led to traffic congestion and a decline in parking space. In some cities in the USA, such as New York, parking can cost up to R170 per hour ($19) – or even more. As a result of these factors, suburban stores, where travelling and parking are relatively effortless, benefitted.
☐ Customer traffic increased as a result of the wide range of product offerings as well as retail mixes in the shopping malls.
☐ Suburban malls were less prone to crime than CBDs.
☐ Suburban malls offered a clean and tidy environment.
☐ Urban populations increased, which resulted in the need for more living space and people were forced to move further away from the cities. The CBDs therefore became too far away for people to do their shopping in the city.

The image projected by the shopping centre attracts a variety of consumers, which benefits the retailers that are located at the heart of the shopping centre (or mall) (Lusch, Dunne & Carver, 2011). When selecting a mall it is important that a retailer consider the make-up, image, preferences and personality of the mall before making a decision about whether to locate there or not.

Freestanding location

Another option open to a retailer is a *freestanding location*. This type of retail location is essentially any stand-alone, unconnected building. This option means exactly what it says: it stands free of others and can be anywhere – in a busy street or in the suburbs all on its own. These outlets generally have sufficient parking, but they attract fewer walk-in customers than those in malls, as this outlet now becomes a destination store. This means that the retailer of a freestanding site has to work harder via marketing efforts to get the customers inside.

6.2   Store atmosphere

Store atmosphere, which can also be called the store environment, refers to the design of the in-store environment, which communicates with the customers through the senses such as lighting, colour, music and smell (Pegler, 2010). These are referred to as store atmospherics. The store atmospherics that appeal to the five senses can be 'layered' into the store to enhance the shopping environment and improve the experience of the customer, as well as build the brand image of the store (Bell & Ternus, 2006). Layering means including several sensory elements, such as sight, sound, touch, taste and smell, to accomplish a particular atmosphere in the store environment.

It has been proven that if the shopping atmosphere is pleasant to the customer this will enhance the buying experience and the Rand spent in the store over time. Creating the perfect store atmosphere has, therefore, become a more important method of retail positioning and a strategic tool that can be used by retailers in their quest for higher profits and market share. A consumer's decision to support a store and to become a loyal customer can be influenced by the atmospherics that prevail in the store. It will also impact on the consumer's views and perceptions regarding the merchandise, service quality and satisfaction of the store. Recent experiential results suggest that signals in the store environment add to customer's perceptions of that specific store (Sharma & Stafford, 2000).

Atmospherics include, but are not limited to, the following:

❑   *Lighting.* A very effective tool used by retailers is lighting. Lighting can be used in many ways – some subtle and others less so. In a restaurant, for example, the lighting may be more subdued to create a romantic atmosphere. In a car dealership the lighting will be very bright to highlight the features of the vehicles being displayed.

❑   *Colour.* Colour can be used in many unique and inventive ways to create a certain atmosphere to help improve a retailer's image and even to set the mood for the customer. Colours such as red, gold and yellow are seen as warm colours and can help to create emotional, lively, hot and active responses, whereas colours such as white, blue and green are regarded as being more sedate or cool, and have a more serene, tender and soothing effect on customers.

❑   *Music.* A major contributor to the atmosphere in a store is the music. The popular saying is that staff should not play the music they like but rather music that will appeal to the customers. The type of store will determine the music to be played. In an upmarket, expensive restaurant the music will most likely be classical and soothing, while in a pub it may be heavy rock music – and loud. Music can direct the pace of the store 'traffic' and it can entice or direct the customer's attention.

❑   *Scent/smell.* Smell has a huge impact on the consumer's emotions, and the smell of a store can lead to a customer either buying or not. People are influenced by the smell in a store or the smell of a product. Second-hand car dealers could, for example, spray a scent in a car that smells like new leather. This smell usually has a positive effect on customers as it makes them feel that the car smells 'new' and therefore is still in good condition. Natural scents create better perceptions in the mind of the consumer than no scent at all. Scented stores give customers the perception that they are spending less time in the store while browsing through merchandise or waiting for an assistant. Scent, combined with music, can have a very positive impact on the impulsive buying behaviour of customers, if used correctly.

The above-mentioned elements must be used in an optimal combination to elicit the best possible reaction from customers in terms of their purchase behaviour. For example, lighting in a retail store involves more than just lighting up an area. If lighting is used effectively it can catch the eye of the consumer and is has been shown that it can positively influence customer shopping behaviour (Pegler, 2010).

A variety of studies have focused on atmospherics and their effects on consumer behaviour (Jang & Namkung, 2009). All of these studies used the Mehrabian-Russell model (M-R model). The M-R model is one of the most effective models to explain the effect that the physical store environment has on consumer behaviour. This model suggests that environmental stimuli lead to an emotional reaction that influences the consumers' behavioural responses. Figure 6.2 is a representation of the M-R model.

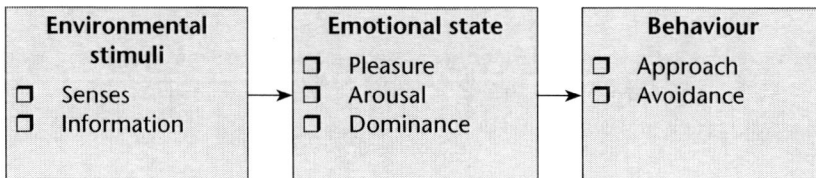

Figure 6.2 The Mehrabian-Russell model

Source: Adapted from Jang & Namkung (2009), p. 451

From this model it is clear that various factors in the environment stimulated some reaction. This may be joy or pleasure of something experienced, which then leads to a specific behaviour related to the emotional state of the consumer. It can, for example, lead to the purchasing of a specific product or a specific action.

6.3 Interior design

It is often said that all the hype created in a marketing campaign can come to zero once the customer walks in the store and the interior does not match the expectation created. Therefore the interior design of a store plays a key role in the shopping experience of the customer. On entering a store the customer will experience certain emotions or feelings. These emotions will be fed by what they see and experience in the store. A number of elements contribute to the overall interior design of the store.

Store design

Store design encompasses all the aspects of visual merchandising, which include visual displays, window displays and interior design, as well as fixtures, fittings and lighting (Morgan, 2008). The main aim of store design is to ensure the retailer's strategy is implemented in such a way that it enhances the goals, vision and brand of the retailer; at the same time it must be consistent with and support the retailer's strategy in meeting the needs of the target market and building a sustainable competitive advantage (Levy & Weitz, 2009).

The brand image and store design go hand in hand, as the design is the view the customer has of the retailer and by implication the brand. Retailers in most instances rely on the design and layout of the store to attract customers to the store to browse and shop. A retailer's store design encompasses different floor plans and store layouts (grid layout, free-flow layout, racetrack layout) and feature areas (displays). A floor plan is a flat illustration of two dimensions, that is, the length and width of an area as seen from above. The most popular floor plans used by retailers are discussed below.

❑ *Grid layout.* The grid layout is a popular layout normally used in supermarkets and discount stores. It is generally preferred by stores that offer self-service. In this layout, shelves are arranged in a grid and all merchandise is displayed in a similar way (Pradhan, 2008). A grid layout permits customers to move without restraint within the area and it uses space effectively. Figure 6.3 illustrates a grid layout.

❑ *The free-flow layout.* In a free-flow layout, the merchandise is arranged in an asymmetrical manner and it allows the customers to move freely throughout the store. This type of layout encourages customers to browse. Figure 6.4 is an illustration of the free-flow layout.

❑ *The racetrack layout.* In the racetrack layout or loop layout, displays are arranged in the shape of a racetrack or a loop with a main aisle running through the store (Pradhan, 2008). This type of layout is used extensively by department stores. Figure 6.5 is an illustration of the racetrack layout.

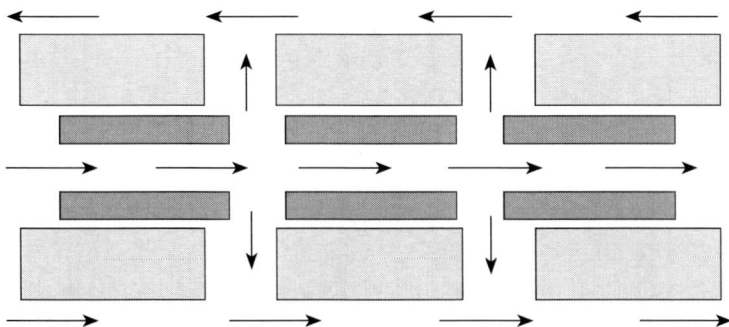

Figure 6.3 Grid layout

Source: Adapted from Pegler. (2010). Visual merchandising and display, *5th edition. New York: Fairchild Publications, pp. 284–292*

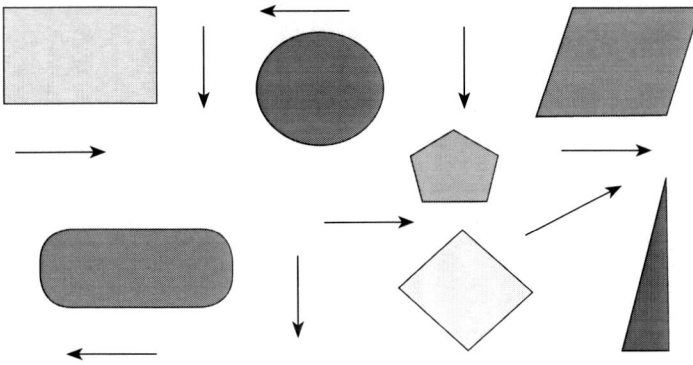

Figure 6.4 Free-flow layout

Source: Adapted from Pegler. (2010). Visual merchandising and display, *5th edition. New York: Fairchild Publications, p. 284.*

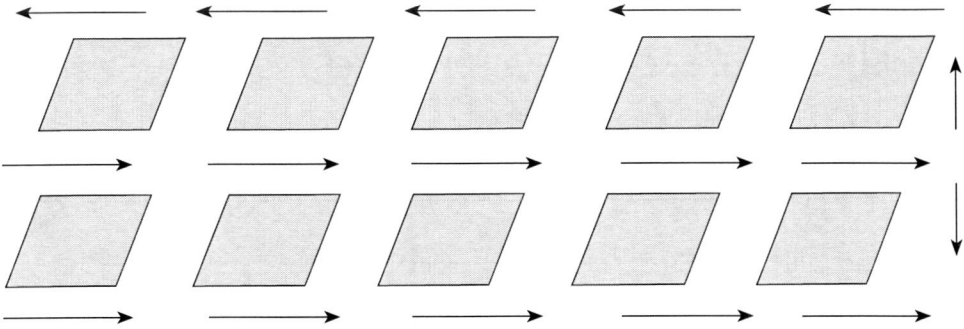

Figure 6.5 Racetrack/loop layout

Source: Adapted from Pegler. (2010). Visual merchandising and display, *5th edition. New York: Fairchild Publications, p. 284.*

Space allocation

What shoppers or customers normally see is the sales floor, but this is not the only element in a retail store with which the planner must contend. The allocation of space in a store is extremely important and must be utilised effectively in order to generate the most sales per square metre. There are five types of space needs in a store: (1) the back room, (2) offices and other functional spaces, (3) aisles, service areas and other non-selling areas, (4) wall merchandising space and (5) floor merchandising space (Lusch, Dunne & Carver, 2011). Each of these is discussed below:

Back room

This space is also referred to as dead space as it is used for the receiving of stock and to keep stock. This space must be limited as the bigger this space, the less sales space there can be. The back room is generally at the back of the store away from the customers and where deliveries can be handled easy. The percentage of space dedicated to the back room varies greatly, depending on the type of retailer and the range of items carried in the store. The trend today is to minimise the amount of inventory in the store, which also means that less space is needed. Costs are saved, as rent is paid for this space as well.

Offices and other functional spaces

Once again these areas are not income generating so they should be placed in areas less suitable for trading. Typically these areas include a staff chill room (tea room), a training room, offices for management staff and bathrooms. Due to the high cost of rental space, many retailers have relocated their management teams to other off-site locations, which are cheaper. This leaves in-store space primarily for selling and receiving (Diamond & Litt, 2009).

Aisles, service areas and other non-selling areas

Designing the layout of a store means making provision for shoppers to move about in a structured way without them feeling cramped or preventing trollies from passing one another comfortably. These spaces are also called non-selling areas or spaces. These aisles also have to be large enough to accommodate peak crowds and people with disabilities. In addition to the aisles, space must be made for dressing rooms, lay-bye areas, service desks and other customer-service facilities. As all these areas take away selling space, the careful placement of these booths and service counters is crucial.

Wall merchandising space

Over time the value of wall space as a marketing tool in a retail store has become more and more clear. In the past it was seen as the perimeter of the store in which trade takes place. Today this has changed dramatically. It is used for shelving as well as to guide shoppers in the store to other trading areas or to display new merchandise. For instance, when walking into a store, a shopper will see children's clothing against a wall, which will immediately indicate where the kids clothing section is located. Walls can therefore be seen as fixtures to hold large amounts of merchandise and provide a visual backdrop for the merchandise on the floor. Walls are used in most layout designs, although a specialist clothing boutique may choose not to use the wall in order to maintain the image of exclusivity (Newman & Cullen, 2002). Wall fixtures are discussed in more detail later.

Floor merchandising space

The actual selling space is called the floor merchandising space and this is an area that has to be carefully planned and filled in order to obtain the best sales results. Generally speaking, retailers make use of bulk fixtures on the sales floor to carry large quantities of merchandise. This can lead to a perception of overcrowding. Many retailers are applying a different approach, namely to display as attractively and effectively as possible the largest amount of stock that customers can comprehend without feeling overwhelmed. In many cases it is more dramatic to display less merchandise and this stimulates higher sales (Lusch, Dunne & Carver, 2011). Various types of fixturing can be used by retailers and some of these are discussed below.

Fixturing

Retail stores need to create fixture designs that are functional as well as visually appealing. Each fixture in a retail store has a purpose or role for either the customer or the retailer – by understanding and working towards these purposes the retailer will be able to improve sales and profitability. Retailers also use different fixtures for different line items according to whether they are prestige, special value or end-of-line items (Newman & Cullen, 2002).

Hardlines

The term hardline is to some extent self-explanatory as it refers to a solid hard structure – something commonly found in supermarkets and discount stores. The hardline fixtures are also referred to as gondolas, so named because they are long structures consisting of a large base and a vertical spine or wall, fitted with sockets or notches into which a variety of shelves, peg hooks, bins, baskets, and other hardware can be inserted. The ends are referred to as gondola ends and are prime spots for promotional items – at a higher price.

Softlines

The softline fixtures are typically synonymous with softer features and items, such as clothing or textiles. Retailers make use of smaller, specialised fixtures, such as the four-way feature rack and the round rack in place of the straight rack that was used extensively in the past. In this way apparel can be better displayed, is more visible and does not appear cluttered.

Wall fixtures

This last type of fixture is designed to be hung on the wall. In order to turn the wall into a merchandisable space, it can be covered with shelving with holes in which to place hooks or pegs – similar to what you get on gondola shelves. In fact it is like mounting gondola shelves without their sides to the wall and attaching shelves, peg hooks, bins, baskets, and even hanger bars to these on which to display goods. In this type of fixture, walls not only hold large amounts of merchandise but also serve as a visual backdrop for the department (Lusch, Dunne & Carver, 2011). These fixtures are higher than the shelves and can be seen from afar by shoppers, helping them to identify departments or sections, and to see new items or special promotions.

Surfacing

Surfacing refers to the fourth component of the interior store design. Surfacing deals with the covering of the floors and walls of the retail outlet. The main aim of surfacing is to provide an aesthetic look to the outlet as well as ensure that it is functional. Some of the materials, such as the tiles on the floors, are more permanent, while others, such as paint, are more easily changed to tie in with short-term needs or promotions (Diamond & Litt, 2009).

Floors

The covering of floors is a serious issue and requires careful planning. This is due to the fairly permanent nature of flooring and the fact that it requires a major operation and inconvenience to change at a later stage. The safety of customers also needs to be considered as a slippery surface can result in injury and potential lawsuits. The floors can be covered in a wide range of coverings, such as carpets, rugs, wood, marble and ceramic tiles, and the choice should be linked to the preferences and comfort of customers and employees.

Walls

Walls can be covered fairly quick and easily – with limited inconvenience to shoppers and staff – and it is fairly inexpensive to create a new look and feel to meet the operational needs of the business. Typically, walls are covered with paint, wallpaper, fabric, wood or mirrors, depending on the required effect or the theme that best suits the corporate goals of the business. Each material imparts a different feeling and must be selected with the overall design concept in mind.

Aspects impacting on the interior have been discussed and now we move on to the external design of the outlet.

6.4   External design

The external design of a store is of immense importance because it is the first impression that motivates a consumer to enter (Diamond & Litt, 2009). The store's exterior influences a customer's impression of a particular outlet and can assist the consumers to evaluate the nature of the store in terms of the type of outlet, the assortment on offer and their inclination to patronise the store or not.

Therefore a shop's exterior design should project and be consistent with the desired store image that the retailer wishes to project to the target market (Cox & Brittain, 2004). Some elements that will influence the perception and that have to be taken into consideration are discussed below.

Store position

The positioning of a store is one of the most crucial decisions a retailer can make. If located in the wrong place there will not be any customers. It is also important that the store is visible, as well as accessible, to the target market. Depending on the type of target market and the type of product sold, retailers should ideally be positioned in a location that is clearly visible from main routes. Furthermore the retailer should evaluate the other stores in the area in terms of their joint drawing power and compatibility and how they can complement one another. The availability of sufficient parking or public transport, and the ease of access to the store are other key factors to consider (Cox & Brittain, 2004).

Architecture

Architectural style is an important element in a retailer's external appearance as it can indicate the size and prestige of the retailer's operations. In many instances, however, retailers have to make do with what they can lease as the design has already been decided upon by the developers. In this case, the responsibility of the retailer is limited to ensure that the store design is compatible with their own ideas and goals. The impression conveyed by a store's outward appearance can, in essence, influence a shopper's judgement on the benefits to be gained from visiting a particular store, and, in such instances, the size and appearance can be the deciding factor. The overall size of an outlet may be important, but it is often the width (particularly window space) that is more essential than the height or depth of the building, as this has an impact on display space, visibility and customer perceptions (Cox & Brittain, 2004).

The store's signage

Store signage is another way of attracting customers into a store. It is an extremely effective method of communicating with customers as it is easily changed, often read and always available, and inexpensive compared to other advertising media (Cant, 2010).

Signage, or the shop's sign, according to Piotrowski and Rogers (2007), is defined as an '…outdoor advertisement on the premises of a store or business describing the product or services provided by the advertiser. Ideally, exterior signs should explain the name, location, and type of merchandise.'

A key benefit of signage is that it aids consumers in recognising the seller (e.g. Mr Price), what sort of merchandise is being sold (e.g. King Pie), where the retailer is located (e.g. Woolworths Sandton), what services and products to expect (e.g. a Pep sign in any town in the country means the same products, service and advantages to customers), or the times at which stores are open (e.g. 8 till late) (Cox & Brittain, 2004).

The storefront

A storefront is the physical exterior of the actual store, which includes construction materials, the store entrance, windows, lighting and everything else to which the shopper is exposed when standing outside the shop. The storefront is used by a retailer to project an image to their customers, such as being a low-price store, trendy, upscale, conservative and so on. Consumers passing through a mall or shopping centre will often evaluate a store by its storefront and hence decide to enter it or not (Berman & Evans, 2010).

According to Cox and Brittain (2004), there are three basic storefront configurations, which are as follows:

1. *The straight front.* This is when a storefront runs parallel to a street or pavement with possibly a break for an entrance into the store. Such a design is seen in Figure 6.6.

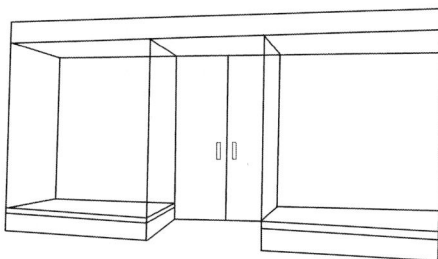

Figure 6.6 Straight front

Source: Piotrowski & Rogers. (2007). Designing commercial interiors, 2nd edition. Hoboken, NJ: John Wiley and Sons, p. 201

2. *The angled front.* This design creates a more appealing and attractive storefront and directs potential buyers into the store. With such a design in place potential buyers are able to view products at a better angle and the design is seen to reduce glare. Such a design is illustrated in Figure 6.7.

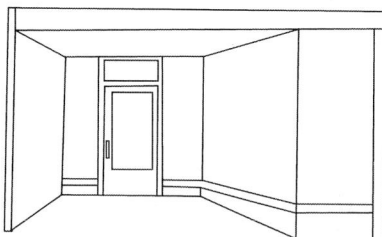

Figure 6.7 Angled front

Source: Piotrowski & Rogers. (2007). Designing commercial interiors, 2nd edition. Hoboken, NJ: John Wiley and Sons, p. 201

3. *The arcade front.* This design is basically a straight-front shape but with numerous recessed windows or entrances. Such a design will create an attractive and relaxing atmosphere surrounding a store and will furthermore provide a potential buyer with numerous protected areas for window shopping. The arcade storefront is shown in Figure 6.8.

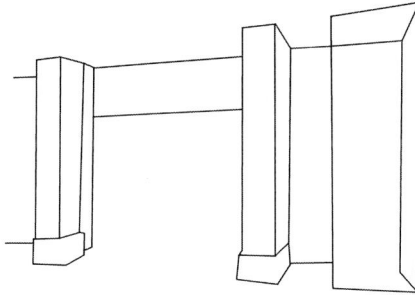

Figure 6.8 Arcade front

Source: Piotrowski & Rogers. (2007). Designing commercial interiors, *2nd edition. Hoboken, NJ: John Wiley and Sons, p. 201*

The store entrance

In order to do any shopping a customer has to pass through a store entrance. As soon as they do this they form a first impression, which will affect the image they have of the store. This impression can be temporary or be of such a nature that it will influence the decision of whether or not to patronise the store again in future.

The entry area plays an important role in developing a store's image and the first four metres of the store are often referred to as the *decompression zone* because potential buyers are adjusting to the new environment – escaping from the busy street or mall, taking off their warm winter coats, closing their umbrellas, as well as forming an overall visual interpretation of the entire store. Customers are often not prepared to assess merchandise or even make any purchasing decision in the 'decompression zone', so retailers should try to keep this area free of merchandise, displays and signage (Levy, Weitz & Beitelspacher, 2012).

According to Varley (2006), the entrance to a store must satisfy two criteria:

❏ That of functionality. This means that it must serve a purpose and function, such as being inviting, informative and so forth.

❏ That of aesthetic appeal. The use of colours and lighting can be used very effectively here to appeal to the sight of customers.

There are numerous ways a retailer could have an entrance into their store, however there are generally four alternative types of store entrances that a retailer could make use of:

◻ *Open entrance.* This type of entrance is used often by large supermarkets and is inviting to customers – a large number of people, as well as those with trollies and disabilities. It does not feel constricted and has a feeling of space and it helps to break down any form of barrier between the store and its external environment. A problem with an open entrance is that it may hinder recognition of the store or its identity, and it has been proven to increase the incidence of theft. This form of entrance is usually found in shopping centres, which protect the store from outside elements.

◻ *Semi-open entrance and closed window displays.* With semi-open and closed window displays the retailer provides easy accessibility to the store, but a window display can still be created, thereby contributing to a store's identity. It also negates a number of the disadvantages of the open entrance as indicated above.

◻ *Funnel or lobby entrances.* A funnel or lobby design, is a design that will allow the consumer to feel as if they are inside the store, without actually stepping over the entrance by using an increased number of window displays.

◻ *Standard door.* This form of design is what will give the retailer a more exclusive feel in the mind of the consumer and allows a retailer to make use of numerous window displays that stand out and communicate the retailer's offering to a passing audience.

Window structures

Windows are used to a large extent to attract customers and entice them into the store, but a window also has other various functions, such as (Cox & Brittain, 2004):

1. To show a representative sample of merchandise sold in the store;
2. To display promotional or seasonal lines;
3. A mixture of both (1) and (2).

Window size and style

The size of a retailer's window can, in essence, affect what they can achieve. The shape and size of windows are not set and it is the retailer's prerogative to decide on the shape and size they want to use to differentiate themselves from other stores and to create their own identity. In terms of size, the bigger the window the more merchandise and more props it will require to fill it. There are a variety of styles of window that can be used, as follows (Morgan, 2008):

◻ *Closed windows.* These windows are usually seen in department stores and have large panes of glass at the front (facing passers-by on the street), and have a firm back wall and two firm side walls, as well as a door. Pep Stores often uses these windows as it offers them an opportunity to display their merchandise and prices to their customers. These windows are often the most exciting to decorate as one can capture a passer-by's attention from the street. It also forces customers to enter the store if they want to see more, as they cannot see inside the store because of the solid back to the window.

- *Open-back windows.* Such windows have no back wall but may have side walls. Many retailers favour such windows as they make the interior of the store visible from the outside and allow customers to see what is in the store, the wall displays and so on.
- *No window.* Shopping arcades are good examples of stores that often do not have store windows. The whole front of a store is seen to be exposed to passers-by and in the evenings a mere lattice is used to separate the store from the passing parade. This can have positive and negative aspects, as some people might not even notice the store or do not want to enter it, while others will enter due to curiosity.
- *Angled windows.* The angled window concept features glass panes that expand from a store's building parameter and end at the entrance to the store, which is set back about two metres. In these instances it is important for the retailer to remember that merchandise should be displayed parallel to the pane of glass and not to the pavement or direction of the street. The reason for this is that customers are more prone to stop and stand in front of the pane of glass before entering the door.
- *Corner windows.* These windows are located on a corner and virtually wrap around a corner. Displayed merchandise should in these cases be dressed towards the middle of the arc. Innovative displays can assist in leading a customer from one side of the window all the way around to the other side and, furthermore, lead them towards the entrance of the store. The corner window design can be seen to benefit from traffic that joins from two different streets (Diamond & Litt, 2009).
- *Arcade windows.* This window design is where the door to the entrance is set back from the windows. In such a design, part of the display should face the pavement or passing street to get the customer's attention, and the other should be set on the return side, leading a customer towards the entrance of the store. In an arcade front window design, a store's entrance is set back about four or more metres from the building parameter (Diamond & Litt, 2009).
- *Showcase windows.* Stores that specialise in small items, such as jewellery or pens, often rely on showcase windows to attract a customer's attention. Such small or minute windows are placed at a consumer's eye level to allow close inspection of the goods.

6.5 Summary

In this chapter we focused on the major aspects of merchandising in retail stores. We started by discussing the location of retailers, and dividing retailers into two broad retail formats, namely store based and non-store based retailers. We explained store atmosphere, emphasising atmospherics, such as lighting, colour, music and scent/smell. We discussed the interior design of a store, taking into consideration factors such as store design, space allocation, fixturing and surfacing. We ended with a discussion on a store's external design, looking at factors such as store position, architecture, store signage, storefront, store entrance and window structures.

Mini case study

Truworths

Truworths International currently comprises Truworths Limited and the international franchise operations.

Truworths Limited is a leading South African retailer of fashion merchandise. The operation has developed a range of specialised retail formats including Truworths Woman, Truworths Man, Daniel Hechter, Inwear and LTD. Key to Truworths' success has been the development of stores as brands and brands as stores. Truworths has become the destination of choice for fashionable individuals in search of quality fashion that makes them look attractive and successful, and feel enthused with confidence.

Retail operations

We strive to provide an enticing, exciting and visually appealing fashion retail environment where our customers can shop effortlessly, assisted by energetic, committed people. It is essential that store ambience reflects and enhances customer confidence in our offering of an innovative and adventurous blend of colour, fabric and fashion styling of international standards.

Regular market surveys indicate that excellent standards of service and visual merchandise presentation have been maintained. This has been achieved in conjunction with an improvement in productivity and profitability.

Merchandise

Truworths is positioned as the country's premier fashion chain, catering for the youthful, quality-conscious South African customer who seeks inspired, innovative and adventurous fashion styling of international standards.

Our merchants have consistently proven their ability to forecast accurately and interpret global fashion trends for the South African lifestyle, earning Truworths the trust and respect of our customers.

Source: http://www.truworths.co.za/about-us

Questions

1. Which store atmosphere elements does Truworths make use of in order to create an exciting and visually appealing fashion retail environment in which their customers can shop effortlessly?
2. Truworths has developed a range of specialised retail locations. Which type of retail location is used most by Truworths stores and why?

6.6 Self-evaluation questions

1. Define the concept of store atmospherics and explain the motivation behind this concept, then name the various cues that are associated with store atmospherics.
2. Music is an atmospheric cue that retailers use to create a mood within their store. However, unlike other atmospheric cues, music can be easily altered. Discuss four reasons why playing music in a store can assist a retailer to attract customers to their store.
3. Discuss the three types of floor layouts. Provide examples of where each floor layout could be used and give reasons for your answers.

6.7 Bibliography

Bell, J.A. & Ternus, K. (2006). *Silent selling,* 3rd edition. New York: Fairchild Books.

Berman, B. & Evans, J.R. (2010). *Retail management: A strategic approach.* 11th edition. Upper Saddle River, NJ: Prentice-Hall, p. 509.

Cant, M.C. (2010). *Introduction to retailing,* 2nd edition. Cape Town: Juta, p. 61.

Cant, M.C. (2011). *The South African retail environment.* Pretoria: University of South Africa.

Colborne, R. (1996). *Visual merchandising: The business of merchandising presentation.* New York: Thomson Learning, p. 26.

Cox, R. & Brittain, P. (2004). *Retailing: An introduction.* London: Pearson Education.

Diamond, E. (2006). *Fashion retailing: A multi-channel approach,* 2nd edition. Upper Saddle River, NJ: Pearson Education.

Diamond, J. & Litt, S. (2009). *Retailing in the twenty-first century,* 2nd edition. New York: Fairchild Books.

Jang, S.S. & Namkung, Y. (2009). Perceived quality, emotions and behavioural intentions: Application of an extended Mehrabian-Russell model to restaurants. *Journal of Business Research,* 62.

Levy, M. & Weitz, B.A. (2009). *Retailing management,* 7th edition. New York: McGraw-Hill/Irwin.

Levy, M., Weitz, B.A. & Beitelspacher, L.S. (2012). *Retailing management,* 8th edition. New York: McGraw-Hill.

Lusch, R.F., Dunne, P.M. & Carver, J.R. (2011). *Introduction to retailing,* 7th edition. Mason, OH: South Western.

Morgan, T. (2008). *Visual merchandising: Window and in-store displays for retail.* London: Laurence King.

Newman, A.J. & Cullen, P. (2002). *Retailing: environment & operations.* London: Thomson Learning.

Pegler, M. (2010). *Visual merchandising and display,* 5th edition. New York: Fairchild Books, p. 181.

Piotrowski, C.M. & Rogers, E.A. (2007). *Designing commercial interiors,* 2nd edition. Hoboken, NJ: John Wiley and Sons, p. 201.

Pradhan, S. (2008). *Retailing management,* 11th edition. Columbus, OH: McGraw-Hill.

Sharma, A. & Stafford, T.F. (2000). The effect of retail atmospherics on customers' perceptions of salespeople and customer persuasion: An empirical investigation. *Journal of Business Research,* 49: 183.

Sullivan, M. & Adcock, D. (2002). *Retail marketing.* London: Thomsons, p. 140–141.

Varley, R. (2006). *Retail product management,* 2nd edition. New York: Routledge. p. 170.

Website

About.com. *Types of retail locations.* (2011). Online. Available from: http://retail.about.com/od/location/a/retail_location.htm. Accessed: 15 April 2011.

7 Product pricing

Jan A Wiid

7.1 Introduction

Bongani and Thandi were looking for office furniture for their new downtown offices. The price quoted to Thandi for office furniture was R35 500, but Bongani paid only R24 500 for his. At first glance it looks as though Bongani got a better deal, but did he?

Thandi's furniture was delivered to her office, she had a year to pay for it, and it was beautifully finished. Bongani, on the other hand, bought a partially assembled desk with no finish on it (he is a do-it-yourself enthusiast). He had to assemble the drawers and bookcases, and then painstakingly stain, varnish and hand-polish the furniture. He arranged for the delivery himself, and he paid cash in full at the time of purchase.

So who got the better deal? The answer is not that simple. When pricing, marketers have to consider not only the tangible goods, but also the associated services and need-satisfying benefits.

Now consider the cabinetmaker who has to set a price for his new furniture. He has to consider how each price will compare to (1) prices for similar furniture made by other manufacturers, (2) other products in the seller's line of office furniture. He also has to consider whether furniture dealers will be able to make sufficient profit from the sales. If the selling price of the furniture does not meet market requirements, or is insufficient to meet the profit objectives of both the retailer and the manufacturer, price promotions in the form of cash rebates or special financing arrangements for buyers may be necessary. Besides these pricing decisions, the cabinetmaker has to decide on what discount to give retailers. In this chapter we examine the concept of price and issues pertaining to basic price determination.

7.2 Meaning and role of price

Pricing is the process of determining the value of a product (the price) that consumers will be willing to pay under particular circumstances at a particular time.

Marketers in general want a satisfactory profit or return on their investments, as well as the highest possible sales volume. These two factors are often in conflict. There are some instances, for example, when it makes sense to maximise profit margins, and other instances when it makes sense to maximise the volume of sales. A high sales volume (turnover) at a lower unit price may be more profitable in the long run than a lower sales volume at a higher unit price.

A price is the value given to something and, in our modern economic system, generally paid in money. We can also say that price is the value of something expressed in terms of Rand and cents, or (in the export market) in other currencies, such as dollars or pounds. It is simply the amount of money paid to purchase a product or a service (Cant, Brink & Machado, 2005). For marketers (sellers) price is essentially a means to achieve the objective of making a profit. For consumers and commercial users it is the means to acquire need-satisfying goods or services. These can take different forms, as indicated in Table 7.1.

Table 7.1 The meaning of price

Form: money offering	What is given in return: need-satisfying goods or services
Price	Physical merchandise
Tuition fee	Education
Rent	Place to live or equipment for a specific time period
Interest	Use of money
Fee	Professional service
Fare	Transportation
Toll	Use of road
Rate	Hotel rooms, taxes
Dues	Membership
Commission	Salesperson's service
Salary	Work of employees and managers
Wage	Work of daily or hourly workers
Bribe	Illegal action

Source: Adapted from Cant, Strydom, Jooste & Du Plessis. (2006). Marketing management, *5th edition. Cape Town: Juta*

Market price can be seen as the price a consumer is prepared to pay to be able to get the need-satisfaction that a product or service can offer. When pricing, marketers consider more than just the tangible goods; they consider a combination of the core product plus services and its need-satisfying benefits. Marketers (sellers) also turn to non-price aspects, such as convenience, brand, quality, uniqueness, customer service and store atmosphere, in an attempt to win customers and minimise the customers' price considerations.

7.3 Price setting

The price setting process is first of all a step-by-step procedure, see Figure 7.1.

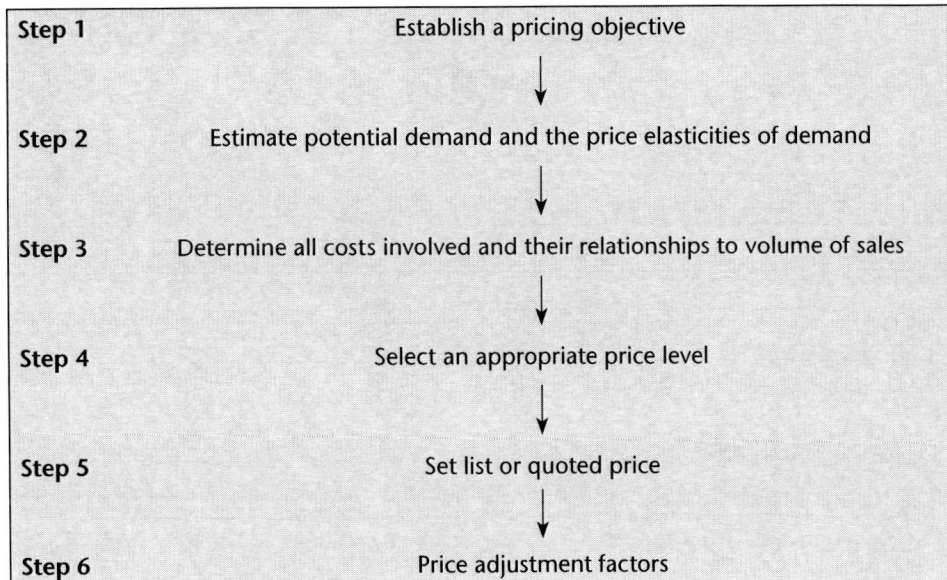

Step 1	Establish a pricing objective
Step 2	Estimate potential demand and the price elasticities of demand
Step 3	Determine all costs involved and their relationships to volume of sales
Step 4	Select an appropriate price level
Step 5	Set list or quoted price
Step 6	Price adjustment factors

Figure 7.1 The price setting process

Source: Adapted from Rix. (2003). Essential marketing skills. *New York: McGraw-Hill*

7.4 Pricing objectives

Pricing objectives are goals that give direction to the whole pricing process (Monroe, 2003). Before marketers can set selling prices for their merchandise, they must set specific, measurable pricing objectives that correspond to their marketing and enterprise objectives (Cant, Brink & Machado, 2005). Pricing objectives can be divided into three categories: profit-oriented objectives, sales-oriented objectives and status quo-oriented objectives.

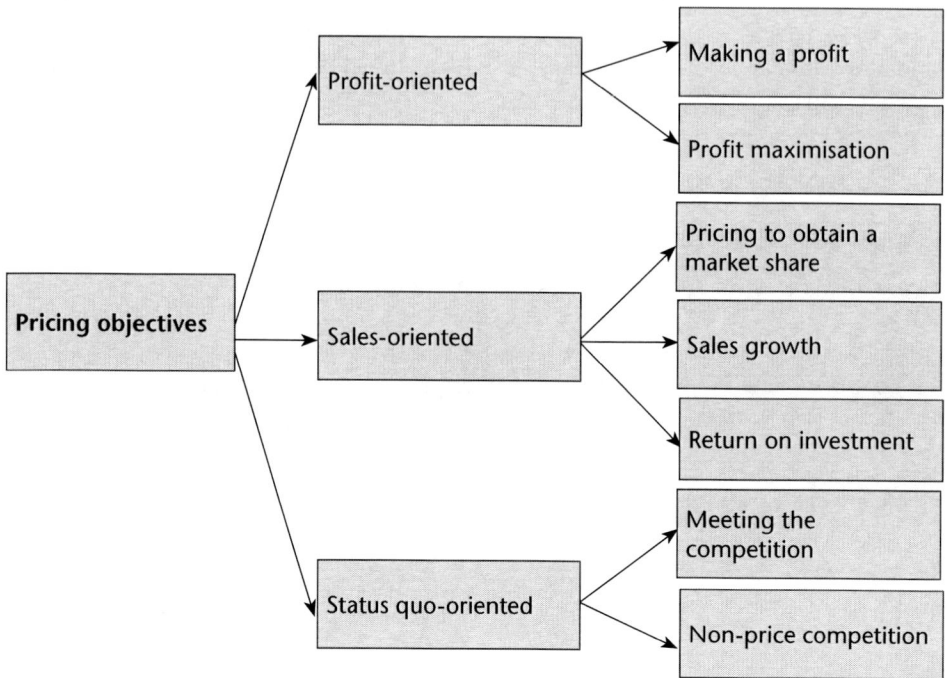

Figure 7.2 The three categories of pricing objectives

Profit-oriented objective

Profit maximisation and target profitability (return) on the investment or on net sales are three profit objectives that are most commonly set for guiding pricing decisions. With profit maximisation as an objective, price objectives are set so that the best possible profit can be earned. The objective of marketers to make a profit involves determining the level at which a price will cover production and distribution costs and at the same time provide a profit (Lamb, Hair & McDaniel, 2012).

Profitability (return) is usually expressed as a certain percentage of profit on invested capital or net sales. Return on investment is the net profit realised for every Rand of capital (facilities, fixtures, equipment, stock and so forth) invested in the enterprise. If the objective is to earn a 15% return on invested capital, it means that the retailer wishes to earn 15% net profit for every Rand of the capital invested in the enterprise. Return on net sales is the percentage calculated by dividing Rand profit by net sales.

Sales-oriented objective

Sales objectives are usually expressed in terms of *sales volume* or *market share*. The primary reason for setting sales-volume objectives is to establish growth in sales or to maintain current sales levels. The aim is to attract buyers for a new or relatively new product and to keep the customers' support for a fairly long time. Attracting 'many' customers with initial low prices may also motivate the customers to develop brand loyalty regarding the product involved.

When setting *market share* as a pricing objective, the enterprise's aim is usually to make it difficult for competitors to compete in the same market or market segments. On the other hand, when an enterprise experiences a decreased market share, lowering price(s) is frequently used to remedy the problem of maintaining a market share.

Sales growth (increase in turnover): In this approach less or no consideration is given to the firm's present competitive situation or to immediate profit considerations, as long as sales volume (turnover) is increasing. This, however, is usually a short-term objective – often used by sellers with a surplus of inventory (stock) to sell off. Other examples of a sales growth objective include after Christmas and seasonal departmental store sales, and 'clearance sales' of existing stock when new products are introduced.

Maintaining the status quo

Status quo price objectives can be objectives directed at meeting or preventing competition, or they can be non-price competitive objectives. The price objectives are directed at imitating the price of the major competitor (Lamb, Hair & McDaniel, 2012). If the price objective is directed at *preventing competition*, prices are set as low as possible to deter additional competitors from entering the market.

In *non-price-competitive objectives* an attempt is made to avoid price competition. Marketers usually prefer to compete on the basis of better products and services, more suitable locations or any other merchandising strategy.

7.5   Factors influencing price determination

The procedure for determining prices in a marketing-orientated manner consists of three stages. Firstly, a *market price* is decided upon. This is the price that most consumers of a particular product will be prepared to pay. This market price (in certain segments of a total market) is directed at a sales volume (turnover) that can be achieved. Secondly, a *target price*, which will meet any price objective of the firm, is calculated, taking into consideration the capital and other costs required to manufacture and market the product. Thirdly, the market price and the target price can be compared and decisions made on a final selling price or prices.

In the process of determining prices several factors can influence the marketer's final decision.

The estimated demand for a product

Demand sets limits on the price for a product. The total number of people who are willing to buy during a given period will vary according to the price charged for a specific product. In most cases there is an inverse relation between a product's price and the quantity demanded (the volume of sales). Normally, the higher the price of the produce, the less one can expect to sell. However, in some cases consumers use price as an indication of the prestige or quality of products and, in such cases, they are induced to buy a product at a relatively high price (Smith, 2012).

A demand curve (see Figure 7.3 for an example) will indicate the reactions of many potential buyers to different prices for the same product. The curve's degree of slope reflects the quantities purchased (volume of sales) at different prices, and the fact that different buyers have different sensitivities to a product's price.

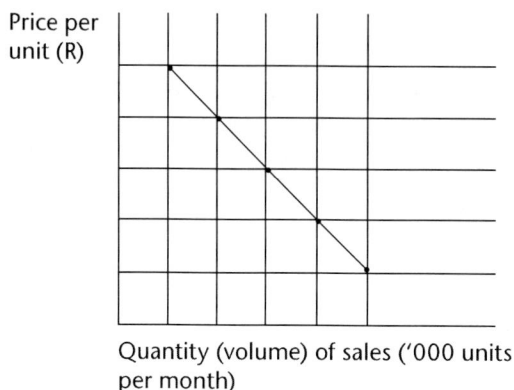

Price per
unit (R)

Quantity (volume) of sales ('000 units
per month)

Figure 7.3 Demand curve for product A

(A demand schedule relates the quantity demanded at different prices.)

Note: This is a very simplified example of the slope of a demand curve.

Factors that could affect customers' sensitivity to price changes are:

❑ *Buyers' perceptions and preferences.* Customers are less price sensitive when they perceive a product as something that provides special or unique benefits, especially when there are poor or no acceptable substitutes. Buyers are also less price sensitive when they regard a product to be one offering high quality, prestige or exclusiveness.

❑ *Buyers' awareness of alternatives/substitutes.* Buyers are usually less sensitive to price differences when they are relatively unaware of competing brands or substitute products, or when it is difficult to compare the quality or performance of alternative brands or substitutes. Conversely, buyers will be more sensitive to price differences when they are aware of and are comparing substitute product brands and other features (Cant, Brink & Machado, 2005).

❑ *The buyer's ability to pay.* Purchasing power consists of the total personal income of an individual, a family or a group after deduction of certain compulsory expenses. Closely related to the ability to buy is the concept of discretionary purchasing power, which is the amount of money a consumer unit has left over after its expenditure on necessities, which can be used to acquire luxury goods and services of all sorts. Consumers are less sensitive to prices when their expenditure for the products or service is relatively low proportionally to their total income. As their income increases consumers spend proportionally less on necessities, such as food, clothing, housing, transport and so on, and proportionally more on items such as household appliances, motor cars, garden furniture, recreation and travel.

Estimating demand involves management practices and aids such as marketing research, market forecasting, as well as the use of a marketing information system.

Cost analyses and pricing

All income from the sales of products or services is achieved at a cost, and costs should therefore, be analysed and controlled. Although all costs must be covered in the long term, products can sometimes be sold at cost or lower than cost to attract consumers to the store. The total cost of a product item or a product line is a composite of all the costs of the activities performed by the various functions in the organisation, such as financing, staffing, purchasing, production, general administration and marketing. An understanding and analysis of product costs is basic to the selection of a pricing strategy.

Various types of costs (Cant, Brink & Machado, 2005)

Fixed costs (FC)

Fixed costs are business expenses that remain constant regardless of the number of products and services that are sold. Such costs continue even if production stops completely. Examples of fixed costs are rent, managerial salaries, property tax, insurance, etc.

Variable costs (VC)

Variable costs are expenses of the business that vary directly according to the number of products or services that are sold. When production stops, for example, all variable production costs stop. When production doubles, for example, all variable production costs double. Examples of variable costs are labour, the cost of all direct materials used in the manufacturing process, sales commission, etc.

Total cost (TC)

The total cost is the sum of the total fixed costs and the total variable costs for a specific quantity produced.

TC = FC + VC

Competition

Sellers must be aware of the prices charged by their competitors. Consumers tend to compare the prices in stores. Another reason why it is important to consider competitors' price strategies is to be prepared for competitors' reactions to their own pricing activities. Before sellers decide to lower their prices to make price competition possible, they should consider other competitive alternatives, for example, competition on the basis of product quality, service or advertising, since price competition may have a negative effect on their profit margin (Cant, Van Heerden & Ngambi, 2010).

Characteristics of merchandise

The characteristics of the merchandise may influence the method of pricing. Seasonal products must be priced according to the season in which they are sold, and their prices have to be marked down at the end of the season to clear out stocks that were not sold. This generally applies to fashion goods. While they are in fashion they can be priced high, but as soon as they go out of fashion they must be sold at a lower price so that stocks can be cleared. The physical appearance of products is also important. If there is a large quantity of perishable products in stock, the prices must not be set too high, so that they may be sold quickly before they perish and can no longer be sold. Unique products may be sold at high prices because consumers of such products are not price sensitive. Product quality is also an important factor, which has to be considered when prices are being determined.

Other factors

The basic price is normally also influenced by some major elements of the marketing mix, for example:

❑ *The product.* The importance of the product in its end use must also be considered. The price of some products is influenced by factors such as whether the product may be leased as well as purchased; whether the product is returnable; whether a trade-in is involved, as is the case of some durable household goods.
❑ *Channels of distribution used.* The types of channels selected and the types of middlemen (such as department stores, supermarkets and speciality stores) used will influence a manufacturer's pricing strategies.
❑ *Promotional methods used.* The promotional methods used (such as the various possible types of advertising media or personal selling) and the extent to which the product is advertised or otherwise promoted by manufacturers or middlemen are important factors to consider in pricing decisions. For example, if some retailers accept the major responsibility for promoting a product, they are normally charged a lower price for a product than if the manufacturer has to carry the major share for promoting the product.

7.6   Basic methods of price setting

By combining all of the available information on potential demand, costs and competition, managers can arrive at a price for a product or service by using one or more of the following pricing methods:

- ❑ Demand-based;
- ❑ Cost-based;
- ❑ Competition-based.

Demand based price levels

Demand as a basis for pricing

Demand as a basis for pricing is also referred to as customer-based pricing. In demand- or valued-based pricing the selling price is set on the perceived worth of the goods or service to its customer, rather than on the actual cost of the product, the market price, competitors' prices, or the historical price. The goal is to align price with value delivered. The following are examples of demand-based pricing. ·

Skimming pricing

This pricing strategy literally means to set a relatively high price for a product or service at first, then to lower the price over time. The firm initially skims the cream off the market demand to recover its sunk costs before the competition steps in and lowers the market price. A great example of skimming occurred with DVD players in the late 1990s and early 2000s. In the late 1990s, when DVD players first came out, they sold for $400 or $500 (between R3 000 and R4 000). By 2001, the price had dropped to less than $100 (less than R1 000) and by 2004 you could buy them for as little as $50 or $60 (under R500) (http://www.witiger.com/marketing/pricingobjectives.htm).

Penetration pricing

Price policies that involve the setting of relatively low prices are called penetration pricing (Smith, 2012). The opposite considerations to skimming pricing are relevant here. This type of pricing policy can also be used to follow after skimming pricing, as explained above. It is a widely used practice to start at a relatively low price during the initial stages so that the product life cycle can be extended, especially via longer first stages, such as the introduction and growth stages. Flexible introductory price strategies when entering the market can be used instead of penetration pricing if the marketer fears that penetration pricing will speed up competitive reactions. Price 'cuts' are used only for a limited period, after which prices are raised to more 'normal' levels. The idea is to attract attention and initial sales growth by an 'introductory sales offer', which can also be regarded as a type of promotional pricing. However, it is often difficult to increase prices immediately afterwards.

Price lining

A pricing line is a certain pricing zone or pricing point for merchandise. In other words, it is the price at which the merchandise is normally sold. This pricing policy eliminates the endless number of prices usually found in a store and replaces these with a series of prices that are set at certain intervals.

For instance, instead of selling dresses at R70,23, R72,65, R78,30 and so on, all dresses in that particular pricing zone are sold at R79. The dresses in a higher pricing zone are all sold at a pricing line of R99, and so on. Therefore the number of different prices at which merchandise is sold is limited (for example all the dresses are only in price categories of R79, R99 or R149).

The advantage of this pricing policy is that it facilitates the buying process for consumers, and because certain prices are popular with consumers, the merchandise is sold more quickly. In addition, the salespeople are sure of prices. Advertising and sales promotion are more effective, and it is easier for the retailer to purchase merchandise. On the other hand, price lining may make it difficult for a store to adjust its prices to meet those of its competitors. A limited number of pricing lines may also create the impression that the store offers only a small variety of merchandise (Stevens & Loudon, 2006).

The objective of a price lining policy is to aim retail selling prices at target market consumers. Retailers must first determine the most suitable pricing zone. A suitable pricing zone is the range of prices that appeals to a certain target market for certain demographic (income, occupation), psychographic (lifestyle, personality), product usage (heavy or light users) or product benefit reasons (economic, social).

Odd-even pricing

Odd-even pricing is the strategy followed where prices are set so that they end on odd numbers. Prices have a psychological effect on consumers, and odd prices are used to encourage consumers to buy. Consumers take a price of 99 cents as being much lower than R1 since they pay more attention to the Rand value than to the cent value. This pricing policy is prevalent in discount stores but not in prestige stores, since this could harm the image of the store (Clemente, 2002).

Multiple pricing

Here, for example, four items are sold for R1 instead of four items being sold for 25 cents each. Consumers are conditioned to think that multiple prices are lower, although this is not always the case. Items that are multiply priced are, therefore, regarded as a bargain.

A multiple pricing policy is used generally for merchandise with a low unit value, which is bought regularly, or to clear stock at the end of a sales season.

Unit pricing

This is the pricing policy in which prices are set per unit of measure. The price is therefore set per kilogram, metre, litre and so forth, to enable consumers to make price comparisons between products of different sizes, shapes and quantities. Usually the price is not marked on the merchandise itself, but the price per unit of measure is marked on the shelf on which the merchandise is displayed.

Bundle pricing

This method involves offering several products for sale as one combined product. For buyers, the overall cost of the purchase shows a savings compared to purchasing each product individually. This method of pricing is very common in the software business (for example, bundling a word processor, a spreadsheet and a database into a single office suite), and in the fast-food industry where multiple items are combined into a complete meal. A bundle of products is sometimes referred to as a package deal (http://www.knowthis.com/principles-of-marketing-tutorials/setting-price-part-2/promotional-pricing-product-bundling/).

Premium pricing

Premium pricing (also called prestige or image pricing) is the strategy of consistently pricing at, or near, the high end of the possible price range to help attract status-conscious consumers. This is done in order to evoke perceptions of quality and prestige of the product or service, such as for high-end perfumes, jewellery, clothing and cars. Rolex and Rolls Royce are examples of companies that make use of this pricing method. Consumers will buy a premium priced product because:

☐ They believe the high price is an indication of good quality.
☐ They believe it to be a sign of self-worth: 'They are worth it.' It authenticates the buyer's success and status; it is a signal to others that the owner is a member of an exclusive group.
☐ They require flawless performance in this application. The cost of product malfunction is too high to buy anything but the best, for example, a heart pacemaker (http://en.wikipedia.org/wiki/Pricing#Demand-based_pricing).

Demand backward

Prices are set by determining what consumers are willing to pay for an item, and then deducting cost to determine if the profit margin is adequate to meet the firm's profit objectives.

Cost-plus pricing

This method involves the setting of a price of one unit of product, equal to the unit's total cost (i.e. fixed plus variable costs) plus a desired profit on the unit (Feinschreiber, 2004). In other words, the cost-plus approach to pricing is to add the cost of producing and marketing a product to the overheads of the product, plus a desired profit margin (a percentage).

Thus, the formula for calculating the price would be:

Price = direct costs plus overheads and a percentage profit added.

The profit margin is a cost-plus figure, which is normally a predetermined percentage. Thus, if a target profit margin is 20% on a product item that has a total cost of R50, the price of the product would be calculated as follows:

Price = total costs (R50) + a profit margin of 20% = R60.

Mark-ups

Mark-up is the difference between the cost of the merchandise and the listed or selling price of the merchandise. To calculate the selling price, the mark-up is added to the cost price. For example, the mark-up on a dress purchased at R400 and sold at R600 is R200. An amount in Rand is therefore added to the cost price, which is sufficient to cover the operating expenses and to realise a profit (Cant, Van Heerden & Ngambi, 2010).

In the above example the mark-up is expressed in Rand, but it is mostly expressed as a percentage of the cost price or the selling price. These percentages can be calculated as follows:

Percentage mark-up on cost price = mark-up in Rand ÷ cost in Rand
The example above:
50% mark up on cost = (200 ÷ 400)%

And

Percentage mark-up on retail selling price = mark-up in Rand ÷ retail selling price in Rand.
The example above:
33% mark up on cost = (200 ÷ 600)%

Different types of mark-up

Initial mark-up and initial retail selling price. When the initial mark-up is added to the cost price, the initial selling price is obtained, for example, if the cost price is R20 and the initial mark-up is R10, the initial selling price is R30. The initial mark-up is, therefore, the first mark-up that is placed on an item of merchandise.

Additional mark-up. In certain cases the initial mark-up might not have been adequate to cover expenses, or to realise a satisfactory profit. An additional mark-up then has to be calculated. If, for example, the additional mark-up is R10, it is added to the initial mark-up and the cost price, and the new retail selling price is then R40.

➲

> *Mark-up cancellations.* A mark-up cancellation is a reduction of the selling price long after an additional mark-up has already been added. This price reduction may take place as a result of a reduction of the competitors' prices, too much stock or consumer resistance to high prices. If the cancellation is R5, the final retail selling price is therefore R35 = R20 + R10 + R10 − R5.
> *Individual or cumulative mark-up.* Individual mark-up is the mark-up calculated for a single item, whereas cumulative mark-up is the mark-up calculated on more than one item, usually on a certain line of merchandise.
> *Maintained or net mark-up.* The maintained mark-up or net mark-up can be used to determine whether price objectives have actually been achieved. This mark-up is the difference between the cost of the merchandise and the price at which it is actually sold. This price may contain various mark-ups and markdowns.

Break-even analysis

A useful tool in both cost- and demand-based pricing is the break-even analysis. A break-even point is the number of units of production at which the income from sales equal the total costs, assuming a certain selling price. Thus, there is a different break-even point for each selling price. Sales revenue of quantities of products above the break-even point result in a profit on each additional unit sold. The higher the sales are above the break-even point, the higher the profit per unit sold. Obviously, sales below the break-even point will result in a loss to the marketer (Nagle & Hogan, 2006).

A method of calculating the break-even point is illustrated in Table 7.2. At each of several prices, we wish to find out how many units must be sold to cover all costs. At a unit price of R100, the sale of each unit contributes R70 to cover overheads. We must sell about 3,6 units to cover the R250 at fixed cost.

Table 7.2 A method of calculating the break-even point

Units	(1) Unit price	(2) Variable cost per unit	(3) Contribution to overheads (1) − (2)	(4) Total fixed cost	(5) Break-even point (4) / (3)
1	R60	R30	R30	R250	8,3 units
2	R80	R30	R50	R250	5,0 units
3	R100	R30	R70	R250	3,6 units
4	R150	R30	R120	R250	2,1 units

In this hypothetical situation the firm's fixed costs are R250 and its variable costs are constant at R30 a unit. (To simplify our break-even analysis, we assume that the variable costs per unit remain constant.)

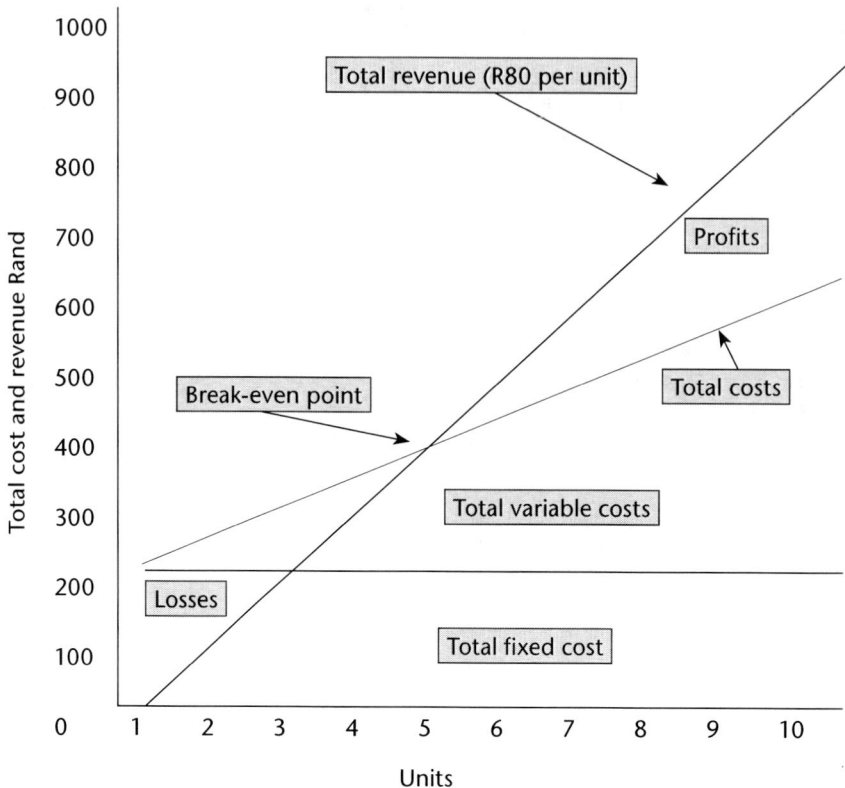

Figure 7.4 Computation of a break-even point

If the company sells five units the total cost is R400 (variable costs: 5 x R30 = R150 plus fixed cost R250). At a selling price of R80 per unit, the sale of five units will yield R400 revenue, cost and revenue will equal each other. At the same price the sale of one unit above five will yield a profit.

Competition as a basis for pricing

In this method the seller uses prices of competing products as a benchmark instead of considering their own costs or the customers' demands (http://www.businessdictionary.com/definition/competition-based-pricing.html). The price range set by the competition is the range that the customers will expect. The major pricing decision that must be made is whether prices should be set lower than, higher than or equal to competitors' prices. Prices should, however, still cover the costs of production and overheads (http://www.ssfp.ca/course/pricing_strat.html).

❐   *Setting prices lower than competitors' prices.* The aim is to realise a large turnover in Rand, as well as to have a high stock turnover rate. To be able to price lower than competitors, the seller must be able to buy merchandise at a lower cost than competitors, their operating expenses must also be lower, and they must also offer the minimum services. Sellers normally have a low-price image.

❏ *Setting prices equal to competitors' prices.* Price is not used as the basis for competition, but the focus is on location, service, promotion and so on. Fixing prices equal to competitors' prices does not mean that the seller must follow every price change of their competitors precisely, but that their prices should fall within the competitive range.

❏ *Setting prices higher than competitors' prices.* If prices are set higher than those of the competition the higher prices must be justified in the mind of the customer by offering other benefits, such as better after-sales service, higher quality products, exclusive products, personal attention to customers, a luxurious buying atmosphere, a large sales staff, a prestigious image, convenient location and longer hours. Consumers must, therefore, believe that the extra service they receive is worth the higher prices, otherwise they will not buy from the shop.

Leader pricing

Leader pricing is practised by intermediaries, such as retailers who aim to attract customers to their stores by advertising and charging relatively low prices on specific items. The price cut is genuine in that the items concerned are freely available at the advertised price. However, the idea is to increase the sale of other products, which have not been specially reduced. In general, the so-called loss leaders are not sold at a loss but below their normal price. Retailers must take care to rotate the products and brand selected so that certain items are not given a low-price image. The idea is to increase the price again after the campaign is over and to select other product items in their place for the next round.

Leader pricing is setting some very low prices – real bargains – to get customers into retail stores. The idea is not to sell large quantities of the leader items, but to get customers into the store to buy other products. Certain products are picked for their promotion value and priced low, but above cost. In food stores, the leader prices are the 'specials' that are advertised regularly, to give an image of low prices. Leader items are usually well-known, widely used items, which are not stocked heavily (such as milk, butter, eggs, tea or coffee) but on which customers will recognise a real price cut.

Set list or quoted price

After all aspects mentioned in the previous sections have being taken into account the listed price is determined. The listed price refers to the price at which the product or service will be sold to the intermediary or the final consumer (Strydom et al., 2004).

7.7 Price adjustments

In this section we discuss trade or functional discounts, quantity discounts, cash discounts and promotional allowances (http://www.knowthis.com/principles-of-marketing-tutorials/setting-price-part-2/price-adjustments-quantity-discounts/).

Trade discounts

Trade discounts are reductions on the prices offered to buyers in exchange for certain functions they will perform in the marketing process. To illustrate this practice: 'A manufacturer may quote a retail list price as R400 with trade discounts of 40% and 10%. This means that the retailer pays the wholesaler R240 (R400 less 40%), and the wholesaler pays the manufacturer R216 (R240 less 10%). The wholesaler keeps the 10% to cover the costs of wholesaling functions and passes on the 40% discount to the retailers.'

Trade discounts are generally offered to distribution channel members who, in exchange for the reduced price, undertake some of the responsibilities (functions for marketing the product). A retailer might, for example, undertake to display the product prominently on their shelves, to display point-of-sale advertising material, talk to customers about the product, provide feedback to the manufacturer and so on.

Quantity discounts

A quantity discount is offered to the buyer for purchasing a greater than usual quantity (bulk) of goods or material to be delivered at one time or over an extended period. Quantity discounts are triggered when a buyer reaches certain purchase levels (http://www.knowthis.com/principles-of-marketing-tutorials/setting-price-part-2/price-adjustments-quantity-discounts/). A hardware store, for example, may charge builders the listed price when they purchase between one and 49 bags of cement, but offer them a 5% discount off the listed price when their purchase exceeds 50 bags of cement.

Price adjustment based on quantity can be offered at the time of purchase or calculated on a cumulative basis:

❐ *Discounts at the time of purchase.* This is a one-time reduction in the list price for a quantity purchased or an order that exceeds a certain level.
❐ *Cumulative quantity discounts* allows the buyer to receive a discount as more products are purchased over time. If a buyer regularly purchases from a supplier they may receive a discount once the buyer has reached predetermined monetary or quantity levels.

Cash discounts

Cash discounts are granted to buyers if they pay cash immediately or undertake to pay cash within a certain period of time (Frensidy, 2008).

A typical example is '2/10, net 30', which means that although payment is due within 30 days, the buyer can deduct 2% if the bill is paid within 10 days. The discount must be granted to all buyers meeting these terms. Such discounts are customary in many industries and help to improve sellers' cash situation, and reduce bad debts and credit collection costs.

Special segment pricing

In some businesses special classes of customers are offered pricing that differs from the rest of the market. Firms offer special segment prices for many reasons, such as building future demand by appealing to new or younger customers; improving the brand's image as being sensitive to customer's needs; and rewarding long-time customers with price breaks. For example, a leading supermarket group offers pensioners 10% discount on all purchases on Wednesday mornings; and some pharmaceutical firms don't charge service fees for members of the South African Police Service when they buy their prescribed medicine from them.

Promotional pricing

Marketers will reduce their prices temporarily below the listed price or sometimes below cost price. Supermarkets for example will price a few products as loss leaders to attract customers to the store in the hope that customers will buy other products at normal mark-ups. Stores also use special-event pricing in certain seasons to draw more customers, for instance during the Soccer World Cup. Stores may simply offer discounts from normal prices to increase sales and reduce inventories, such as clothing stores' end of the season sale.

Advanced purchase discount

This is a discount offered to consumers for buying products or services well in advance. Many hotels, for instance, offer a percentage savings (e.g. 20%) on standard rates for booking accommodation in advance (e.g. 21 days).

Geographical pricing

When a marketer sends a product to distributors or final consumers over a distance, they may modify their final selling prices to cover expenses for these geographical locations or distances (http://www.witiger.com/marketing/pricingobjectives.htm).

The geographical distances between buyers and manufacturers or other types of marketers, means that the marketer has to decide on who will be responsible for transport costs. Prices may be higher to cover the higher shipping costs. Alternatively, marketers charge all customers the same prices regardless of location, because each customer picks up their own costs, free on board (FOB). Marketers can charge the same price plus freight to all customers, regardless of their location. A number of terms are used in geographical pricing:

❏ *FOB* – this is the price out the factory door – you come and get it.
❏ *CIF* – the cost at our factory plus the insurance and freight to ship it to you.
❏ *ZONE* – if you live close, it is cheaper, if you live further away, we add in shipping costs.
❏ *Basing-point pricing* – all customers are charged freight from a specified billing location.
❏ *Freight-absorption pricing* – the seller pays all shipping costs to get the desired business.

7.8 Summary

Pricing is a difficult task for sellers, since there are so many factors that influence pricing decisions. These factors include the cost price of merchandise, competitors' prices and many more. It is, therefore, necessary for sellers to understand and be able to apply the calculation of mark-ups and markdowns and develop a pricing policy (fixed or variable pricing policy, odd-cent pricing policy, multiple pricing policy, and so on), to achieve price objectives. These price objectives must correspond to the firm's marketing and enterprise objectives, and include the general sales, profit and competitive objectives. Selling price can be adjusted by means of markdowns, discounts and mark-ups.

Mini case study

Apple Computers
The edge that Apple enjoyed in the marketplace in terms of ease of use was erased when Microsoft launched Windows 95. This put Apple in a difficult position and forced a review of both its strategic and marketing decisions. One of the key decisions areas was the pricing decision.

Apple had challenges in all four of its market segments. In the home segment, it had gained market share but had not matched Packard Bell, the market leader. Apple had also lost share in the education and corporate segments, despite its new line of Power Macs. Apple had made gains in the government sector, but this sector's potential was not as great as the others were.

The options Apple considered were:
❏ Price at or below competitors to attract more household buyers. This depended on accurate forecasts of demand and reliable supply of products. The risk with this strategy was the potential for intense price competition that could damage the company's profit position.

↪

- Apple could offer leading-edge PCs with advanced graphics and multimedia capabilities to the sophisticated computer user, especially those in the corporate market. The superior capabilities of the product compared to competitive products should allow for higher prices.
- Apple could license its basic design and operating systems to other manufacturers so that lower-priced clones of Apple PCs could be marketed. If this was successful, Apple could attract more software developers to produce software for Apple operating systems rather than Windows systems. The better the software, the more customers are attracted to a product. The risk was that if the cheaper clones were very successful, it could result in the sales of Apple's own brand declining sharply.
- Apple needed to improve its presence and image with software developers, large corporations and government agencies that wanted to build large networks of compatible PCs. It also wanted to double its overall market share to 20%. In early 1996, Apple responded to these issues by replacing its chief executive Gilbert Amelio. He quickly announced a price cut of around 10% on Macintosh Performa computers and a licensing agreement allowing Motorola to build Apple-style PCs.

7.9 Self-evaluation questions

1. Which pricing objective does Apple seem to be following?
2. If Apple wants to launch a new product on the market, what type of demand pricing will they follow?
3. What is the mark-up in percentage that Apple adds to their products, bearing in mind that it cost them R1 060 to manufacture the iPhone 4, which they sell in store for R5 900?

7.10 Bibliography

Cant, M.C., Brink, A. & Machado, R. (2005). *Pricing management,* 2nd edition. Cape Town: New African Books.

Cant, M.C., Strydom, J.W., Jooste, C.J. & Du Plessis, P.J. (2006). *Marketing management,* 5th edition. Cape Town: Juta.

Cant, M.C., Van Heerden, C.H. & Ngambi, H.C. (2010). *Marketing management.* Cape Town: Juta.

Clemente, M.N. (2002). *Marketing glossary: Key terms, concepts, and applications in marketing management, advertising, sales promotions, public relations, direct marketing, market research, sales.* Glen Rock, NJ: Clemente Communications Group.

Feinschreiber, R. (2004). *Transfer pricing methods: An applications guide.* Toronto: John Wiley & Sons.

Frensidy, B. (2008). *Financial mathematics.* Jakarta: Penerbit Salemba Empat.

Lamb, L.W. Hair, J.F. & McDaniel, C. (2012). *Essentials of marketing*, 7th edition. Mason, OH: South-Western Cengage Learning.

Monroe, K.B. (2003). *Pricing: Making profitable decisions.* New York: McGraw-Hill.

Nagle, T.T. & Hogan, J.E. (2006). *The strategy and tactics of pricing: A guide to growing more profitability.* Upper Saddle River, NJ: Prentice Hall.

Rix, P. (2003). *Essential marketing skills.* New York: McGraw-Hill.

Smith, T.J. (2012). *Pricing strategy: Setting price levels, managing price discounts, and establishing price structures.* Mason, OH: South-Western Cengage Learning.

Stevens, R.E. & Loudon, D. (2006). *Marketing planning guide*, 3rd edition. New York: Best Business Books.

Strydom J.W. (ed.). (2004). *Introduction to marketing,* 3rd edition. Cape Town: Juta.

Websites

http://www.businessdictionary.com/definition/competition-based-pricing.html

http://www.knowthis.com/principles-of-marketing-tutorials/setting-price-part-2/price-adjustments-quantity-discounts/

http://www.knowthis.com/principles-of-marketing-tutorials/setting-price-part-2/promotional-pricing-product-bundling/

http://www.ssfp.ca/course/pricing_strat.html

http://en.wikipedia.org/wiki/Pricing#Demand-based_pricing

http://www.witiger.com/marketing/pricingobjectives.htm

8 Merchandise advertising

Colin N Diggines

Learning objectives

After studying this chapter you should be able to:

☐ Discuss the communication process and its impact on retail promotions;
☐ Identify and define the five main components of the promotion mix;
☐ Discuss the components of the advertising strategy;
☐ Describe the steps to follow when creating retail advertisements;
☐ Discuss various advertising media a retailer can select from for use in an advertising campaign;
☐ Describe the various sales promotional techniques that a retailer can use when engaging in sales promotions;
☐ Discuss publicity with special reference to types of publicity, the development of a publicity story, the advantages of publicity and the objectives of publicity.

8.1 Introduction

There is little point in having a store in a fantastic location, with a concept that appeals to a large audience, if consumers do not know of your existence. Retailers have to inform consumers of their existence and then motivate them to visit the store. Consumers have to be informed about the existence of the store, its location and more or less what it offers, and be persuaded to visit it. This can be done through retail advertising. We discuss the objectives of the advertising function, its composition and execution in this chapter. We also address the topics of sales promotion and publicity.

The marketing mix of the retailer consists of the product, price, distribution and marketing communications mix. Marketing communication is defined in Cant, Strydom, Jooste and Du Plessis (2006: 438) as 'the process by which the marketer develops and presents an appropriate set of communications stimuli to a target audience with the intention of eliciting a desired set of responses'. Marketing communication includes basic activities such as advertising, personal selling, sales promotion and publicity.

8.2 Retail promotions

Promotion involves providing the customer with information about the retailer's store and the product offering. It also entails influencing the customer's perceptions, attitudes and behaviour towards the store and product offerings. Promotion is thus a communication process that focuses on supplying information and persuasion.

The communication process

Communication is the transfer of meaningful messages between the sender (in this case the retailer) and the receiver (target customers). This process of communication is illustrated in Figure 8.1. As can be seen from this figure, this process follows a complete circle in that the sender of the message relies on receiving feedback from the receiver to ascertain whether or not the message was received by the receiver, and whether or not it was received correctly and the desired behaviours achieved. The entire process is affected by 'noise', which can interfere with how the message is received and interpreted by the receiver. This noise can be in the form of attention distracters, such as other people talking to you, excessive exposure to advertisements, or even stress, where a person is not listening to the messages properly because their mind is elsewhere.

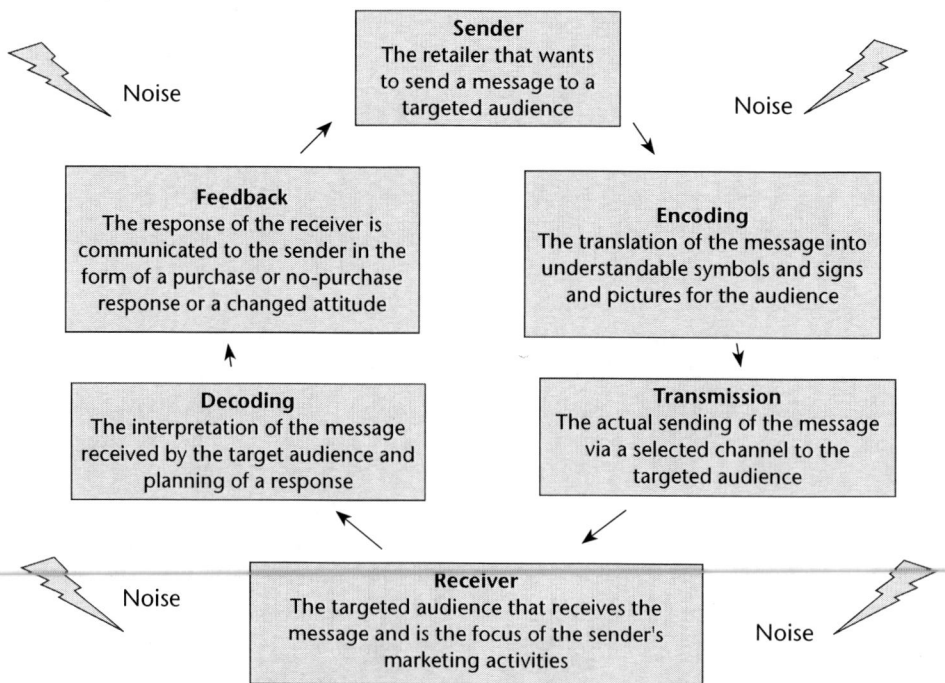

Figure 8.1 The communication process

Source: Adapted from Koekemoer. (2010). Introduction to integrated marketing communications. *Cape Town: Juta, p. 34*

The promotion mix

When communicating with the targeted audience, it is customary to use a number of communication elements in combination to ensure that the message reaches the targeted audience. Each of these elements must complement and supplement each other to ensure that the consumer receives a consistent message. The combination of these communication elements is referred to as the promotion mix. The promotion mix consists of the following main elements:

- *Advertising* is indirect, non-personal communication conveyed by the mass media and paid for by an identified retailer.
- *Personal selling* involves direct, face-to-face communication between a retail salesperson and the customer.
- *Store displays* involve direct, non-personal, in-house presentations and displays of merchandise with product-related information.
- *Sales promotions* are direct and indirect, non-personal methods of persuasion, which give the customer additional value. Their effect is of a short-term nature.
- *Publicity* is indirect, non-personal communication (positive and negative) conveyed by the mass media, which has not been paid for by an identified sponsor.

8.3   Retail advertising

Retail advertising includes all types of non-personal communication in respect of the store, merchandise, service and ideas by an identified retailer. The characteristics that distinguish advertising from other types of promotion are contained in Table 8.1.

Table 8.1 Characteristics of the different types of promotion

	Advertising	Personal selling	Store display	Sales promotion	Publicity
Mode of communication	Indirect Non-personal	Direct Face-to-face	Direct Non-personal	Indirect Non-personal	Indirect Non-personal
Regularity of activity	Regular	Regular	Regular	Irregular	Irregular
Flexibility	Unvarying Uniform	Personalised Tailored	Unvarying Uniform	Unvarying Uniform	Retailer has no control
Feedback directness	Indirect feedback	Direct feedback	Indirect feedback	Indirect feedback	Indirect feedback
Control of message content	Controllable	Controllable	Controllable	Controllable	Uncontrollable
Sponsor identity	Identified	Identified	Identified	Unidentified	Identified

↪

	Advertising	Personal selling	Store display	Sales promotion	Publicity
Cost per contact	Low to moderate	High	Varies	Varies	No cost

Source: Compiled from Cant & Van Heerden (eds). (2010). Marketing management. Cape Town: Juta and Strydom. (2011). Introduction to marketing, 4th edition. Cape Town: Juta

The influence of advertising

The influence of advertising can be discussed from two perspectives, namely its influence on customers and its influence on the total market.

The influence of advertising on consumers

Consumers go through a series of steps before accepting an offer. According to Russell Colley's 1961 DAGMAR model (Defining Advertising Goals for Measured Advertising Results), consumers move from total unawareness of the store and the product offer to buying behaviour or action, via the following steps:

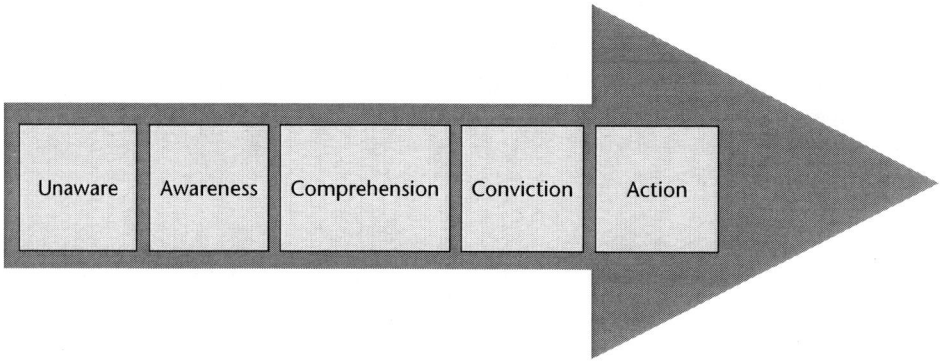

Figure 8.2 Consumer acceptance model

Source: Adapted from http://drypen.in/advertising/dagmar-defining-advertising-goals-for-measured-advertising-results.html. Accessed: 24 February 2012

Through advertising, together with other aspects of the marketing mix, the retailer can help the consumer to move through these steps. Advertising plays a particularly important role during the awareness and comprehension phases. In terms of awareness, the advertiser needs to ensure that the consumer is not only aware of the product, but that they consider it to be a solution to a need they have. At the comprehension stage the consumer needs to have sufficient information on the retailer or product so that when the consumer engages in decision-making they see that store or those products as the preferred solution. This is achieved through effective advertising.

The influence of advertising on the total market

As a result of the mass media used, advertising influences a large number of people simultaneously. The ultimate effect of advertising is often strengthened by personal communication between consumers. This phenomenon is known as the two-way flow of communication and can be illustrated as follows:

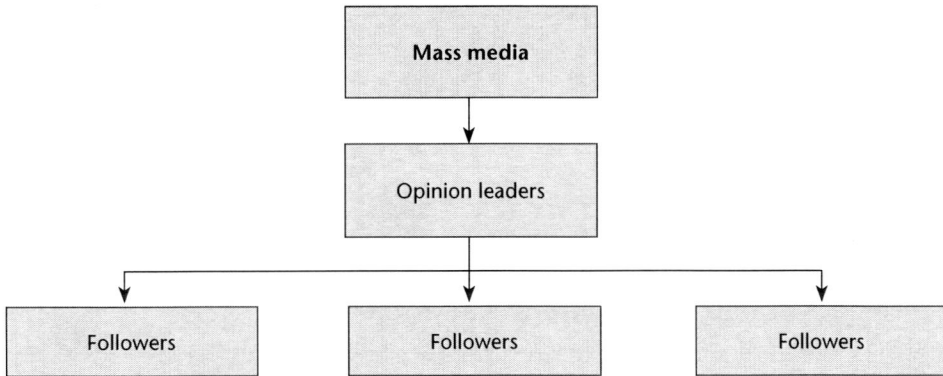

Figure 8.3 The two-way flow model of communication

Source: Adapted from http://www.utwente.nl/cw/theorieenoverzicht/Levels%20of%20theories/macro/Two-Step%20Flow%20Theory.doc/. Accessed: 12 March 2012

According to the above model, the first step involves the flow of communication from the media to the opinion leaders. The attitudes, opinions, preferences and actions of these opinion leaders influence other consumers. The second step involves word-of-mouth communication between the opinion leaders and the followers in the group. According to this model of communication, retailers should, therefore, try to reach and persuade opinion leaders. It is difficult to identify opinion leaders and deal with them as a separate market segment, however. The following methods are recommended when deciding how to deal with opinion leaders:

❑ Create opinion leaders by supplying particular people with free samples and information about products.
❑ Work through influential people in the community, for example television personalities and public figures.
❑ Create advertisements that depict conversations about the store and the products.
❑ Develop advertisements with 'conversation value'.

Different types of advertising

Advertising is aimed mainly at getting customers into the store and at creating a specific image of the store. To achieve these two objectives, retailers usually use three types of advertising, namely product advertising, institutional advertising and co-operative advertising.

Product advertising

Product advertising offers specific merchandise for sale and invites customers to come in and buy the product immediately. An example of this is a theme about products that are new, exclusive and of exceptional design and quality. Announcements of sales and special promotions are also types of product advertising. Checkers Hyper uses this, for example, when promoting their 'Heyday' specials.

Institutional advertising

Institutional advertising presents the store in general as a 'pleasant place to shop'. The store creates a particular image through art, copywriting, typography and its logo. The retailer can thus create an image as a fashion leader, a price leader, a leader with regard to the variety of merchandise, and so on. Woolworths, for example, uses 'welcome to the difference' to create a specific image of its stores and to stand out from its competitors.

Co-operative advertising

With co-operative advertising, the manufacturer prepares the advertising material and allows a particular retailer to insert their store's name and address on the advertisement. The manufacturer and the retailer then share the advertising costs.

8.4   The development of an advertising strategy

An advertising programme must be systematically planned, organised, executed and controlled. It thus requires the retailer to determine what they want to achieve with the advertising, establish the organisational structure necessary for objective implementation, develop means by which these objectives can be achieved, and measure the degree to which these objectives have been achieved. The components of this advertising strategy are illustrated in Figure 8.4.

Planning the advertising function

The first step in developing the advertising strategy is to engage in planning. The two key elements addressed here are the determination of advertising objectives and the development of the advertising budget.

1. Planning the advertising function	2. Organising the advertising function	3. Executing the advertising function	4. Controlling the advertising function
A. Determine advertising objectives ❑ Store image ❑ Store positioning ❑ Traffic generation ❑ Special events ❑ Average purchase ❑ Sales and profits B. Developing advertising budgets ❑ Advertising budgets ❑ Advertising expenditures ❑ Budget considerations ❑ Budgeting methods	A. Establishing advertising departments B. Using advertising specialists	A. Creating advertisements ❑ Advertisement purpose ❑ Basic message ❑ Communications approach ❑ Total advertisement B. Selecting advertising media ❑ Media characteristics ❑ Newspaper advertising ❑ Magazine advertising ❑ Radio advertising ❑ Television advertising ❑ Sign advertising ❑ Direct advertising	❑ Controlling the strategy implementation

Figure 8.4 The components of the advertising strategy

Source: Adapted from Koekemoer. (2002). Promotional strategy: Marketing communications in practice. *Cape Town: Juta, p. 70*

Advertising objectives

❑ *The nature of advertising objectives*

Successful execution of the advertising function requires the determination of definite advertising objectives. Objectives must be based on:

- A clear definition of the target audience;
- A clear exposition of the reaction of the target audience to be generated;
- Quantitative expression of objectives;
- A projection of performance as a result of advertising;
- Understanding of the role of advertising with regard to the rest of the promotion programme;
- Recognition that the objectives are demanding but achievable;
- Recognition of the time limit.

The specific objectives of an advertising campaign depend mainly on four factors, namely how the retailer wants to influence the target market's decision-making, the nature of the product offering, other marketing efforts and promotion variables of the retailer, and the competitive conditions.

- ❏ *The types of advertising objectives*
  - *Store image.* In order to obtain and retain sufficient regular customers, the retailer must create some unique image of the store in the minds of the target market. This unique image can, for example, be based on size, merchandise specialisation, clientele fashion leadership, quality of merchandise or price levels. Think of the different images created by retailers such as Woolworths and Pep Stores.
  - *Store positioning.* Positioning is the way in which customers see the enterprise in relation to its competitors. The retailer must therefore position their store in such a way that they can obtain a maximum competitive advantage.
  - *Generating traffic.* Traffic refers to the number of customers who visit the store and the frequency of their visits. The retailer can generate traffic by creating a specific reason for customers to visit the store, for example, through theme promotions at Easter, special offers and demonstrations. If we accept that a higher frequency of visits will necessarily lead to an increase in sales, the retailer can measure the results of their advertising efforts by the number of customers visiting their store every day.
  - *Special opportunities.* As we have already said, the retailer can try to increase their clientele by creating special reasons for the customer to visit their store. Through advertising, the customer is made aware of special offers and opportunities that will make it worthwhile for them to visit the store. Checkers Hyper Heydays are an example of this.
  - *Increased average purchases.* Although advertising is often aimed at recruiting new customers, the retailer can also try to increase the average purchases of existing customers. A record must be kept of existing customers, since these customers have already shown a favourable attitude to the store involved. Advertising efforts concentrated on these customers can encourage them to buy more regularly and to buy more merchandise each time they visit the store.
  - *Sales and profits.* Retailers often measure the success of advertising by the levels of sales or profit. Factors such as price, quality of merchandise, general economic conditions, competition and so on, also influence the volume of sales and profitability. Therefore, advertising alone cannot be held responsible for generating sales and profit. Examples of advertising objectives are listed in Table 8.2.

Table 8.2 Advertising objective examples

Close sales to prospects already partly sold through past advertising efforts
❏ Perform the complete selling function.
❏ Announce a special reason for 'buying now'.

Close sales to prospects already partly sold through past advertising efforts
☐ Remind people to buy.
☐ Tie in with some special buying event.
☐ Stimulate impulse sales.
☐ Create awareness of product existence.
☐ Create a brand image.
☐ Provide information regarding product benefits.
☐ Correct false impressions.
☐ Build familiarity with a product or trademark.
☐ Build confidence in a company.
☐ Place advertiser in a position to select preferred dealers.
☐ Secure universal distribution.
☐ Establish brand recognition.
☐ Hold market share against competition.
☐ Convert competitors' customers to advertiser's brand.
☐ Convert non-users of the product to users of the product and the brand.
☐ Increase usage rate among present customers.
☐ Advertise new uses for the product.
☐ Persuade the prospect to visit a showroom.
☐ Induce the prospect to sample the product.
☐ Aid the sales force in getting accounts and orders.
☐ Build morale of the sales force.

Budget decisions

The budget decision is of cardinal importance owing to its impact on the effectiveness of the advertising effort. When planning the advertising effort, the following two questions should be asked:

☐ How much must be spent to achieve the set advertising objectives?
☐ How much money is available?

The size of the budget determines the scope of alternative strategies from which the retailer can choose. The determination of an optimum budget is very complicated. A budget that is too small restricts the number of alternatives from which the retailer can choose, while a budget that is too large can lead to waste of money. Each retailer's budget is based on their unique situation and is determined by:

☐ The objectives of the advertising programme;
☐ The attempts needed to achieve these objectives;
☐ The retailer's ability and willingness to finance the advertising effort.

Table 8.3 identifies the leading advertisers (in terms of Rand spend) in South Africa for the year 2010. Take note of the mix between individual manufactures and retailers.

Table 8.3 Top 10 advertisers in South Africa for 2010

	South Africa's leading advertisers in 2010
1.	Unilever South Africa
2.	Shoprite Checkers
3.	Pick n Pay
4.	Vodacom (Vodafone)
5.	MTN
6.	KFC
7.	Standard Bank
8.	Coca-Cola
9.	Cell C
10.	SAB Miller

Source: Adapted from http://www.adbrands.net/za/sabmiller_za.htm. Accessed: 14 March 2012

Organising the advertising function

The next step in the development of the advertising strategy is the organisation of the advertising function.

Establishing advertising departments

In smaller enterprises, the owner-manager or their partners are responsible for dealing with the advertising function. It is obviously highly unlikely that this person would be an expert in advertising. A smaller retailer, such as this, is advised to use advertising specialists, media representatives and advertising agencies. Larger retailers often have small advertising departments consisting of an advertising manager, a few artists, copywriters and production specialists. Retailers use mostly printed media, which can then be handled by their own advertising department, while any broadcast advertising is handled with the aid of agencies and the staff of the television and radio stations. Some of the largest retailers have comprehensive advertising and sales promotion departments. These retailers still concentrate mainly on the printed media, however, and use advertising agencies for broadcast production and scheduling.

The use of external advertising specialists

Retailers can use freelancers, advertising agencies and media representatives. Freelance advertising involves artists, copywriters or photographers, who produce advertisements on a part-time basis. Media representatives are employees of newspapers, and radio and television stations, and it is their responsibility to sell advertising time and space. These representatives can also arrange the production of advertisements. The advertising agency offers specialisation, creativity and objectivity. The task of these agencies includes the initiation, preparation, production, placement and evaluation of advertising campaigns for the products or services of the client. Different criteria influence the retailer's choice of agency. Research done by Jansen van Rensburg, Venter and Strydom (2010) showed which criteria are the most important when clients select an agency. The findings of this research are illustrated in Figure 8.5.

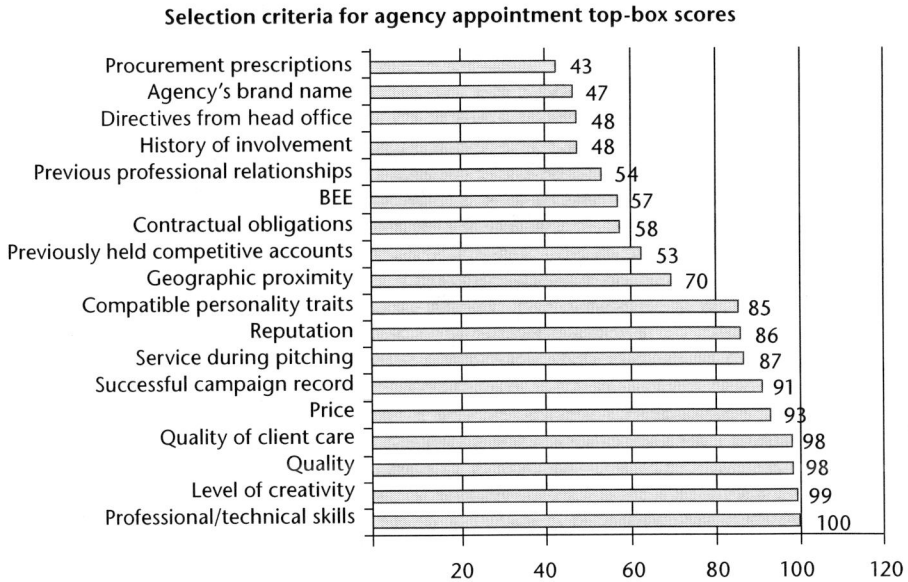

Selection criteria for agency appointment top-box scores

Criterion	Score
Procurement prescriptions	43
Agency's brand name	47
Directives from head office	48
History of involvement	48
Previous professional relationships	54
BEE	57
Contractual obligations	58
Previously held competitive accounts	53
Geographic proximity	70
Compatible personality traits	85
Reputation	86
Service during pitching	87
Successful campaign record	91
Price	93
Quality of client care	98
Quality	98
Level of creativity	99
Professional/technical skills	100

Figure 8.5 How clients select an agency

Source: Jansen van Rensburg, Venter & Strydom. (2010). Approaches taken by South African advertisers to select and appoint advertising agencies. Southern African Business Review: *14(1): 21*

Executing the advertising function

The third step in the development of the advertising strategy is to execute the advertising function. This involves developing the advertisement and selecting the most appropriate media for placement.

Creating retail advertisements

To develop effective advertisements, the retailer must remember the following steps:

❐ Determine the purpose of the advertisement;
❐ Decide on the basic message;

❑ Select the communication approach;
❑ Develop the total advertisement, part by part.

The purpose of the advertisement

Individual advertisements can have a variety of objectives, for example to advertise the store as a whole, to make the customer aware of special offers, to highlight specific products and so on. An individual advertisement also has an 'institutional' component, however. To be able to utilise the benefit of both special-purpose advertising and institutional advertising, the retailer may use a special theme or product in the advertisement, but retain the same style throughout.

The basic message

Persuasive communication, such as advertisements, consists of two basic elements, namely what is said and how it is said. The message used must be based on the needs of the target market and the ability of the specific product to meet these needs. These two elements are known as the appeal or impact of an advertisement. The basic message must not emphasise the properties of the product, but rather the benefits the customer will derive from that product. The retailer must also decide what they are going to advertise. It is naturally more cost-effective to advertise a variety of products than just a single product. The effectiveness of the advertisement can also be increased when a range of related products is advertised.

The communication approach

The emphasis in the communication approach falls on how something is said. Retailers can follow rational or emotional approaches in their advertisements. A rational approach involves facts, descriptions and logical reasons to convince the customer to visit the store. It tells the consumer what they can expect from the product or service.

The emotional approach is aimed at the consumer's feelings, ego and so on. In this case, the advertisement creates a mood and taps into the emotions and feelings of the consumer in order to persuade them to connect with the product/service on offer. From a product perspective, think of SABMiller's advertisement for Castle Lager, which focuses heavily on friendship and sharing that feeling.

Other approaches that can be used include a humorous approach, a fear-inducing approach, a testimonial approach, or even a fantasy approach. The effectiveness of the approaches depends, inter alia, on the nature of the product and the target market at which the message is aimed.

The total advertisement

The total advertisement consists of the heading, the illustration, the copy, the logo and the layout. Every component works together to initiate consumer action.

The heading of the advertisement draws the attention of the consumer, provides information, selects readers and arouses curiosity. The heading should, therefore, indicate to the reader what the rest of the advertisement will offer.

The illustrations in an advertisement help to achieve comprehension. The copy is what is actually said in the advertisement and develops comprehension, identification and action.

The logo is the characteristic sign of the enterprise, which appears on all advertisements to create recognition and evoke feelings.

The purpose of the layout is to capture the consumer's attention and then lead them through all parts of the advertisement.

Selecting the advertising media

The selection of the particular medium or media to use for an advertisement is an extremely important decision. When making this decision the retailer must consider what they want to achieve with the advertisement, who their target audience is and which medium/media is the most appropriate to reach this targeted audience.

Media characteristics

When the retailer selects the media for the advertising effort, they must consider the following characteristics of the different media:

- *Communication effectiveness.* The medium's ability to make an impact on the target market as required by the retailer.
- *Geographical selection.* The medium's ability to concentrate on a specific geographical area.
- *Audience selection.* The medium's ability to aim the message at a specific audience in a population.
- *Flexibility.* The number of different approaches and 'extras' that can be used in the medium, for example, by including coupons, stamped envelopes and so on.
- *Impact.* How well the medium encourages certain behavioural reactions in the specific target market.
- *Prestige.* The amount of status that customers attach to a medium.
- *Immediacy.* The ability of a medium to convey a well-timed or newsworthy message.
- *Lifespan.* The period for which the announcement or advertisement will continue to generate sales.
- *Coverage.* The percentage of the given market reached by the advertisement.
- *Cost.* This must be regarded in absolute and relative terms.
- *Frequency.* The number of times the same viewer or reader is exposed to the same advertisement.

Different advertising media

Knowledge of the different types of advertising media and their application possibilities in the retail environment is of cardinal importance to the retailer. This section will briefly consider the different media available to the retailer.

1. Newspapers advertisements

Newspapers enable retailers to reach many customers at a minimum cost at relatively short notice. Newspapers are geographically bound, so are ideal for the smaller retailer. There are two main types of newspapers: the weekly – one to three editions per week; the daily – four or more editions per week. The advertisements that appear in weekly papers have a longer lifespan, but the repetitive effect of advertisements in dailies can be more advantageous.

The specific target market will determine the type of printed media to be used by the retailer. For example, consider the difference in the readers of the *Daily Sun* versus the *Business Day*.

2. Magazine advertisements

Magazine advertisements in retailing are limited mainly to large retailers, for example, Truworths, Woolworths and Pick n Pay. Magazines are aimed at a specific demographic market, while, as we have already said, newspapers are geographically bound. Magazine advertising can, therefore, be aimed more at a specific target market; for example, when a clothing range, such as Hilton-Weiner or Truworths, advertises in fashion magazines, such as *InStyle, Elle* or *Cosmopolitan*.

3. Radio advertisements

Like newspapers, radio is a flexible medium and has the advantage of being relatively cheaper than television or glossy magazines. The retailer must be aware of the different target markets of each radio station so that they can correlate these with their own target market. The biggest disadvantage of radio as an advertising medium is the short lifespan of the actual message. Another disadvantage is that consumers often have the radio on in the background, so they are not concentrating fully on everything that is being said.

4. Television advertisements

Television has an advantage over all the other media because it combines images, sound and movement when the retailer's message is presented. The retailer can again aim their message at different market segments according to the different television channels or programmes. The BBC Home Channel on DSTV will have a different audience from that of e.tv, for example. Television covers a wider geographical area, however, and this can lead to wasted advertising exposure for the retailer serving a small market area.

5. Outdoor advertising

Outdoor advertising refers to open-air posters, bulletins and advertisements along the road. Brevity is of the utmost importance since the reader does not usually have much time to read the message. As a result, the copy must be in large print and easy to read.

6. Transit advertising

This type of advertising can be regarded as 'moving advertising boards', and the same principles apply here as for outdoor advertising. Examples are the advertisements displayed on buses and company vehicles.

7. Speciality advertisements

Speciality advertisements can be defined as any usable item on which an advertising print is affixed and given to customers or potential customers without any obligation. Examples of items used for speciality advertisements include ties, calendars, pens, diaries and so on. The retailer must ensure that the items selected are unique and suitable for the target market.

8. Direct mailing advertisements

Direct mailing can be regarded as the most flexible advertising medium, since it can be sent to any desired number of people. The most popular type of direct mailing is the 'personal letter'. Other alternatives are catalogues and circulars. The basic principle of success with any direct mailing campaign is the mailing list. Advertising money can be wasted, however, if the article does not reach the correct person. The retailer must therefore ensure that their mailing list is as correct as possible. Direct mailing campaigns should focus on obtaining an immediate response from the targeted audience – 'buy now!'

9. Donation advertising

As indicated by the name, donation advertising involves a financial donation by a firm or group where no advertising profit is expected. Examples of this are advertisements in concert programmes or in high school yearbooks.

10. Other media

Other media also available to the retailer include skywriting, advertisements in the *Yellow Pages* and advertisements in cinemas.

11. Internet and interactive media

These media have the potential to reach a very finely defined target audience with customised messages. They provide the retailer with opportunities to gather data and develop a database, and they are excellent for engaging the customer and gaining customer involvement. Issues of privacy and security are a major concern, however.

Evaluating the advertising function

The evaluation of the effectiveness of advertising includes, among other things, determining the effectiveness of the copy, illustrations or layouts, evaluating the specific media and measuring the achievement of advertising objectives. In order to be able to determine the effectiveness of advertising, the retailer must set specific, measurable advertising objectives. Instruments and methodology must be developed to determine whether advertisements meet these advertising objectives. As already mentioned earlier, it is difficult to determine the effectiveness of advertisements since so many internal and external factors influence the impact of advertising. Increases in sales, customer traffic and number of sales are very important yardsticks of success for advertising. The most appropriate yardstick, however, is to compare the gross profit on additional sales (generated by the advertising effort) with the cost of advertising. One way of using this yardstick is illustrated in Figure 8.6.

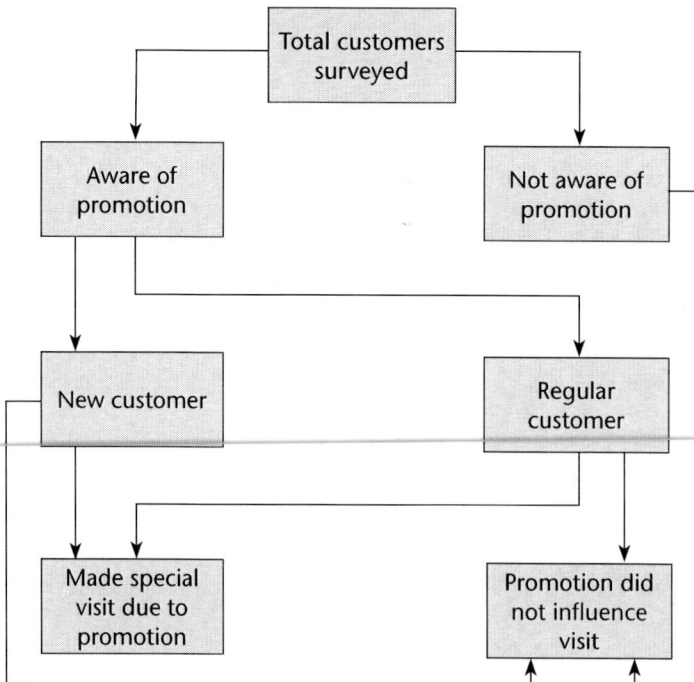

Figure 8.6 Determining whether promotion succeeded

Source: Based on discussions in Blythe (2006). Essentials of marketing communications, *3rd edition. Harlow: Pearson*

8.5   Sales promotion

Sales promotion includes such a large variety of techniques that it is difficult to define. In general, sales promotion can be described as all promotional activities except advertising, personal selling and publicity, and is any direct incentive that offers an extra value or reward to the customer to stimulate fast and immediate purchase behaviour. The objectives of sales promotional techniques are to

- Attract the customers' attention;
- Provide information for customers;
- Provide an incentive that is meant to be of value;
- Extend a definite invitation to buy now, to convince non-consumers to try a product;
- Encourage bigger purchases by present consumers.

It is important to realise that sales promotional activities play only a supplementary role and that they must not be used as a replacement for other marketing communication elements. Many different sales promotion techniques can be identified. Some of the most common ones are discussed below.

Coupons

Coupons are certificates that are distributed by manufacturers to consumers through newspapers, magazines, direct mail, and in or on packets. They are redeemable at retail outlets and give the customers a specific price reduction on a certain product item. Coupons are advantageous for retailers as they attract customers to the store. Retailers must understand the following principles of coupons and keep them in mind:

- Coupons are best used with products that are in the introductory stages of their life cycle.
- Coupons are best used for products that are purchased regularly, and by selectively choosing target consumers who are most likely to use coupons, the retailer can effectively increase traffic within their store.

The growth of the Internet and other mobile technologies has given rise to the electronic coupon. In this case the consumer receives the coupon via cellphone, e-mail, or downloaded from a website. Groupon is a company that has grown significantly in the past year and focuses on coupons for retailers and other products. It is interesting to go to Groupon's website and to read up on their business model.

Free samples

The presentation of free samples is one of the most effective marketing communication techniques to encourage consumers to try new or improved products and to purchase them regularly. Samples are small reproductions of the full-sized product so that consumers can express their own opinion on the characteristics of the product after the sample has been used for a trial period. The retailer must remember that only products with low unit costs, and that are small and are regularly purchased can be used as samples.

Premiums

Premiums are merchandise items that are offered free to customers or at a reduced price (self-liquidating premium) as incentives to promote the purchase of a specific product. This sales promotional technique is used, particularly, by cosmetic companies to promote purchases of cosmetic products, by offering a gift to the consumer when they purchase one of their cosmetic products for a certain value. Alternatively, they offer cosmetic products of the same brand at a reduced price if other items of that brand are purchased. The objective of premiums is to make customers aware that the store exists, introduce them to what the store has to offer, promote immediate purchases, create excitement and enthusiasm in consumers, and generally increase sales and traffic in the store.

Trading stamps

Trading stamps are printed stamps that the retailer offers the customers in exchange for their patronage. These stamps can be exchanged by customers for certain merchandise items or, in certain cases, for cash.

Competitions and sweepstakes

Competitions require the entrant to use a certain degree of skill that is measured against that of other participants (for example, solving a puzzle, completing a sentence, suggesting a name for a product or store), while sweepstakes are games of chance. Winners are chosen at random by drawing an entry form. They are usually aimed at making an advertisement more interesting, drawing attention to a certain store, creating an atmosphere of excitement, supplying an extra selling aid, giving new life to the image of a brand, or to synchronise the competition with an event that is receiving a lot of publicity.

Specialities

Gifts in the form of pens, pencils, calendars, matches and T-shirts bearing the retailer's name or slogan are given to customers to stimulate their interest in the store. These gifts are given to customers to build long-term relationships between them and the store.

Tie-ins

Tie-ins are used to attract the attention of consumers to various offers in a store. Here a retailer can work together with another enterprise to make special offers to customers. For instance, free tickets to movies are offered if a certain dish is ordered in a restaurant.

Tie-ins can take various forms, such as a tie-in with a public holiday, a sporting event or other products, to name just a few examples.

Strengths and weaknesses of sales promotions

As a method of marketing communication, sales promotions have strengths as well as weaknesses. These strengths and weaknesses are given in Table 8.4.

Table 8.4 Strengths and weaknesses of sales promotions

Strengths
☐ A positive attitude towards the product is stimulated within consumers.
☐ Consumers feel that they are getting something extra.
☐ Immediate action can be stimulated via sales promotion.
☐ This medium is most adaptable.
☐ It is a multipurpose medium. For example, it can be used to introduce a new product, to support a sales message or to attract attention, to convince or result in action.
☐ Sales promotion is exceptionally effective when a new product is being introduced, when product improvements are being announced, when intensive distribution is required, and when it supports an advertising campaign.
Weaknesses
☐ Results of sales promotions are short term in nature.
☐ Sales promotions cannot be used without the support of other marketing communications methods.
☐ A specific sales promotion method cannot be used continuously.
☐ Too many sales promotion efforts can be disadvantageous for the image of the brand.
☐ The effect of a sales promotion method can be eliminated easily by competitors.
☐ Sales promotion methods are often viewed as a form of bribery.

Source: Compiled from Cant & Van Heerden (eds). (2010). Marketing management. *Cape Town: Juta*

Table 8.5 identifies specific advantages and disadvantages of the sales promotion techniques that were discussed. Each of these needs to be taken into account when deciding which technique to use in a specific campaign.

Table 8.5 Strengths and weaknesses of specific sales promotion techniques

Method	Strengths	Weaknesses
Coupons	❏ More effective than a direct price decrease ❏ The price is only temporarily decreased ❏ A greater psychological effect than normal price decrease ❏ More regular and larger volume of purchases are encouraged ❏ Introduces new products ❏ New consumers can be convinced to try the product	❏ Competitors can easily eliminate the effect of coupons ❏ Consumers of coupons are already loyal supporters of the product ❏ Fraud can result ❏ Retailers are not always willing to co-operate ❏ Many coupons are not redeemed – this leads to waste
Competitions	❏ Attract consumers to stores ❏ Causes consumers to be involved and interested in the product ❏ Attention is focused on the firm/product	❏ Consumers are lax in executing the task that the competition requires of them ❏ Poorly planned competitions can cause the consumer to react negatively to the product ❏ Requires an aggressive advertising campaign to introduce the competition ❏ Effect is short term in nature
Free samples	❏ Consumers are given the opportunity to test the product ❏ Can be used as an offensive or defensive mechanism ❏ Suitable for the introduction of new products or to attract new consumers to the product	❏ Very expensive promotion method ❏ Not suitable for expensive and slow-moving items ❏ Wasting of the product occurs (as much as 20% of the samples are wasted) ❏ Potential consumers are not always reached; samples often end up in the wrong hands
Premiums	❏ Effective in stimulating the support of a store or a product ❏ Support is not directly linked to a price discount; the consumer receives something of value in return for their support ❏ Repeat purchases are encouraged ❏ Stimulates impulsive buying	❏ Not all products are suited for this type of sales promotion ❏ Difficult to select a suitable premium article that is exceptional ❏ Causes additional administrative burden and costs ❏ Repeat purchases decrease as soon as consumers have collected enough premium articles

Source: Compiled from Clow & Baack (2010). Integrated advertising, promotion, and marketing communications, 4th edition. Harlow: Pearson

8.6 Publicity

Publicity is defined as 'a type of promotion that relies on the public relations effect of a news story carried usually free by mass media. The main objective of publicity is not sales promotion, but creation of an image through editorial or "independent source" commentary. While the publicist can control the content of the story, he or she may not have any control over its placement or interpretation by the media' (http://www. businessdictionary.com). In other words, any reference to an enterprise, a product, or a service, or store personnel in the mass media, except an advertisement, is called publicity. Publicity can be beneficial or negative for a retailer.

Publicity is free in the sense that media, such as television and newspapers, report on newsworthy items regarding an enterprise without charging the enterprise a fee, as in the case of advertising. The retailer should, therefore, try to generate favourable publicity about the enterprise as it can lead to increased sales and a good reputation.

Types of publicity

Publicity can either be planned or unplanned. In planned publicity the retailer has some measure of control over the news item that is published by, for example, making available press releases, press conferences, photographs and letters to the editor. Unplanned publicity can irreparably damage the reputation and financial structure of the enterprise. The growth of social media sites, such as Facebook, YouTube and Twitter, for example, has presented consumers with a large, global platform, which can produce either very positive or negative publicity for any retailer. Retailers are under more scrutiny than ever before and they need to manage their actions carefully to limit the damage that these social platforms can cause.

Developing a publicity story

A publicity story is a story or message about the product or enterprise and includes the following Ws:

❏ *Who*: the enterprise or people involved;
❏ *What*: the important event;
❏ *When*: the date and time;
❏ *Where*: the place;
❏ *Why*: the reason for the event.

Before the publicity story is developed the retailer must establish what objectives they want to achieve through it. Do they want to stimulate the demand for certain merchandise items or do they want to promote the image of the enterprise? They must also establish what kind of stories the media accept and the criteria they use to decide whether to place a story or not. Publicity stories dealing with new and unusual events, store innovations, improvements in working conditions, the opening of new stores and so on, usually attract the attention of the media. Publicity must also be newsworthy, unusual, appeal to a large part of the public and be credible. The retailer must also decide in which media the story should be placed, for example, newspapers, magazines, radio or television.

Advantages of publicity

Publicity has at least three advantages over other methods that retailers use to communicate with their customers. Firstly, the public perceives news items to be more credible than advertisements, personal selling or sales promotions, which they perceive as methods intended to persuade them to buy. Consumers therefore regard news items as factual, objective and true. Secondly, consumers are more likely to read a news item about a retailer than read an advertisement from the same retailer. Lastly, publicity is presented in a dramatic way, which captures the attention and emotions of the reader.

Other advantages of publicity are that it is free for the retailer and that a large audience is reached.

Objectives of publicity

The objectives of publicity are to make the consumer aware of a retailer and their merchandise. It seeks to make a favourable impression on current customers and potential customers, and to generate interest in a store. Publicity also has the goal of increasing traffic and sales within the store, and building consumer confidence in the store. A key objective is to establish a lasting and favourable reputation of the store.

8.7 Summary

In this chapter we focused on the communication process. Advertising is part of the promotion mix and can greatly influence individual customers, as well as the total market. In this regard we looked at various types of advertising, namely product advertising, institutional advertising and co-operative advertising.

The advertising function must also be thoroughly planned if it is to achieve the set objectives. This planning includes determining advertising objectives and making budget decisions. With regard to the organisation of the advertising function, the retailer must decide to what extent they can establish advertising departments, and whether or not they will use external advertising specialists. We also discussed creating retail advertisements and selecting advertising media, and evaluating the effectiveness of retail advertising.

Finally, we looked at how sales promotion and publicity are effective marketing promotional tools, which retailers can use to achieve their objectives, to encourage consumers to make purchases and to positively influence the attitude of consumers towards a store and its merchandise. Coupons, premiums, trading stamps, competitions and gifts are examples of sales promotional devices, which can be used to draw customers to a store and to increase sales. Although many retailers neglect publicity, it is one of the most beneficial communication devices that can be included in the retailer's total marketing communication strategy. Retailers can generate favourable publicity by making available press releases, photographs, letters to the editor, and so on.

Mini case study

Read the following case study and work through the questions that follow:

New Cambridge Food store opens its doors in Soweto as part of Massmart's aggressive expansion into food retail

100 stores and R1 billion in turnover. That's the vision Massmart has for Cambridge Food by the end of 2015. This ambitious plan is fuelled by the brand's winning hybrid strategy of bringing quality, value-for-money products and excellent service to the transport nodes of the country, where convenience and low cost are key.

Soweto supermarket

Overlooking the Bara Taxi Rank in Soweto, Cambridge Food was officially declared open for business on Wednesday, 25 May. The 3 450 m² hybrid store, which caters for both retail and wholesale customers, is anchored by its extensive service departments which greet customers as they enter the store. It is only the fourth Cambridge Food store to be built from scratch as part of Masscash's (a division of Massmart) growing focus on and expansion in food retail. Other previously independent stores, such as the Astor Cash & Carry chain, Savemoor and JD's Cash & Carry, have been bought by Masscash and converted to the bright yellow and pink of Cambridge Food.

A market of opportunity

Cambridge Food started as a small butchery operation in KwaZulu-Natal and gradually began to incorporate groceries into the offering. Massmart bought Cambridge Food in December 2008 and stores have started popping up in Gauteng, predominantly in CBD areas near taxi ranks and townships to take advantage of the mass commuter traffic each day.

Traditionally, the township market has been neglected by the major supermarket groups and serviced by independent butcheries, but this has changed in recent years as they realised the great opportunity for expansion.

Contemporary and vibrant stores

'Although Cambridge Food started life as a regional chain, the brand has strong equity throughout the country in the lower LSM market,' says Andrew Stein, marketing executive designate at Cambridge Food, and they are able to ride on this wave of success as they expand. 'We have retained the best of the original business and brought it together with the best of Massmart's retail experience to provide our customers with a unique service offering,' he adds. The pink, blue and yellow colours of Cambridge Food are certainly visible throughout the store, as well as assisting the hybrid store to stand out from the retail landscape. ➲

The store is spacious and natural lighting creates an airy atmosphere. 'It's all about creating a shopping environment that is fresh, fun and exciting for our customers and that stands out against our "more conservative" competition,' says Stein.

Focus on service

As customers enter the store, they are greeted by a line of service departments along the right wall, starting with a new concept Sausage Bar (the Cambridge Food sausage is renowned). 'Service departments are our top priority. At Cambridge Food, the store is anchored by service departments and supported by dry groceries – versus the competition, who seem to do it the other way around,' says Stein. They've invested heavily in the home meal replacement (HMR) or 'Hot Foods' offering and emphasis has been put on making a tasty, affordable and culturally appropriate offering.

There is a 'meal of the day' every day and customers have a wide choice between fried chicken, pap and stews, samp and beans, etc. 'We're giving our customers the food from the street … but at a better price, of a higher quality, and in a modern shopping environment,' he says. A bit of theatre has also been added to the hot foods department with staff ladling the steaming pap out of a huge potjie pot. Customers can also choose to have steak, chops and wors cooked by one of the chefs on the grill right at the counter. The in-store bakery produces fresh bread each day (sold for just R3.49 a loaf), as well as a variety of confectionery, with cream cakes and snowballs being favourites amongst the customers.

Butchery heart of business

Without moving away from the core business of the original Cambridge Food model, the butchery in the Soweto store is very impressive, with the counter taking up most of the back wall. Again, the offering is culturally specific, and offal, walkie-talkies and boerewors lie side by side.

A central meat plant services the Cambridge Food stores in Gauteng with all their pre-packed and over-the-counter needs. Nick Catling, head of the plant, says they are currently doing around 400 tons out of the 1 500 m² production area.

Customer specific ranging and pricing

Throughout the store there is a strong pricing message with promotional posters and shelf talkers throughout. As a hybrid store, Cambridge Food services both retail and wholesale customers and pink signs in every category indicate the bulk price of the products.

There is a strong KVI presence in the store but every Cambridge Food store's product mix does differ slightly as it is tailored to suit the specific store and specific local market. 'For example, in the Soweto store we don't stock mustard,' says Stein. 'Our philosophy is to provide narrower ranges so that we can push bigger volumes and pass the price benefit on to our customers.'

The cross-merchandising throughout the store is also very effective and will no doubt fuel many impulse purchases. They have also set up a trader help desk to assist the wholesale customers with price negotiations and keep them up to date with the current specials and promotions. Stokvels are also encouraged to form relationships with the store and social grants are distributed in-store.

Private label has a strong presence in the KZN stores already and this will be brought to the Gauteng stores soon, says Beverley Levitt, head of private label at Cambridge Food. The house brands will range across most categories and boost the Cambridge Food marketing strategy of combining good value and quality for all South Africans.

Source: http://www.supermarket.co.za/SR_Downloads/S&R%20June%202011%20Cambridge%20 storewatch.pdf. Accessed: 25 February 2012.

Questions

1. How would you go about promoting the new Cambridge Food store opened in Soweto? Give reasons for your answer.
2. Given the target market of Cambridge Food stores, outline the practical steps you would follow when creating the retail advertisement for Cambridge Food stores.
3. Which advertising medium/media would be most appropriate for Cambridge Food stores to use when advertising their new store? Discuss your reasons.
4. Would sales promotions be appropriate for use in a Cambridge Food store? Give reasons.
5. How would you utilise publicity to announce the opening of the new Soweto Cambridge Food store?

8.8 Self-evaluation questions

1. Discuss the communication process and its implications for the retailer.
2. Describe the five main components of the promotion mix.
3. How does advertising influence customers and the total market?
4. Discuss the difference between product advertising, institutional advertising and co-operative advertising.
5. Discuss the components of the advertising strategy.
6. Identify the various types of advertising objectives that can be developed.
7. Discuss the steps the advertiser goes through when creating the retail advertisement.
8. Explain the various media characteristics a retailer should consider before selecting the medium or media for an advertising campaign.
9. Discuss the various advertising media that a retailer can use for an advertising campaign.

10. Describe the various sales promotional techniques that a retailer can use in a promotions plan.
11. Discuss the strengths and weaknesses of sales promotion as a promotional tool.
12. Discuss how publicity can be used to the benefit of a retailer.

8.9 Bibliography

Blythe, J. (2006). *Essentials of marketing communications*, 3rd edition. Harlow: Pearson.
Cant, M.C. & Van Heerden, C.H. (eds) (2010). *Marketing management*. Cape Town: Juta.
Cant, M.C., Strydom, J.W., Jooste, C.J. & Du Plessis, P.J. (2006). *Marketing management*. Cape Town: Juta.
Clow, K.E. & Baack, D. (2010). *Integrated advertising, promotion, and marketing communications*. 4th edition. Harlow: Pearson.
Jansen van Rensburg, M., Venter, P. & Strydom, J.W. (2010). Approaches taken by South African advertisers to select and appoint advertising agencies. *Southern African Business Review*, 14(1): 21.
Koekemoer, L. (2002). *Promotional strategy: Marketing communications in practice*. Cape Town: Juta.
Koekemoer, L. (2010). *Introduction to integrated marketing communications*. Cape Town: Juta.
Pride, W.M. & Ferrell, O.C. (2010). *Marketing*, 15th edition. Mason, OH: Cengage.
Strydom, J. (ed.). (2011). *Introduction to marketing*, 4th edition. Cape Town: Juta.

Websites

http://www.adbrands.net/za/sabmiller_za.htm Accessed: 14 March 2012.
http://www.businessdictionary.com/definition/publicity.html Accessed: 24 February 2012.
http://drypen.in/advertising/dagmar-defining-advertising-goals-for-measured-advertising-results.html Accessed: 24 February 2012.
http://www.marketingpower.com/_layouts/Reference/Bestpractices.aspx Accessed: 9 March 2012.
http://www.supermarket.co.za/SR_Downloads/S&R%20June%202011%20Cambridge%20storewatch.pdf Accessed: 25 February 2012.
http://www.utwente.nl/cw/theorieenoverzicht/Levels%20of%20theories/macro/Two-Step%20Flow%20Theory.doc/ Accessed: 12 March 2012.

9

Visual merchandising

Colin N Diggines

9.1   Introduction

We have all been into a shop and purchased something. Did you notice the way the items were displayed? Did you notice the lighting? Did you listen to the music that was playing? Each of these elements are carefully planned to entice you into the store and encourage you to purchase.

While retailers can entice customers to their stores by effective advertising, it is the visual presentation of their merchandise (the display of the merchandise) that motivates consumers to enter the store and to buy the products on offer. In the world of today, where self-service has become the norm in retail stores, visual merchandising plays an increasingly important role in influencing consumers to buy. In this chapter we discuss the topic of visual merchandising. We begin by outlining the key concepts and issues relating to the development of displays and display equipment, before moving on to the actual development of a display. Here we focus on planning displays and then preparing and installing them on the retail floor. Each component plays a crucial role in attracting the customer's attention, creating a pleasant shopping experience and making it desirable to buy from the selected retailer in the long term.

Lastly, we look at the topics of design, colour and lighting. Because a person's sense of sight gives them more information than any other sense, visual merchandising is the most important medium retailers can use to influence customers. We look specifically at how the elements of design can be used to achieve the retailer's set objectives.

9.2   The role of the visual merchandiser

In the past, those people responsible for dressing mannequins and decorating store windows, and the store in general, were not involved in the planning of visual merchandising. Nowadays, however, the visual merchandiser is an important member of the decision-making team and is very much involved in the process of planning visual merchandising.

The current generation of visual merchandisers need the qualities of creativity, imagination and sales skills. While a customer is shopping, their attitude towards the store and their impression of it are influenced by the store's interior appearance. It is, therefore, the visual merchandiser's duty to create and uphold a consistent and positive image for the store.

As in the past, visual merchandisers must use space, colour, lines, design, lighting and movement to make both the store and its displays visually attractive to customers. In addition, nowadays it is important to appeal to all five of the consumer's senses, not just their vision. Visual merchandisers are, therefore, sometimes responsible for the planning of background music, aromas and any other aspects that will appeal to all the customer's senses.

9.3   Display objectives

The principal objective of all visual merchandising activities is to increase the sales of products and services. Depending on the objectives, a distinction can be made between promotional and institutional displays. Let us consider each of these.

Promotional displays

When the retailer's objective is to promote the sales of specific merchandise or services, promotional displays are used. The attractive way in which specific merchandise is presented in promotional displays motivates customers to buy that merchandise. A good promotional display stimulates the impulse to buy and reminds buyers about items they need. It also exposes customers to new products and the latest fashions and, in addition, suggests new uses for existing products.

Institutional displays

When the retailer's objective is to promote the store's image rather than specific merchandise, institutional displays are used. World Aids day displays and displays featuring environmental issues are examples of institutional displays. Such displays of issues of public interest suggest that the retailer cares about the community's welfare. This in itself promotes the image of the enterprise.

9.4 Functions of a display

The primary function of displays is to increase the store's sales. An effective display should also perform the following additional functions:

❏ Displays must attract the attention of consumers. This can be achieved through the effective use of colour, dramatic lighting and the incorporation of moving parts in the display.

❏ Displays must arouse and hold the customers' interest. It is not sufficient merely to attract customers' attention – their interest must also be aroused and retained.

❏ Displays need to stimulate the desire of consumers to examine the merchandise displayed more closely – for instance, by asking to look at them or try them on. The display must, therefore, arouse the consumers' desire to such an extent that they want to buy.

Some generic functions of retail displays include:

❏ Maximise product exposure;
❏ Enhance the appearance of products;
❏ Stimulate interest in the products;
❏ Exhibit product information;
❏ Facilitate sales transactions;
❏ Ensure the security of products;
❏ Allow for the storage of products;
❏ Remind customers about products that they planned to buy;
❏ Generate additional sales of impulse items.

Retail displays should also reinforce the store's image and create an atmosphere of excitement around a promotional event.

9.5   Different types of displays

The discussion of displays can be divided into three categories: window, in-store and point-of-purchase displays. Each of these is used within a retail store to build an overall image and create a 'feel' for the store.

In-store displays

In-store displays can be divided broadly into selection, special and audiovisual displays.

If a retailer uses self-selection and self-service, merchandise is presented to customers in selection displays. The retailer's whole range of merchandise is put on mass display in aisles and wall units (shelves, counters, tables and so on) to expose the consumer to the retailer's complete range of merchandise. Such displays are usually open, so that customers can inspect the merchandise. The chief function of this type of display is to give customers access to the merchandise and encourage self-service. To be effective, selection displays need to present the goods in logical selling or usage groups, in a simple, well-organised arrangement, in a clean and neat condition, and arranged in an attractive, informative and safe manner.

A special display is one that presents merchandise in such a way that it attracts special attention and leaves a lasting impression on consumers. Such displays are normally situated in areas where they receive maximum exposure, for instance, at the end of an aisle, on top of a counter, on free-standing units in places where customer traffic is heavy, near points of payment and at store entrances and exits. Special displays focus on items that have the ability to entice consumers into the store, strengthen the store image, improve the store's sales volume, and increase its net profit. Such items are advertised, best-selling, high-profit fashion articles, and articles that cause impulse buying and complementary buying behaviour.

Modern technological innovations enable retailers to use the new technology in displays to inform customers about the merchandise available and to demonstrate it to them. They can use modern projection techniques to project images onto a wall, which serve to lure customers through the store.

In-store displays can take different forms, depending on the merchandise to be displayed and the amount of space available. An open display enables customers to touch and examine the merchandise. In such a display, merchandise is exhibited openly on a counter, shelf, table or mannequin.

Closed displays allow customers to only look at the merchandise, without being able to touch it. This type of display is used where, for instance, the merchandise is fragile and easily damaged, expensive or easy to steal.

A shadow box is usually found behind a counter and stands alone. A small, well-lit display area resembles a shallow box and is open on one side. It displays merchandise in a more dramatic manner. A ledge display is one where merchandise is exhibited on store walls, ledges or room partitions. This type of display offers the advantage that every possible space is used for display, so as not to clutter the aisles. A flying display features items suspended from the ceiling by means of wire, hangers or other props. A dump display is used for small, unbreakable items, which are placed in large containers to create a bargain image.

Point-of-purchase displays

A point-of-purchase display is an in-store special display, but it is discussed separately because of its importance and popularity.

Point-of-purchase displays are popular because of their ability to stimulate on-the-spot buying behaviour. Such displays are located where the merchandise is displayed for sale. These displays can take any of the following forms: banners, cards on counters, video screens, counter displays, audio recordings, samples of products and so on. Point-of-purchase displays should be informative, rather than merely decorative. They should, therefore, tie in with the retail business's advertising campaigns in the various media, rather than be an independent communication medium.

Window displays

Window displays form an integral part of the exterior of a store and are intended to entice customers into the store. Such displays usually take one of three forms: a promotional, an institutional or a public service display.

☐ *Promotional window displays* promote particular items. A dress in the window of a clothing store is an example of a promotional display.

☐ *Institutional window displays* promote a store in its entirety. A 'back to school' display in a store window is an example of an institutional window display.

☐ *Public service window displays* promote items and ideas that are unrelated to the store as such, for example Child Welfare Society displays.

Various window display areas can be used by retailers.

☐ *Elevated windows* are built into walls several centimetres above ground level to prevent damage and to enable merchandise to be placed at the eye level of passers-by. This type of window display is used especially by retailers selling jewellery.

☐ *Shadow boxes* are small solitary windows or are part of a larger window and are principally used to display small items of merchandise, such as jewellery and cosmetic products. The advantage of corner windows is that consumers can observe such displays from two directions.

☐ *Island windows* are freestanding displays in the middle of a store entrance, offering the advantage that goods can be viewed from all angles.

The back of the window display areas discussed above may be open, closed or semi-closed. Open windows are those that present an open back, enabling customers to see right into the store. This may motivate them to enter the store and look around. Closed windows have a backing that isolates the display from the store interior. This type of window has the advantage of focusing the consumer's full attention on the display. Semi-closed windows are closed at the back up to the level of the average person's line of vision, and above that they are open. Such windows are often used by pharmacies and hardware stores.

9.6   Elements of a good display

Creating a good display is not an easy task. To be able to communicate the intended message effectively, the retailer must carefully plan and consider each element of a display. The elements of a display include, among others, the merchandise, the location of the display, colour, background material, lighting and signage. The following guidelines should help the retailer to create effective displays:

❑ *A good display requires a theme.* A theme is the idea or group of ideas, which are repeated, and which unify all the displays throughout the store, thus creating continuity. In addition, it is the retailer's means of making a strong statement about the products for sale.

❑ *A good display must be distinctive.* To attract attention, the display must stand apart from others. The market situation determines what is truly distinctive.

❑ *A good display must be appropriate and tasteful.* What is considered appropriate and tasteful changes as people assume a more liberal outlook. Viewers have to decide for themselves what is appropriate and tasteful. A thorough knowledge of the store's target market is therefore necessary, so that a display matches the preferences of the target market.

❑ *A good display should be clean, neat and attractive.* Every display should be checked at least once a day to ensure that nothing is in need of repair or adjustment.

❑ *A good display must provide information.* The visual impact of the display itself should convey most of the information. A controversial issue is whether prices should be included in a display or not. This decision depends on the type of store and the expectations of its target market.

❑ *A good display needs to be simple.* Since a customer has only a few seconds to look at the display in passing, it must be kept as simple as possible. For example, there must not be too many different items in a single display. It should have a single focal point, since more than one focus can be confusing and can diminish a display's effectiveness.

❑ *A good display should show merchandise in use.* By displaying merchandise being used, the retailer suggests a possible buying motive to people who need a motive.

❏ *A good display must convey an appropriate store image.* Displays help to give a store its own personality or image. If the retailer wants to project an image of quality or prestige, the display should uphold that image.

❏ *A good display must be safe.* Displays can sometimes be dangerous and injure customers. Conscious efforts are constantly required in the area of safety; particularly in today's litigious society.

❏ *A good display must not pose a security threat.* A display must be built in such a way that items cannot easily be stolen from it. Ways of eliminating theft from displays include the following:

  ■ Display only one of a pair.
  ■ Display merchandise in a set pattern so that it will be obvious if something is missing.
  ■ Never use expensive items if cheap ones will work just as well.
  ■ Never drape goods over chairs or the arms of mannequins without attaching them firmly.
  ■ Use enclosed cabinets in less secure areas.

❏ A display that attracts attention must contain the following features: *contrast, repetition, movement, harmony, balance, rhythm* and *proportion* (refer to Table 9.1).

Table 9.1 Using displays to attract attention

❏ Display elements must be evaluated to determine how well they attract and hold the attention of passers-by.
❏ Contrast is one way to attract attention. Contrast is achieved by using different colours, lighting, form, size, shape, lettering or textures.
❏ Repetition attracts consumer attention. Duplicating an object reinforces and strengthens the impression. For instance, displaying 20 tennis rackets, creates an image of a store selling a wide assortment of merchandise in that category.
❏ Physical motion is a powerful attention getter, as is dominance. If an item is much larger than other items in a display, it will be the dominant item and will draw attention to the entire display.
❏ Once attention has been harnessed, the next step is to direct that attention to the intended message.
❏ Harmony and graduation are used frequently to accomplish this.
❏ Harmony refers to the unification of merchandise, lighting, props, shelf space and show cards to create a pleasing effect. Balance, emphasis, rhythm and proportion work to focus attention on the central point.
❏ Formal balanced displays, in which one side is duplicated by the other, tend to produce feelings of dignity, neatness and order. Informally balanced displays, in which one side does not exactly match the other, tend to generate excitement and are less stuffy.
❏ Rhythm refers to the eye's path after initial contact with the display. The objective is to hold the eye until the entire display is seen.
❏ Design specialists use vertical lines to create the image of height, strength and dignity.
➲

- ☐ Horizontal lines suggest calmness, width and sophistication; diagonal lines create action, and curved lines suggest continuity and femininity.
- ☐ Proportion concerns the relative sizes of the display's various objects. Attention can be directed to the desired focal point by arranging items in a graduated pattern from small to large.
- ☐ The proportion concept also involves the positioning of objects in patterns. Popular display patterns include pyramids, steps, zig-zags, repetition and mass.
- ☐ The image of height and formality is created with pyramids, while the zig-zag is a popular method of displaying clothing to create an aura of excitement.
- ☐ Repetition arrangements are used primarily in shelf merchandising situations. Merchandise items are placed equidistant from one another in a straight, horizontal line.
- ☐ The mass arrangement is the placement of a large quantity of merchandise in either neatly stacked lines or in jumbled dump bins to convey the image of a sale item.

Source: Adapted from http://www.redcliffe.co.uk/point_of_sale/boost-your-sales.htm. Accessed: 27 February 2012

9.7 Visual merchandising in a full-service retail store

In a full-service retail store the aim of displays is to entice customers into the store and to create the right atmosphere for the sales person to take over the selling process. In full-service department stores or large speciality stores, each department usually has one or more displays in which new or attractive merchandise sold in that department is displayed. Such displays are generally located in areas frequented by most customers, for example near the entrances. These displays can also be set up on ledges, in shadow boxes, in and on counters or in display cabinets. The way in which these displays have items grouped together and labelled with the necessary information helps both the sales person and the customers, by showing them what is new and in fashion. Creative window displays are particularly useful in full-service stores to entice customers into the store.

Service enterprises, such as banks, hotels and restaurants serving takeaways, also need to pay careful attention to their use of visual merchandising to sell their products and services.

Just as visual merchandising and the use of colour are important in self-service stores to persuade customers to buy, they are equally important in full-service retail stores, since customers reveal the same buying behaviour in full-service stores that they learnt by shopping in self-service stores.

9.8 Visual merchandising in a self-service retail store

With the emergence of self-service, visual merchandising has become increasingly important. The reason is that merchandise sold in a self-service retail store has to sell itself. Products therefore compete with one another in the sales area for consumers' attention to motivate them to buy that specific item. For this reason, manufacturers are competing increasingly with one another on the design and packaging of their products, as well as the design of point-of-purchase displays and materials.

In self-service retail stores, such as Edgars, Checkers Hyper and Builders' Warehouse, visual merchandising is used to attract customers' attention and help them to make their purchases, with minimal or no assistance from sales staff.

Point-of-purchase display

The most effective type of display that can be used in a self-service retail store is a point-of-purchase display. A point-of-purchase display is one that is aimed at encouraging impulse buying. It can take any of the following forms: posters, price cards, samples of products, video advertisement spots, or any other device that focuses the customers' attention on the product. These point-of-purchase displays tie in with the manufacturers' product advertising campaigns and repeat the messages that consumers hear over radio and television, and see in magazines. The manufacturer supplies the materials for a point-of-purchase display to the retailer. The aim is to promote sales of the manufacturer's product at the point of sale. Supermarkets use point-of-purchase displays at the ends of the aisles, in particular where products such as canned foods, paper serviettes and biscuits are incorporated into the display. Displays of sweets, magazines, breath-mints and razor blades at the points of payment are also point-of-purchase displays, and are aimed at encouraging impulse buying.

Dump displays

Dump displays are another feature used in self-service retail stores to exhibit small, unbreakable merchandise. A dump display is a large container into which this merchandise is placed to create a bargain image. The merchandise displayed in this way is usually products that are purchased regularly, reduced in price or seasonal (for example, sweets and toys).

Gondolas

Gondolas are movable shelving units on which merchandise can be displayed. They are used in grocery stores, in particular. They are usually arranged in rows to form the aisles along which customers move while shopping. Since these shelving units are movable, they facilitate changes in the layout of self-service stores.

Endcaps

Endcaps are display units located at the ends of aisles in self-service retail stores. High-profit merchandise and seasonal products are frequently displayed here.

9.9　Display equipment

Display equipment consists of props on which merchandise can be displayed to showcase the products and to project the store's image. The most important factor to be considered when choosing display equipment is whether the store provides full service or self-service. Self-service stores use props that make the merchandise accessible to customers and enable them to touch and examine the goods. Examples of props used in self-service stores are counters that are open on all sides, and open shelves that are not enclosed behind a counter. In full-service retail stores, in which sales staff attend to customers, preference is given to closed counters, shelves behind counters that are staffed by sales people and any other props that restrict customer access to the merchandise.

The nature of the merchandise also largely determines the props to be used. Expensive jewellery, for example, must be displayed in closed counters, while staple products, such as tea and coffee, should be displayed on open shelves, since this facilitates self-service.

Display equipment can take various forms. Examples are imitations of human figures, representations of the whole or part of the human figure, and various types of stands, stages, platforms, counters and shelves. Similarly, pedestals can be used for draping or elevating the merchandise, and for displaying it on walls, counters, display cabinets, floors and so on. In order to facilitate the effective preparation of a display, retailers must be familiar with the different types of props available.

The use of mannequins

Men, women and children mannequins can be used to display an entire outfit. These mannequins are available in a wide variety of materials, such as plastic, plaster of Paris, velvet, rubber, wood, metal and papier-mâché. The design of these mannequins ranges from lifelike replicas of human figures with styled hairstyles to abstract representations of human forms.

When selecting mannequins, the image of the store must be borne in mind. For example, if the store's target market is fashionable teenagers, the use of conventional lifelike mannequins would not be appropriate.

Full-figure mannequins are not the only ones available for displaying merchandise. Representations of certain parts of the human body are also used, for example:

- ❐　A form of a woman's torso – used especially for displaying swimsuits, jackets, lingerie, blouses and skirts;
- ❐　A form of a woman's head and shoulders – used especially for displaying jewellery, scarves, hats and hair ornaments;
- ❐　A form of a woman's hand – used especially for displaying gloves, jewellery, scarves and watches. It can also be used to drape merchandise such as blouses and skirts;

- A form of a woman's leg – used to display stockings and socks;
- A shoe form – used to display shoes and sandals;
- A man's suit form – used to display men's suits and sports jackets;
- A woman's blouse form – used to display women's blouses, sweaters and lingerie.

Adjustable stands

Adjustable stands are props that can be adjusted to different heights and to which various attachments can be secured to display dresses, blouses, lingerie, stockings, tablecloths, hats, scarves, gloves and bed linen.

Stages and platforms

A wide variety of stages and platforms are used to display merchandise at various heights and levels. These stages and platforms come in different shapes and sizes and are made from materials such as plastic, transparent plastic, wrought iron, wood, chrome and brass.

9.10 Anthropometrics and visual merchandising

Ergonomics (anthropometry) measures human characteristics and functions, and establishes the way in which the human body and brain work. The results of these scientific studies in the human sciences are then applied by ergonomists to solve practical problems in the design and manufacture of products and systems.

The physical and psychological characteristics of people need to be taken into account in visual merchandising. For example, the height of an average person has an influence on the height at which shelves should be placed in a retail store. Ergonomics (anthropometry) must, therefore, be taken seriously in visual merchandising and the layout of a store. These aspects should receive attention in the planning and design stages.

Information about, among other things, the characteristics of the human body and brain is required for the effective design of visual merchandising and store layouts. This information includes particulars about the size, strength and form of the human body. Information is also required about how human height varies within a population, and between the different populations and nationalities. Differences in body weight and shape are also important. People of the same height and sex may differ in arm length, sitting height, hand size or any other body measurement. Information about the height of the customers is, therefore, not enough in itself. Information on the extent to which measurements, such as arm length and hand size, differ is also important in the design of store layouts and visual merchandising.

In contrast to information about the measurements of the human body (static anthropometry), information is also needed on how these measurements of the human body influence its performance. For example, the distance a person can reach with their arm is related to the length of their arm, but does not equal their arm length.

Information on the functions of the human senses, that is touch, taste, smell, sight and hearing, is also needed. For example, information such as how large an object must be before it can be seen, what colours are easily distinguished, and how much contrast there must be between a figure and its background for the figure to be seen, is all very important for retail stores.

Store design demands more than information on the average height and measurements of the target group. It also requires information on the range of body measurements within the target group. The majority of people in a group are near the average for the particular group, but a suitable proportion is appreciably above or below the average. It is accepted practice to provide for 90% of the target group who are near the group average, and ignore the 10% of the target group who range the furthest above or below the average.

For the positioning of shelves or any other storage surfaces, information is also required about the maximum possible distance that a person can stretch upwards. Thiberg calculated regression lines and correlation coefficients for the ratio between the length of the human body and the height of reach. The following is the ratio between height of reach and the length of the human body:

Maximum height of reach = 1,24 x body length.

If it is necessary for the customer to be able to see to the back of the highest shelf in order to see the object they wish to take, the highest shelf should not be higher than:

Men: 150–160 cm
Women: 140–150 cm.

The situation in every retail store and the body measurements of each store's target group of customers differ. It is beyond the scope of this book to address this topic in further detail. When a retail store's visual merchandising and store layout are designed, these aspects must receive attention and the help of specialised ergonomists should be obtained for this purpose.

9.11 The influence of displays on consumer purchasing decisions

The consumer goes through five mental stages before making a purchase. These five mental stages are attention, interest, desire or need, conviction and action (AIDCA). The goal of all displays is to guide potential customers through these five mental stages. The following discussion demonstrates how displays should guide customers through these five mental stages prior to a purchase being made.

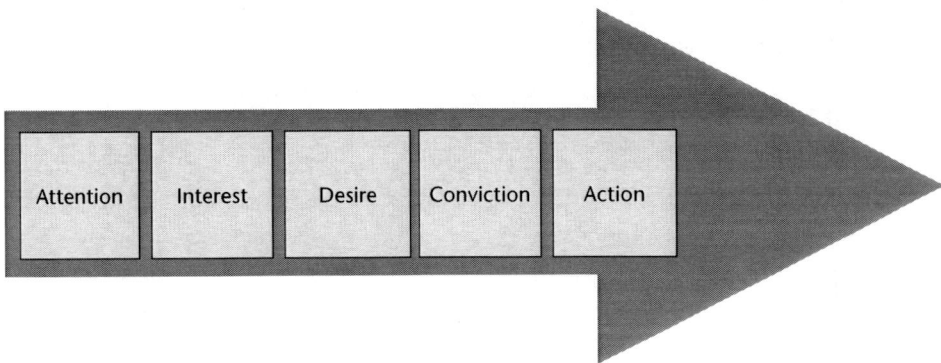

Figure 9.1 Stages in making a purchasing decision

Attention

A distinction can be made between voluntary and involuntary attention. Consumers give a display their voluntary attention when they view it with the idea of learning more about the merchandise they are planning to buy. Involuntary attention is given when customers give unintentional attention to a display. The display must be of such a nature to attract their attention away from their current focal point.

A display can attract attention by emphasising the item displayed and by giving the viewer a reason to give more attention to the display. A display that is unusual and surprising will attract a potential customer's attention and persuade them to view it more closely. This effect can be achieved by using movement, contrasts, sound, lighting, colours and so on.

Interest

The display must relate to the interests and concerns of the consumer in some way. Sometimes a display tells a story – this is an effective technique to arouse and hold customer interest. A display will stimulate interest only if it emphasises the product and suggests a reason for continued attention. The use of pictures and mannequins can arouse customer interest still further, by inviting the viewer to identify with the display.

Desire or need

The consumer's desire or need for a product is stimulated by relating the item emphasised in the display to the consumer's own needs and desires. This is usually achieved through the theme of the display. The written copy on the show card can also help to make consumers aware of their need. The display must therefore persuade consumers that they will be lacking something if they do not own the product displayed. This sense of missing out on something can be induced by demonstrating the features, benefits and applications of the product, by explaining the necessity for it and also by suggesting that owning it will lead to satisfaction.

Conviction

A good display convinces consumers that they want to own the product. This conviction is created by displaying the product as it would be used. A display of dinnerware can be designed to show the dinnerware on a beautifully decorated dining-room table, with mannequins seated for a candlelit dinner. The viewer is now able to visualise themselves sitting down to their own candlelit dinner using this dinnerware. The price on the show card can then reinforce their conviction to buy the dinnerware.

Action

In a self-service retail store, the action objective of displays is to persuade the consumer to buy the item displayed without any further assistance from sales staff. The attractiveness of the item or its packaging can convince the consumer to buy it. The information on the package or the label, as well as the price tag and information on the show card, can also convince the consumer to take action and buy the item.

By contrast, the action objective of displays in full-service retail stores is to bring consumers into the sales area, where the sales staff can take over the selling process. Similarly, the goal of window displays in speciality shops and department stores is to persuade viewers to enter the store, where the sales person can then take over the transaction. Window displays must, therefore, provide viewers with the necessary information to know where the merchandise can be purchased and then persuade them to go there.

9.12   The development of a display

The development of a display can be divided into 11 distinct stages. These stages can be grouped into four main activities, namely planning the display, preparing the display, installing the display and monitoring the display. This is highlighted in Figure 9.2. We shall discuss this process according to each main activity. It must be remembered that the steps in planning, preparing and installing a display are sequential with the activities in the previous step needing to be completed before moving on to the next.

Steps in planning a display

When planning a display, the following steps must be carried out before the preparation phase is put into operation:

Step 1: Check the display schedule.
Step 2: Choose a theme.
Step 3: Draw a sketch.

Planning a display
- ☐ Step 1 – Check the display schedule
- ☐ Step 2 – Choose a theme
- ☐ Step 3 – Draw a sketch

Preparing a display
- ☐ Step 4 – Choose the merchandise
- ☐ Step 5 – Choose the props
- ☐ Step 6 – Order the show cards
- ☐ Step 7 – Draw the final sketch

Installing a display
- ☐ Step 8 – Dismantle the current display
- ☐ Step 9 – Prepare the display area
- ☐ Step 10 – Mount the new display

Monitoring the display
- ☐ Step 11 – Check to ensure the display is maintained and that the display is effective

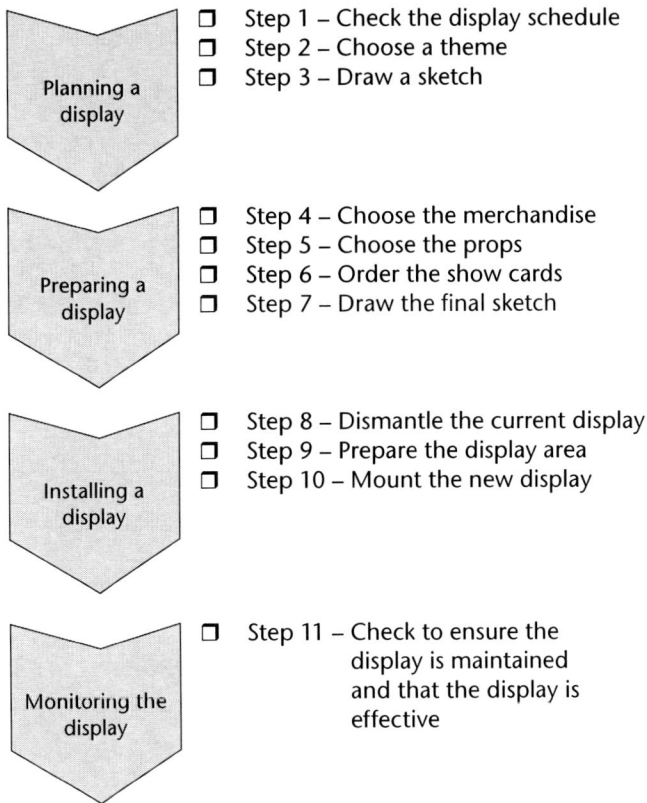

Figure 9.2 Steps in the development of a display

Good planning is a prerequisite for an effective display. The following points need to be kept in mind when planning a display:

- ☐ The type of retail store;
- ☐ The store image;
- ☐ The types of consumers wanted as customers;
- ☐ The season of the year;
- ☐ The display cycle of the merchandise;
- ☐ The space assigned to the display.

Step 1 – Check the display schedule

A display schedule for medium and large retail stores allocates specific display areas to selected categories of merchandise for fixed periods. For example, the display schedule may indicate that for December, a certain window display area has been allocated for the display of ladies' swimwear. The format of the display schedule can vary from store to store and can also include, for example, the type of fixtures/props to be used, the information to be conveyed on the show cards, and a floor plan of the display area. Display schedules are usually set for a period of six or 12 months.

Before further planning of a display occurs, the visual merchandiser must check the display schedule to ascertain which display areas have been allocated to which merchandise categories for the period concerned.

Step 2 – Choose a theme

Every display, regardless of its type or location, should have a basic theme or a clear message to convey to the viewer. It is essential that the entire merchandise display be built around a central theme or idea that passers-by can immediately grasp. This theme must tie in with the overall marketing communication theme of the store.

A theme can, for example, be based on a particular season (such as spring), a festive period (such as St Valentine's Day) or an important event. This central theme or idea, around which the entire display is built, is very important to a display and before the other elements of the display are planned, a decision about an appropriate central theme must first be made.

Step 3 – Draw a sketch

After a theme has been chosen for the display, a rough draft of its design must be prepared on paper. The design must include the following aspects:

- Prepare the floor plan of the display, drawn to scale.
- Show the position of the props and mannequins.
- Show the possible floor coverings and background material that can be used.
- Show the vertical position of the show cards, props and merchandise.

This is only a preliminary sketch of the display. The design can be finalised only once the merchandise and props have been chosen.

Steps in preparing a display

After the display has been planned, preparations can be made to install it. The following steps are taken in the preparation phase:

Step 4: Choose the merchandise.
Step 5: Choose the props (fixtures).
Step 6: Order the show cards.
Step 7: Draw the final sketch.

An empty display area leads to lost sales. Before the current display is removed, the merchandise, props, show cards and lighting equipment for the new display must be ready, so that they can be installed immediately once the old display has been dismantled and the area cleaned. To do this, co-operation between the various visual merchandisers is essential.

The timing must be planned in such a way that both the dismantling of the old display and the installation of the new one are performed while the smallest possible number of customers are in the store. The installation of a new display should preferably take place after closing time or before opening time. To ensure that the new display will be installed on time, the necessary attention must be given to all the steps in the preparation phase.

Step 4 – Choose the merchandise

It is important that the right merchandise be selected for display. The most attractive and the best-selling items should be chosen. The merchandise chosen must be representative of the merchandise category that is being promoted and must emphasise the theme of the display. When selecting merchandise, it must also be remembered that sufficient stocks of the merchandise selected must be available to meet the anticipated consumer demand.

When deciding how much merchandise should be put on display, the price of the goods must be used as a guideline. A display of expensive designer clothing, for example, may include only a single item, while a display in a discount store tends to include scores of the same kind of item to create a bargain image. When selecting merchandise, the colour scheme to be used must also be borne in mind.

Step 5 – Choose the props/fixtures

Different kinds of props can be used in a display. Structural props are those that support other props or merchandise, such as platforms, panels, screens and pillars. Functional props, such as mannequins, easels and stands, are used to support the merchandise. By contrast, decorative props, such as flowers, mirrors, curtains and pictures, are used only for decoration.

Structural props are used to create the basic dimensions of the display. Platforms are used to display the merchandise and the decorative props on different levels. Pillars can be used to frame the display or to give it a strong vertical appearance. Panels and screens can be used to form walls or the background.

Merchandise is draped over the functional props, which are tailored to show it off at its best. The props selected are important since they must contribute to improving the appearance of the merchandise and encouraging its purchase. However, they must not overshadow the merchandise. The props must also tie in with the chosen theme. So, for example, beach umbrellas and beach chairs can be used in a display of swimwear, using the theme of a summer holiday at the seaside.

The possible colour scheme must also be remembered in the selection of props and background material in order to achieve colour harmony. These props can be bought or hired from companies that specialise in such props.

Step 6 – Order the show cards

Show cards should answer possible questions that customers may have when they view the displays. These cards furnish information about the merchandise, such as its price, its positive features and how to use it, and why it should be bought immediately. Show cards in store window displays can also show the name of the store and where the relevant merchandise is located in the store.

The size of the show card and the information to be included depend on the type of display. If the show card has to contain a great deal of information, the following guidelines can be used to prepare the copy:

❑   Concentrate on one thought or idea, so that customers can immediately grasp the message.
❑   Provide information. Refer to the latest fashions or newest products. Show the product's uses.
❑   Word the copy in such a way that the largest possible group of customers is attracted by it.
❑   Make the copy convincing to coax customers into buying.
❑   Give accurate information.
❑   Use brand names and so forth to increase customer confidence.

It is important to order the show cards in good time so that they are ready for use when the display is installed.

Step 7 – Draw the final sketch

After the merchandise and props to be used in the display have been chosen, the final design of the display can be put on paper. The elements and principles of design, the arrangement patterns to be used, the different colour schemes and the lighting must now be incorporated in the formal design of the display.

The following aspects must, inter alia, be included in the final sketch:

❑   A floor plan of the display area, drawn to scale.
❑   The positions of the merchandise, mannequins and other props.
❑   An indication of the background material and floor coverings to be used, and their colours.
❑   The position of the show card is to be shown.
❑   The position and type of lighting equipment to be used must be indicated.

Steps in installing a display

Once the planning and preparation have been completed, the display can be installed. Display procedures and practices differ according to the type of store concerned, the merchandise to be displayed and the purpose of the display. There are, however, basic steps that are taken in the installation of any kind of display:

Step 8: Dismantle the current display.
Step 9: Prepare the display area.
Step 10: Mount the new display.

Step 8 – Dismantle the current display

Before the new display can be installed the one currently occupying the display area must first be removed. If the old display is dismantled during shopping hours, the activities must, as far as possible, be cordoned off with screens or curtains, so that customers cannot see what is happening. This also helps to minimise disruptions. The merchandise must be removed carefully to prevent damage so that it can be taken to the sales floor to be sold.

The merchandise and props used in a display must be signed for. The visual merchandiser is, therefore, responsible for the prompt return of the merchandise and props obtained from the dismantled display to the place from which they were borrowed.

Step 9 – Prepare the display area

After the old display has been removed, the display area must be cleaned before the new display is installed. The background, walls and ceiling must be checked to establish whether they are clean and neat. Any nails, adhesive or other material from the previous display must be removed, the floor and windows must be cleaned, and care must be taken to ensure that the lighting fixtures are in working order.

Step 10 – Mount the new display

During the actual mounting of the display, the structural props must be positioned first, then the functional props, and thereafter the decorative props. The next step is the preparation of the mannequins, stands and merchandise prior to their installation in the display. The final task is to place the accessories. While mounting the display, care must be taken not to damage the props and merchandise, because valuable time and money can be wasted in replacing them.

Once all the merchandise, props and accessories are in place, the display must be checked. Make sure that all the merchandise, props and accessories are in their correct positions, the lighting equipment is in position, and that it works as it should.

Monitoring the display after installation

Accurate records must be kept of each display's contribution to sales. These records can then be used when deciding on the allocation of display space for the coming year, in selecting merchandise for display and as a source of ideas for new displays.

The display must be checked and maintained regularly if it is to remain effective. The display must be kept clean and the merchandise always neatly displayed. The lighting equipment must be checked every day to ensure that all the lights work properly.

In self-service stores, customers take the items they want from the displays so these items must be replaced regularly, since empty shelves have a negative effect on customers. The display must always be kept clean and neat, and a display of fresh produce must be inspected regularly so that old stock is replaced with fresh produce.

Our attention now moves to the design aspect of visual merchandising.

9.13   The elements and role of design

Knowledge of the elements of design is important; since each of these elements can influence the way in which consumers react to a display. A positive reaction from consumers to a display can stimulate their interest and arouse in them the desire to buy the product or service.

The elements of design

The elements of design are highlighted in Figure 9.3. Each of the elements of design, that is, line, shape, size, texture, weight and colour, will be discussed in the section that follows. The issue of colour and its use will be discussed later.

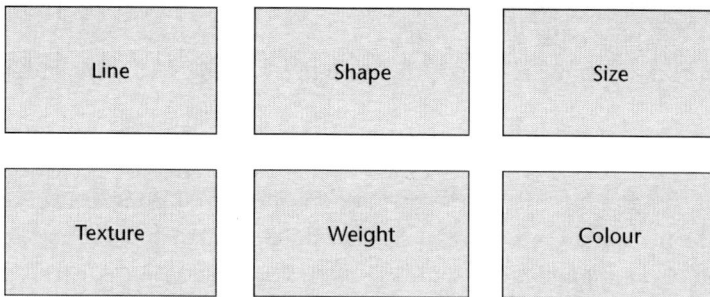

Line	Shape	Size
Texture	Weight	Colour

Figure 9.3 The elements of design

Line

Line is the physical outline of merchandise or is formed by the way in which the merchandise is arranged. It creates a certain mood or impression in the consumer. Vertical lines create a dramatic and formal mood and produce a sense of power, self-confidence and pride, whereas curved lines suggest an informal mood and are associated with femininity. Diagonal lines communicate a sense of action and horizontal lines create a sense of peacefulness, quiet and calmness. The mood that the visual merchandiser wants to create will determine the type of lines used.

Shape

Cubes, triangles and circles are a few shapes commonly used in displays. Similar shapes used together in the display create a sense of harmony. Different shapes used together suggest contrast and are used to attract attention.

Size

Displaying merchandise of the same size together can create a harmonious mood, whereas contrast can be achieved by placing merchandise of different sizes together. Small merchandise will not be noticed if it is displayed in a large window.

Texture

Texture refers to the texture of the surface of the product or display unit. Textures vary from shiny to dull, smooth to rough. Different textures can be used in a display to create contrast and emphasise the texture of the merchandise. For example, by displaying genuine silk scarves against a rough background, the smooth texture of the merchandise is emphasised.

Weight

The weight of an item can be the real weight or the suggested weight of the item. Dark objects appear heavier than light objects of the same size. If colour and size are used together, the consumer's impression of the weight of a certain item in the display can be influenced. Actual and visual weight can also be used to move the consumer's attention from one item to the next in a display.

Colour

Colour is one of the most important elements of a display, since it has certain biological and emotional effects on a person. For example, orange makes one hungry (a biological effect) and yellow and brown make one feel comfortable (an emotional effect). Colour therefore plays an important role in visual merchandising in a retail store, because it has certain biological and emotional effects on consumers, which can motivate them to buy. The use of colour and its influence on consumers is discussed later in this chapter.

9.14 Principles of design

When the elements of design, that is, line, shape, size, texture, weight and colour, are arranged according to the basic principles of design, the result is a good display. The principles of design define how the elements of design must be combined to create unity and order.

Creating unity

Unity is created by one main theme or idea dominating or being emphasised. The other elements in the display contribute to the main idea.

If the objective is to increase sales, unity in visual merchandising is very important. The display must, therefore, have a central point that emphasises the sales message. Emphasis refers to the point of a display that is dominant. It is the point at which the consumer makes eye contact with the display and from where their eye moves to the rest of the items in the display. A display of jewellery will have the most important item, for example a necklace, in the centre of the display area and other items, such as bracelets and rings, will be placed to emphasise the necklace.

Position of the dominant element

The dominant element of a display can be placed either near the optical centre of the display or in the upper left corner of the display for emphasis. The optical centre is halfway between the left and right sides of the display and slightly higher than the lower half of the display. If the dominant element of the display is placed on the optical centre, customers will make eye contact with the display here, and their eyes will then gradually move to either side of the dominant element. They will, therefore, also see the other elements. If the dominant element is placed in the upper left corner of the display, the customers' eyes will move from left to right of the display, as when reading.

Emphasising the dominant element

The dominant element can be emphasised by surrounding it with similar or contrasting colours, lines, shapes and textures. The dominant unit can be emphasised by making it larger, brighter, darker or lighter than the surrounding elements of the display.

Achieving order

Achieving order in a display means that all the elements are arranged in a simple sequence so that the sales message is communicated immediately to passers-by.

The proper combination of all the principles of design, in other words, emphasis, contrast, balance, harmony, proportion and rhythm, creates displays that make consumers stop, look and buy.

The principles of design

The principles of design are emphasis, contrast, balance, harmony, proportion and rhythm. These are represented in Figure 9.4.

Emphasis	Contrast	Balance
Harmony	Proportion	Rhythm

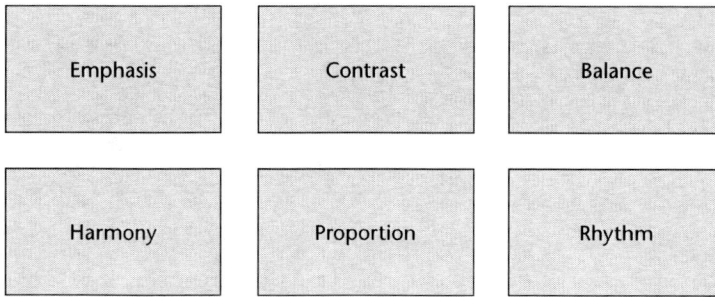

Figure 9.4 Principles of design

Emphasis

Emphasis refers to the point in a display that is dominant. The point that is emphasised in a display is the place at which the viewer makes eye contact with the display. The viewer's eye moves over the display from this point, and for this reason it is better to emphasise only one point in the display. Too many areas of emphasis will cause the display to lack unity and confuse the viewer.

If the display can be approached from more than one direction, there must also be a secondary point of emphasis that leads the viewer to the dominant item being displayed, for example, in displays in corner or island windows.

Contrast

The combination of different shapes, sizes, lines, textures and colours that emphasise difference is called contrast. The dominant unit in a display may be larger, brighter, darker or lighter than the background and the surrounding units. This emphasises the dominant unit and draws the viewer's attention to it.

Contrast can be used to create an exciting, stimulating and informal buying atmosphere.

Balance

Two types of balance can be distinguished: formal and informal balance.

Formal balance means that the left side of the display is a mirror image of the right side. One or more identical items are placed on both sides of the axis, which forms the centre of the display. The arrangement is symmetrical and can be used in most types of displays, since it is easy to design.

Informal balance means that different items of varying sizes, shapes and so on are grouped together in such a way that the whole display appears to be balanced. More weight is placed on one side of the display than the other to create an interesting effect.

Harmony

Harmony is the combination of similar elements of design, that is, lines, shapes, sizes, weights, colours and textures, in a pleasing arrangement. Harmony is usually associated with a quiet, peaceful, luxurious and formal buying atmosphere.

Proportion

Proportion is the relationship between the items with regard to size. The size of the display area must be proportionate to the size of the merchandise displayed in this area. Perfume and jewellery cannot therefore be displayed in a large area in relation to their size, and neither can large items, such as refrigerators, be displayed in small areas. The size of the show cards must also be proportionate to the size of the display area and the merchandise displayed.

Rhythm

Rhythm in a design is the sense of movement created by the way in which the various elements of design are arranged together. Rhythm can be created through repetition, gradation and interruption. Repetition is the frequent use of a certain element of design in the display. In a display of paper serviettes, for example, serviettes of the same size and colour can be used to create repetition and rhythm.

Rhythm can also be created by arranging the items in order of size with the smaller items in front and the larger items at the back of the display. This arrangement suggests gradation or progression, which is the gradual change in size and colour of the items in the design.

An interrupted rhythm can be obtained by inserting an item in the design that differs in size, shape and colour from the rest of the items. This interruption of the rhythm in the display can arouse the interest of the customers.

9.15   The arrangement of a display

The arrangement of a display involves the arrangement of the merchandise in interesting and stimulating patterns to create rhythm, harmony and contrast within the display. Merchandise in a special display can be arranged in a pyramid, zig-zag, step, fan, repetition or radiation pattern. Figure 9.5 illustrates these patterns.

Pyramid

A pyramid arrangement is a triangular display of merchandise in a vertical (ascending) or horizontal (level) shape. The pyramid starts with a broad base and tapers to a point on the highest level. The vertical pyramids can be two- or three-dimensional and are used mainly for merchandise in boxes or tins. The base of a horizontal pyramid is placed towards the back of the display and the point of the pyramid is at the front. The pyramid arrangement is used mainly in supermarkets, pharmacies and hardware stores, because a large quantity of the same merchandise can be grouped together.

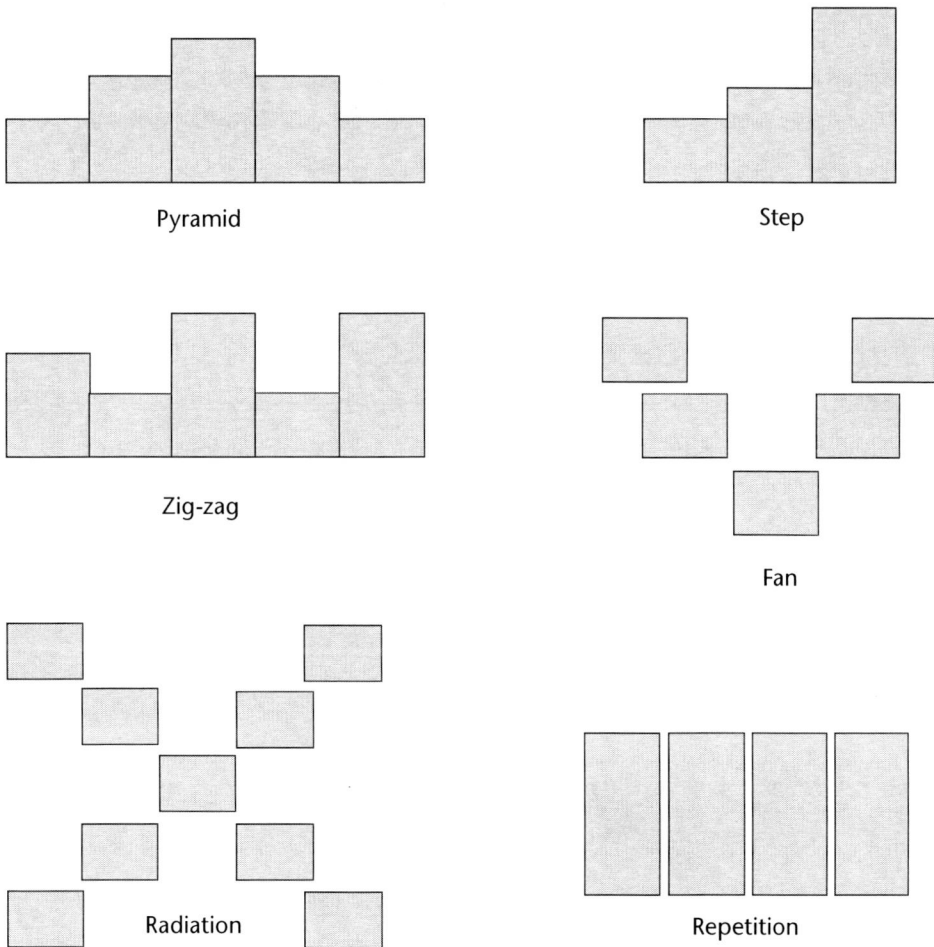

Pyramid

Step

Zig-zag

Fan

Radiation

Repetition

Figure 9.5 Patterns for the arrangement of merchandise

Source: Adapted from http://www.slideshare.net/kotharivr/visual-merchandising-5256539. Accessed 1 March 2012

Zig-zag

In a zig-zag arrangement no display levels are at the same height. This pattern is regarded as more flowing, graceful and feminine, and is particularly suitable for displaying jewellery, cosmetics and shoes. Department stores use the zig-zag pattern mainly for displaying shoes and clothes, such as sweatshirts, shirts and skirts, in an open display.

Step

The step arrangement is a series of steps. This pattern leads the consumer's eye in a direct line from bottom to top. A wide variety of merchandise can be arranged in this pattern. This is a harmonious type of display that creates a sense of movement.

Fan

In a fan arrangement the merchandise is spread out upwards and sideward from a small base. The consumer's eye is drawn to the top and sideways. This pattern is particularly suitable for clothing and sporting equipment.

Radiation

In a radiation pattern the merchandise units are arranged in rays spreading outwards from a central point. This arrangement creates interest because there is one dominant point from which the other elements of the display radiate outwards.

Repetition

In a repetition pattern items that are similar in nature are arranged in the same way according to size and space or angle. This pattern is used for classical styles of clothing and professional wear.

9.16   The psychology of colour

Enterprises are becoming increasingly aware of the value of colour in preventing accidents and increasing the productivity of workers and sales.

The colour of an object makes the first impression on a person when they look at it. In most cases, the colour of the object is the aspect of the object that attracts the consumer's attention, holds their interest and motivates them to buy the item.

Every colour usually suggests certain feelings and concepts to people and leads to an emotional reaction. This does not mean that every person perceives colours in the same way or reacts to them in the same way. However, most people do have similar reactions to colours. Retail shops can use this knowledge of the effect of specific colours to influence customers in their buying behaviour.

Warm and cool colours

Warm colours, such as yellow, red and orange, are those that motivate customers to approach an object. In other words, people generally would rather approach and examine an object if it has a warm colour than if it has a cool colour. For this reason, researchers have recommended that retail shops use warm colours in their display windows, entrances and areas on the selling floor associated with impulse buying. A negative aspect associated with warm colours is that customers will not spend too long in a shop decorated with warm colours. Warm colours are used very successfully in displays to emphasise certain items and to lead the customer's eye to the main item. Warm colours make an object appear larger and closer than it really is. They also give the impression of a comfortable and informal atmosphere.

Cool colours, such as blue, green and purple, have a calming effect on people and motivate consumers to spend more time in the shop because they create a peaceful atmosphere. These cool colours can be used in shops in which customers need to spend more time thinking about each purchase. On the other hand, cool colours also create a formal, distant and aloof impression. Cool colours make an object appear smaller and further away than it really is.

When used properly, warm and cool colours can create a relaxed and stimulating buying atmosphere.

The messages of colour

Table 9.2 identifies certain associations and symbols that consumers link to certain colours. Retailers need to plan the use of colour to obtain the optimum effect in terms of their store atmosphere.

Table 9.2 Meaning of colour

Warm colours			Cool colours		
Red	**Yellow**	**Orange**	**Blue**	**Green**	**Violet**
Love	Sunlight	Sunlight	Coolness	Coolness	Coolness
Romance	Warmth	Warmth	Aloofness	Restful	Retiring
Sex	Cowardice	Openness	Fidelity	Peace	Dignity
Courage	Openness	Friendliness	Calmness	Freshness	Rich
Danger	Friendliness	Gaiety	Piety	Growth	
Fire	Gaiety	Glory	Masculine	Softness	
Sinful	Glory		Assurance	Richness	
Warmth	Brightness		Sadness	Go	
Excitement	Caution				
Vigour					
Cheerfulness					
Enthusiasm					
Stop					

Source: Adapted from http://www.slideshare.net/kotharivr/visual-merchandising-5256539. Accessed: 1 March 2012

Table 9.3 summarises the psychological, temperature and distance effect of different colours on consumers in a retail shop.

Table 9.3 Effects of colour

Colour	Psychological effect	Temperature effect	Distance effect
Violet	Aggressive and tiring	Cold	Very close
Blue	Restful	Cold	Further away
Green	Very restful	Cold-neutral	Further away
Yellow	Exciting	Very warm	Close
Orange	Exciting	Very warm	Very close
Red	Very stimulating	Warm	Close
Brown	Exciting	Neutral	Claustrophobic

Source: Adapted from http://www.scribd.com/doc/38791716/Visual-Merchandising-Color. Accessed: 8 March 2012

Black and white are neutral colours and can be used with brown to soften the effect of brightly coloured displays.

9.17   The importance of colour quality

Colour has three important qualities that must be considered when planning colour combinations: the hue, the value and the intensity or chroma.

- *The hue* of the colour is the name of the colour, for example red, yellow or green.
- *The value* of a colour is how light or dark it is. A light tone of a colour is a tint and is obtained by mixing the colour with white. A darker tone of a colour is a shade and is obtained by mixing the colour with black.
- *The intensity or chroma* of a colour is its purity or brightness. A pure colour, for example red, shows up brighter than when it is mixed with other colours.

9.18   Primary, secondary and tertiary colours

Figure 9.6 is a representation of the colour wheel. The colours in the colour spectrum always occur in the same order: red, orange, yellow, green, blue and purple.
The colour wheel consists of primary, secondary and tertiary colours.

- The *primary colours* are yellow, red and blue. They are primary colours because they cannot be created by mixing other colours together. All the other colours in the colour spectrum can be obtained by mixing the primary colours together. For example, green can be obtained by mixing blue and yellow, and orange can be obtained by mixing red and yellow together.
- The *secondary colours* are orange, purple and green. These are obtained by mixing two primary colours together.
- The *tertiary colours* are obtained when a primary and a secondary colour next to each other on the colour wheel are mixed together, for example yellow-green, blue-green, blue-purple, red-purple, red-orange and yellow-orange.

❏ Black and white are *neutral colours* and are used to obtain tints or shades of a colour, for example brown is obtained by mixing orange and black. Brown is also regarded as a neutral colour.

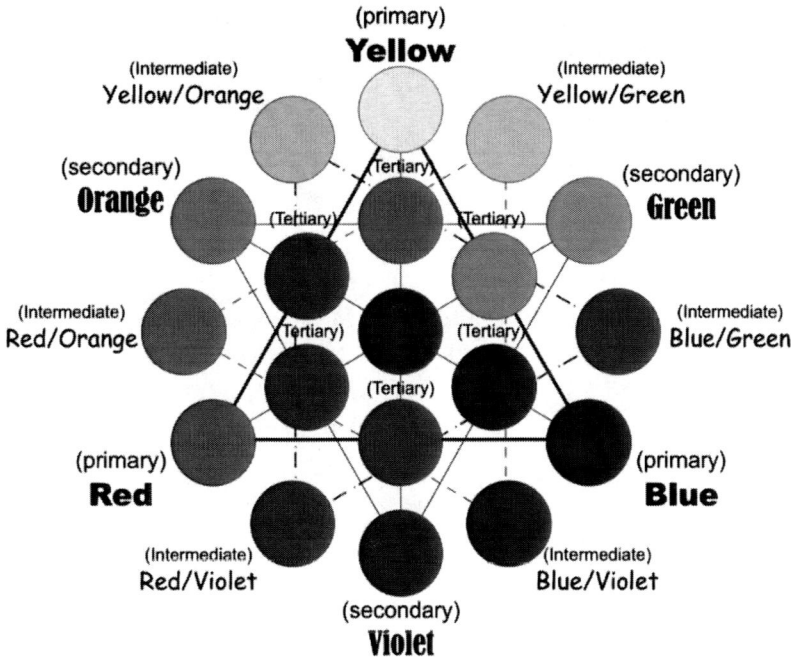

Figure 9.6 The colour wheel

Source: http://erinkruger.files.wordpress.com/2011/11/color-wheel-brown-2.jpg. Accessed: 8 March 2012

9.19   Colour schemes

An endless number of colour combinations can be obtained by mixing different colours.

Different colour schemes or colour combinations can be used for displaying merchandise. There are monochromatic, analogous, complementary, split-complementary, double-split complementary and triadic colour schemes.

Monochromatic colour scheme

One colour is used in a monochromatic colour scheme. The tones of the colour may differ and, for example, vary from dark blue to light blue, and the brightness of the colours can differ. A display of men's shirts, for example, can be in a monochromatic colour scheme if all the shirts with a blue tone are displayed together. Black, white and brown can also be used with the chosen colour since they are neutral colours.

Analogous colour scheme

An analogous colour scheme is where more than one colour is used and colours are selected that are next to each other on the colour wheel, or analogous. Consider the colour wheel in Figure 9.6. As you can see, orange and yellow are next to each other on the colour wheel and are therefore analogous. When they are used together, it is an analogous colour scheme. The same applies for blue and green, red and purple, and so on. Three adjacent colours are generally used in an analogous colour scheme, but up to five adjacent colours can be used.

Different tones of two colours, as well as black, white and brown (the neutral colours) can also be used together in an analogous colour scheme.

Complementary colour scheme

Complementary colours are directly opposite each other on the colour wheel. If you look at the colour wheel in Figure 9.6 you will see that purple (violet) and yellow, blue and orange, red and green, and so on, are directly opposite each other and are therefore complementary colours. If these colours are used together in a display, a complementary colour scheme is used.

Various tints and shades of two complementary colours can be used together to create colour harmony. Complementary colours are contrasting colours and can be used together to create contrast in a display.

Split-complementary colour scheme

In a split-complementary colour scheme, three points on the colour wheel are grouped together. For example yellow, which has purple as its complementary colour, has the colours adjacent to its complementary colour (purple) as its split-complementary colours. The split-complementary colours of yellow are therefore blue-purple and red-purple and these three colours together form a split-complementary colour scheme. Refer to Figure 9.7, which is a diagrammatic representation of the different colour schemes according to the colour wheel.

Double-split complementary colour scheme

In a double-split complementary colour scheme four points on the colour wheel are used, for example the two colours adjacent to yellow, that is, yellow-orange and yellow-green, can be combined with the two colours adjacent to purple (yellow's complement), that is, red-purple and blue-purple.

Triadic colour scheme

A triadic colour scheme is created by using three colours that form an equilateral triangle on the colour wheel. Red, yellow and blue used together form a triadic colour scheme.

Complementary	Analogous	Triadic

Split-complementary	Double split-complementary	Tetradic

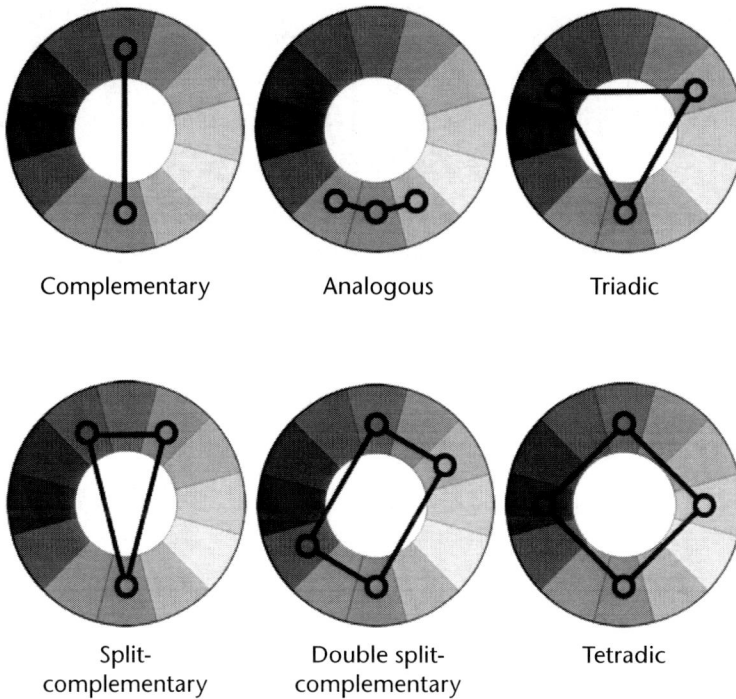

Figure 9.7 Colour schemes and harmonies

Source: http://www.tigercolor.com/color-lab/color-theory/color-theory-intro.htm. Accessed: 8 March 2012

9.20 Hints for the use of colour in visual merchandising

The following colour hints are general industry standards:

- ❏ Yellow is very visible and therefore it is a good colour for price labels.
- ❏ Red can also be used very successfully to indicate the price of items on sale merchandise.
- ❏ Keep the colour scheme simple. Rather use a monochromatic or one-colour scheme, because too many colours may confuse the viewer.
- ❏ Look for clues in the colour of the merchandise itself or its packaging when deciding on a colour for a display.
- ❏ Be careful when using bright colours and contrasts. Bright colours should not be used excessively. Many bright colours may attract the attention of consumers, but they can also confuse them and distract them from the merchandise displayed.
- ❏ Try to balance the colours and achieve colour harmony in the display.
- ❏ Select colours that will create the mood to suit the occasion.
- ❏ Allow sufficient space around a colourful item and make sure that the colours do not clash. Open spaces around an item to emphasise the item.

❏ Light colours are easy on the eye and create the impression that the display is deeper and the display area is larger than it really is.

❏ Emphasise the contrast between the merchandise and the background. Contrasting colours make the display more interesting and can be achieved through lighting.

The following colour-specific suggestions should be kept in mind:

❏ Red is one of the most stimulating colours and should therefore be used very carefully. Red should be used to emphasise something rather than as a background. An exception to this rule is the use of red in restaurants because it stimulates the appetite and, of course, the use of red in St Valentine's Day and Christmas displays.

❏ Yellow, like red, is a very stimulating colour that should be used carefully. The advantage of yellow is that it can be seen from a distance so it is useful for signs and in poorly lit areas. Yellow is a colour that children like so it can be used effectively in toy sections and children's clothing sections.

❏ Orange should be used sparingly, since it is very bright and can easily clash with other colours. It can be used to emphasise particular items, but must not be used as a basic background colour. Orange is another colour for children so it too can be used in toy and children's clothing sections.

❏ Blue can be used to create a peaceful and calm atmosphere and can be used in men's sections, since this colour is associated with masculinity.

❏ Green can be used very successfully to make small areas appear larger, since it is associated with space. Green is a colour that is acceptable to most people and therefore has many uses.

❏ Purple must be used carefully, because it has a depressing effect on consumers. It can, however, be used to create a particular effect.

❏ Light colours make a room or object appear larger, whereas dark colours make them appear smaller.

❏ It is better to use light, neutral colours, for example beige, for fixtures, since these colours are regarded as warm and soft and do not distract the attention from the merchandise displayed.

You will not be able to keep everyone happy as it is not possible to satisfy everyone's colour preferences. When planning the colour schemes to be used to promote the sales of merchandise, the colour preferences of the target market (the regular and potential consumers of that specific item or the regular and potential customers of the shop) should be considered.

9.21   The importance of lighting

Lighting, air conditioning and heating are standard features in any office, shop or factory. In retail stores this equipment not only creates a comfortable working environment, but also indirectly supports the selling effort by making the shop attractive to customers.

The lighting is easily the most important equipment in a retail store and plays a vital role in visual merchandising. Some retailers tried to reduce their overhead expenses by using dimmer lights, but they had to revert to brighter ones because they found that dim lighting had a negative effect on their businesses. Lighting is also very important in a display. It is of no use to select the best merchandise, display equipment, background material and so forth, if no attention is given to the lighting of the display. Good lighting draws the customers' eyes to the merchandise displayed and brings out the best features of the products.

Good lighting has the following advantages:

- It attracts the attention of customers and makes the interior of the shop visible to passers-by.
- It emphasises the true colour, texture and other qualities of the merchandise. It is important not only in displays, but also in changing rooms and at the checkout points.
- Lighting helps to separate the shop visually into different sections.
- Lighting promotes the neatness and cleanliness of the shop.
- Lighting can be used to project the image desired by management.

9.22   Types of lighting

Three main categories of lighting can be distinguished: primary, secondary and atmospheric lighting.

Primary lighting refers to the general lighting of the shop as a whole, including the aisles, escalators and so on. Self-service shops illuminate the shop more than speciality shops, which prefer softer lighting. Discount shops prefer cool lights, whereas prestige shops use mostly warm white lights. The strength of the primary lighting is an important factor to be taken into consideration when determining the intensity of the lighting required for indoor displays.

Secondary lighting is used to emphasise the merchandise. Spotlights and floodlights are used to support the primary lighting in window displays, and shelf, cabinet and freestanding displays.

Atmospheric lighting is special lighting used to create a certain atmosphere or mood. For example, coloured or flashing lights can be used to create a certain mood.

Spotlights mounted behind a screen, a frame in a window, or on the floor are best used to highlight the focal point of the display. These spotlights will draw the customers' attention to the focal point of the display, set the right mood and lead the customers' eyes to the show card displaying all the necessary information. White spotlights should preferably be used because they throw a direct, bright and colourless beam at an object. Although coloured lights can be very effective in a display, they must be used selectively because they can have a negative effect if not used correctly. The colour of the merchandise changes if the wrong colour lighting is used. For example, a red dress can be illuminated with a red light to highlight its colour, but a light of a different colour will change the colour of the dress. In other words, if you want to highlight the colour of merchandise, you must use a light of the same colour as that merchandise.

9.23   The intensity of lighting

The more difficult it is to see detail in a display, the stronger the lighting has to be in the display. The lighting in a display should be between two and five times stronger than the primary lighting used in the store. If particular items need to be emphasised in a display, extra lighting needs to be used, and this should be two-and-a-half times stronger than the lighting usually used in a display. The lighting equipment should be far enough away from the displayed merchandise to illuminate all vertical surfaces effectively.

9.24   Artificial lighting

Many retailers use fluorescent lighting in their stores because it is very economical. It is used mainly for the general illumination of the store and creates a cool effect. Retailers who want to project a certain atmosphere, for example shops selling high fashion clothing, do not use fluorescent lighting.

Incandescent light bulbs found in most houses can also be used effectively in retail shops by mounting them in a variety of fixtures. These light bulbs can be mounted on walls or on the ceiling, or even in candlesticks. Incandescent light bulbs and spotlights can be used to create a warm effect. This type of artificial lighting uses more electricity so it is more expensive to use than fluorescent lighting. An alternative is LED light bulbs. These use considerably less electricity.

To illuminate an entire display, incandescent or LED light bulbs or fluorescent lighting can be used. In both cases, the light fittings should be hidden away in the ceiling and the lights should be on day and night. Only white light bulbs should be used, and if it is necessary to create a coloured effect, spotlights should be used to highlight certain parts of the display. Retailers also use track lighting systems that can be moved easily to areas in which they are needed.

Whichever type of lighting is used, it must suit the type of retail store. Because lighting plays such an important role in retailing, most retailers use lighting specialists to assist them in the selection and placing of suitable lighting equipment.

9.25   Summary

In this chapter on visual merchandising, particular attention was given to displays, colour and lighting. In the greater scheme of things, it is the visual presentation – the display of the merchandise – that motivates consumers to enter a store and to buy. This point alone emphasises the importance of the visual merchandiser in the retail setting.

In the discussion of displays we looked at the functions of displays and the different types of displays that are available to the retailer. A distinction was made between visual merchandising in a full-service retail store and a self-service retail store. We also highlighted the elements that contribute to a good display. In a full-service retail store, the purpose of displays is to entice customers into the store and to create the right atmosphere to enable the sales person to take over the selling process. In self-service retail stores, visual merchandising is used to help customers with their purchases, and to attract their attention with little or no assistance from sales staff. We then moved on to the different types of equipment that are available for displaying merchandise, and briefly discussed the topic of anthropometrics. The next topic we addressed was the development of a display. We highlighted that this process consists of certain consecutive steps, each of which can be divided into four phases: the planning, preparation, installation and monitoring of a display.

The third topic we discussed was the elements and role of design. A visually attractive display that achieves the objectives of sales and attracts the attention of consumers must combine the basic elements and principles of design in the arrangement of the display. The elements of design were identified as line, shape, size, texture, weight and colour. The principles of design describe how the elements of design should be combined to create order and unity and include emphasis, contrast, balance, harmony, proportion and rhythm. Next we considered the arrangement of a display and discussed the various patterns that could be used, namely pyramid, zig-zag, step, fan, repetition or radiation patterns.

We addressed the psychology of colour and considered the messages of colour and how various colours can be used to create the most appropriate setting and feel within the retail store. We emphasised that visual merchandisers have to understand how people experience colours, the qualities of colour, and different colour schemes that can be used to influence the buying behaviour of consumers. We concluded with a look at lighting and its role in visual merchandising, the impact and types of lighting and the use of artificial lighting.

Mini case study

Read the following case study and work through the questions that follow:

Famous Fournos

Fournos Bakery was started in 1989 as a tiny rotisserie chicken and rolls outlet on Oxford Road in Rosebank, Johannesburg, by a master artisanal baker and the present managing director, who also has a sound baking background. That was almost 20 years ago. From the start, all developments, upgrades and product range changes and additions have been customer-driven. Today, the privately owned family business consists of 10 stores, with nine based in the Johannesburg region and one in Centurion, that offer bakery, deli and coffee shop products and services. Specific locations include Bedfordview, Benmore, Dunkeld, Centurion, Fourways, Little Falls, OR Tambo International Airport, Rosebank, Southgate and Woodmead. Their mission is to 'provide a range of top quality bakery products, a selection of deli items and a coffee shop menu that offers our customers value for money and outstanding service'.

➲

The key products on offer include:

- Breads and rolls
- Croissants
- Pastries and confectionery delights
- Cakes and tarts
- Quiches
- Pies and savoury bites
- Biscuits
- Greek speciality pastries and biscuits
- Dough
- Deli offerings (unique by store)
- Platters.

In 2012, Fournos won its 14th Best Bakery in Joburg award at the Leisure Options Awards, which Debi van Flymen, operations manager for Fournos, believes reflects the consideration and care its customers have been shown since the beginning. 'Our customers are our life blood. We listen to them all the time and apply their suggestions and requests as far as we possibly can. The fact is that we don't get trapped watching our competition to see what they're doing; we look to our customers and what they want for our direction. It's the way it's always been. We see everyone as our target market – from the construction worker picking up a couple of R1,40 rolls for lunch to the office executive ordering regular massive platter orders.'

She says Fournos's driving passions are quality and freshness of product, value for money, and service. 'All our baked products are made using traditional baking methods and without flavourants, colourants, preservatives or stabilisers – and have been since the first rolls came out of the oven.'

While the bakery is the cornerstone of Fournos, the company's offering has expanded to include deli, coffee shop, food platters, ice cream, pasta making, and much more. The bakeries produce about 85 bread and bread roll products, and more than 230 lines. The famed Fournos croissants are produced in vast quantities by hand, and daily sales across all shops have reached mind-boggling quantities.

Bread is also mixed by hand. 'We believe that a baker should have a connection with the dough to feel exactly what's needed to get it right all the time. For instance, on a rainy day, the mix will be a bit different to on a dry, sunny day,' she says.

The high baking standards set by the two founders are still maintained as they are deeply involved in training bakers to consistently achieve the same standards. Maintaining consistency of quality across the group is absolutely crucial.

Fournos employs more than 600 people and is enormously proud of its phenomenal staff retention record. It's one of the fundamental reasons for its success, maintains Van Flymen. 'Our team is passionate about our business – the quality and service excellence. It's constantly inspiring.' Fournos store managers are responsible for understanding their own customer bases, what their preferences are, and when their peak periods are, and to deliver on those expectations.

In identifying sites for Fournos bakeries, Van Flymen says there are two main criteria. The location must be in a neighbourhood with an office component to service both families and office needs, and customers must be able to see the sky when they sit and eat. 'That's an important piece of the puzzle,' she maintains, 'as it eliminates a sense of claustrophobia and being enclosed that some malls can project.' Even Fournos outlets based in malls are on the outskirts with access to outside seating.

Merchandising, as with everything else in Fournos Bakery, is done with extreme care and attention to detail. Each store is designed according to store layout and customer comfort levels. The company follows general merchandising principles, but each store is unique, and everything is taken into account – with an eye on flexibility to enable the store to adapt, change and grow as the need arises.

And when all is said and done, Van Flymen waxes lyrical about the core of the business – freshly baked bread. 'Bread is food for the soul. All over the world, bread is an important part of many meals in some form or another. There is something about a loaf fresh out of the oven that is intoxicating – and being in the business of making really good bread is a privilege we treasure.'

Source: http://www.supermarket.co.za/SR_Downloads/S&R%20Jan%202012%20Bakery.pdf
Supermarket and Retailer, January 2012 edition. Accessed 2 February 2012

Extracts from the Fournos website:
Deli

We work hard to procure the best quality meats, cheeses, olives, and pickles from every corner of the world and honour the 'local is lekker' principle too by featuring outstanding local products. Our delis also feature many items we make ourselves.

Choose your roll, bread or croissant and our friendly, professional deli staff will create your unique masterpiece. Consider yourself the conductor as you let them know what to pile on! So many choices from the gourmet to the everyday to suit all appetites and budgets. Your edible masterpiece will be music for your mouth.

A wide variety of salads grace our deli counters where you can help yourself to what's on offer. Regular favourites include Greek village salad, bean salad, potato salad, butternut and poppy seed salad, avocado salad, pasta salad and more!

We also stock a range of dips and spreads that include our divine homemade chicken liver pâté, olive tapenade, pesto, tzatziki, hummus, tahinasalata (sesame dip) and melitzanosalata (brinjal dip). These are stunning accompaniments to our bread and cold meat selection.

⮑

Don't forget to explore the daily deli specials in each Fournos location – we receive regular raves about dishes like oxtail, chicken schnitzel, calamari, lamb chops, spiced rice, and a wide variety of pastas. This is the perfect choice for the busy professional, soccer Mom or anyone needing a night off from cooking.

Each Fournos branch has a unique deli offering that caters to the individual customer base of the shop. Come and browse the shelves at your nearest outlet.

Coffee shop

We take our coffee seriously at Fournos and we proudly use Illy coffee! Just like baking, coffee hovers in the space where the spheres of science and art converge. Whether your cup of coffee is a traditional filter coffee or you opt for an espresso, cappuccino, or latte – our trained baristas showcase their talents in every cup. In addition to the leaded variety, we offer de-caffeinated coffee in all our branches. For you non-coffee drinkers, we offer a delightful range of teas, hot chocolate, and Milo.

Source: www.fournos.co.za. Accessed: 6 February 2012.

Questions

1. Fournos is a food retailer. Taking their products into account, how would you utilise the different types of displays in their Fourways store (visit the Fournos website for more detailed information if required).
2. How would you use displays to move customers through the mental stages a customer goes through before making a purchase?
3. Describe the process you would follow when developing the display for the cakes and tarts in a Fournos store.
4. Considering the nature of the products on sale in a Fournos store, describe how you would make use of the principles of design when developing displays in their stores.
5. Visit the Fournos website and view their products. Describe how they have used the arrangement of colour to display their merchandise.
6. Would lighting play a role in the visual merchandising at a Fournos store? Explain.

9.26 Self-evaluation questions

1. Distinguish between promotional displays and institutional displays.
2. Outline the functions of a display.
3. Describe the different types of displays that a retailer can use in its visual merchandising.
4. Discuss the elements that contribute to a good display.
5. Distinguish between visual merchandising in full-service retail stores and visual merchandising in self-service retail stores.

6. Describe the various types of display equipment and props that retailers can use in displays.
7. Discuss the application of anthropometry to visual merchandising.
8. Explain how displays guide customers through their five mental stages before a purchase is made.
9. Discuss the steps in the development of a display for a fashion clothing retailer.
10. Explain the steps in the preparation of a display.
11. Discuss the steps in the installation of a display.
12. Describe the elements of design and their impact on visual merchandising.
13. Discuss the various principles of design and how they are used to attract the customer's attention.
14. Describe the different arrangement patterns that can be used in a display.
15. Discuss the topic of the psychology of colour in visual merchandising with specific reference to the messages of colour and the effects of colour.
16. Distinguish between primary, secondary and tertiary colours and then discuss the colour schemes that can be used for a display.
17. Explain how lighting can be used in visual merchandising with reference to the advantages of lighting, the types of lighting and lighting intensity.

9.27   Bibliography

Berman, B. & Evans, J.R. (2012). *Retail management: A strategic approach,* 11th edition. Harlow: Pearson Education.
Cant, M.C. (ed.). (2010). *Introduction to retailing,* 2nd edition. Lansdowne: Juta.
Cox, R. & Brittain, P. (2004). *Retailing: An introduction*, 5th edition. Harlow: Prentice Hall.
Dunne, P.M. & Lusch, R.F. (2008). *Retailing,* 6th edition. Mason: Thomson.
Levy, M. & Weitz, B. (2012). *Retailing management*, 8th edition. New York: McGraw-Hill.

Websites

http://erinkruger.files.wordpress.com/2011/11/color-wheel-brown-2.jpg Accessed: 8 March 2012.
http://www.fastmoving.co.za/marketing Accessed: 8 March 2012.
http://www.fournos.co.za Accessed: 6 February 2012.
http://www.ies.org/lighting/applications/interior-retail.cfm Accessed: 8 March 2012.
http://www.redcliffe.co.uk/point_of_sale/boost-your-sales.htm Accessed: 27 February 2012.
http://www.scribd.com/doc/38791716/Visual-Merchandising-Color Accessed: 8 March 2012.
http://www.slideshare.net/kotharivr/visual-merchandising-5256539 Accessed: 1 March 2012.
http://www.supermarket.co.za/SR_Downloads/S&R%20Jan%202012%20Bakery.pdf *Supermarket and Retailer,* January 2012. Accessed: 2 February 2012.
http://www.tigercolor.com/color-lab/color-theory/color-theory-intro.htm Accessed: 8 March 2012.

Index

triadic colour schemes 198–199
tropika case study 63–64
Truworths case study 120–121
turnover 94–97
   high 96–91
   increases 127
   increasing by merchandising 97

U

unemployment 10, 11–12
unit inventory control systems 87–88, 91
unit pricing 133
unity in design 190
universal product coding 17
urbanisation 12–13

V

value adding 7
vehicle sales 10
vending 4
visual control systems 88
visual merchandising 170

in full-service stores 176
in self-service stores 176–177
use of colour in 199–200

W

wall fixtures 113–114
wall merchandising space 111, 112
walls 114
Walmart case study 69
weaknesses 26
web 19
weight in design 189
wholesaling 72–73
   vs retailing 1–2
window displays, types of 173–174
windows, styles of 118–119
women, working 15

Z

zig-zag displays *193–194*
ZONE 140